AMAZON REVIEWS

★★★★★ **Secret to success — consulting case interviews.** In graduate school, I browsed [illegible] books on consulting case interview preparation. This was the only book I read. The clear, consistent way of thinking through how to manage case interviews made sense. Rather than focusing on formulas, frameworks (e.g., Porters Five Forces), or just examples, Cosentino classifies cases into sensible categories and coaches the student through how to think about answering. Additionally, he gives valuable tips on how to get comfortable in the interview.

The true proof; however, was that I interviewed with the two top strategy consulting firms and received offers from both. I would highly recommend this book to anyone considering interviewing with top strategy consulting firms.

★★★★★ **Outstanding prep for case interviews.** *Case in Point* is in my view the best book of its type on the market. The top firms vary their cases from interviewer to interviewer; Cosentino's book provides a good system for tackling any case that you're presented. This book got me extremely well-prepared for my interviews. I just received a summer associate offer from what's arguably the top consulting firm, despite my non-business background.

★★★★★ **This is excellent.** This is probably the best consulting book on the market for undergrads looking to get a job in a top consulting firm after college. I own the *Vault Guide to the Case Interview* and felt this was MUCH better because it gives you a system to follow, not just a bunch of random structures and cases. Cosentino does a great job of putting all these pieces together in a very useful book.

★★★★★ **Great book for consulting preparation.** Cosentino's compilation of cases is a superb way to prepare for management consulting case interviews. Not only does he provide a wide variety of cases (from market-sizing to acquisition opportunity to dipping profits) he also offers several helpful frameworks for approaching consulting cases in general. I would highly recommend this book to anyone planning to do consulting interviews (and they're tough!).

★★★★★ **Having a job interview? Use this book: it's a must.** I used this book as a tool to prepare for interviews, and it really helped me. In this tough period, I followed the Ivy Case Method proposed, and it didn't fail. The book presents in a very readable way what to expect in an interview and how to create your best strategy. I'm usually very skeptical about these kinds of books, but I must say that Cosentino is able to attract the reader and through anecdotes and concrete examples, to keep the reader's interest till the last page. Definitely a must.

★★★★★ **Got me a consulting job!** I was VERY nervous about getting a good job after school. I compared several interview guides and found some to be incomplete and others to be too long and confusing. Cosentino's *Case in Point* was easier to understand and covered the key techniques/frameworks behind case interviews. I practiced the sample cases and I eventually got a job in strategy consulting.

I am positive that *Case in Point* and *CQInteractive* coupled are the most complete source for case interview preparation currently on the market. While *Case in Point* teaches how to approach the toughest cases in a systematic but creative way, *CQInteractive* takes you to the driver's seat and gives you first hand experience on virtually all types of questions you will face in interviews, with the convenience of the Internet. We have acquired and distributed *Case in Point* and *CQInteractive* to all club members, and both are undeniably among the most important resources used by them to excel in case interviews and secure offers from the most prestigious management consulting companies.

Paulo da Silva
VP of Member Education, Wharton MBA Consulting Club '07

Also by Marc P. Cosentino

The Harvard College Guide to Consulting Case Questions

The Harvard College Guide to Consulting

The Harvard College Guide to Investment Banking

Case In Point

Complete Case Interview Preparation

SIXTH EDITION

10th ANNIVERSARY EDITION

Marc P. Cosentino

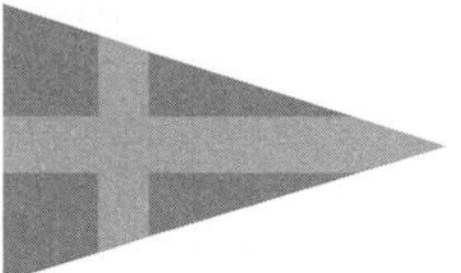

Published by Burgee Press, Needham, MA

Acknowledgments

Special thanks are due to Lynda Knoll Cotter and Semil Shah who contributed cases.

Thanks are owed to all the students from around the world who contributed thoughts and case questions especially Adrian Cighi, Agnés Noël, Basil Waite, Deepa Gupta, Emily Cosentino, Eric Edwards, Gonzolo Zubieta, Javier Luzarraga, John Loken, Memphis Gator, Mukund Jain, Sebastien Desreux, Tatum Bell III and Veronica Chau.

Burgee Press
P.O. Box 920654
Needham, MA 02492

As with all case questions, we assume facts not in evidence, as well as generous assumptions. Familiar companies are used as examples because of the power of their brand and their familiarity to the general public. Information concerning the actual companies cited as examples may not be accurate. This information was based on research but should not be used as reliable, up-to-date data.

Edited by Chris Glasser

ISBN 978-0-9710158-5-2
Library of Congress Cataloging-in-Publication Data:
Case in Point: Complete Case Interview Preparation / Marc P. Cosentino — 6th ed.
Library of Congress Card Number 2001117521

First Printing, 1999
Printed in the United States of America

Second Edition 2001
Third Edition 2004
Fourth Edition 2005
Fifth Edition 2007
Sixth Edition 2010

Contents

The mind is wondrous. It starts working the second you're born and doesn't stop until you get a case question.

Dedication

To my college friends Suzie, Lorin, Margot, Cowboy, Tony, Elizabeth, Sco, Buttsey, Terry and Charlie.

Time of my life, a lifetime ago.

1 : Introduction

In Q4, the number three US wireless carrier slipped further behind its rivals in the number of customers, even as profits rose 35%. What do you think is going on?

Consulting firms are in the business of renting out brains. Consultants get paid to synthesize massive quantities of foreign data, toss out the irrelevant information, structure an approach to a given client issue and hypothesize logically and creatively before people of power and influence (like bigwigs at the wireless company). That's why consulting firms put so much weight on the case question — because it allows them to judge how logically and persuasively a potential consultant (i.e., you) can present a case. In essence, a case interview is a role-playing exercise.

In order to nail a case interview, you need to know both how to prepare and how to perform. This book will help you do both. It walks you through the overall consulting interview, teaches you how to conduct your research, tells you what the consulting firms are looking for in a candidate, explores the various types of case questions and then introduces you to the Ivy Case System©.

As a career officer at Harvard for over eighteen years, I've helped more than ten thousand of the nation's top students prepare for case interviews. During this time, students have tirelessly memorized individual frameworks and have then struggled to decide which one(s) to apply. All the while, the case questions given by consulting firms, as well as by a growing number of companies in various industries, have become increasingly complex. The standard frameworks of the past, while still valuable, aren't enough to solve these sophisticated cases. I've developed The Ivy Case System© in order to simplify things. This system will allow you to make an impressive start (without a long and awkward pause) and ensure that you approach the answer in an organized and logical way. The difference between a framework and a system is that a framework is a tool; a system is a process with all the tools built in. The Ivy Case System© is the most sensible and comprehensive case interview strategy you can learn.

Keep in mind that case questions help educate you during your job search by acting as a self-imposed screening device. Is this the type of work you want to be doing? Is this the type of environment in which you can learn and flourish? You need to ask yourself, "Do I enjoy problem solving? Do I enjoy these types of questions and issues?" Case questions can and should be fun.

The best way to prepare is to hunker down and (i) read this book and don't skip any pages; (ii) attend all case question workshops sponsored by consulting firms or your career services office; (iii) practice with your econ professor, roommates, friends and anyone you know who worked or is currently working in consulting (see The Roommate's Guide, page 170); and (iv) read this book again and don't skip any pages.

Sounds like you had better start reading . . .

2 : The Interview

Relax, it's worse than you think. If you figure the odds of getting chosen for an interview, having all the interviewers like you, and making it through seven to ten cases, you'll be spending next semester's tuition on lottery tickets. But you know what? You faced much tougher odds when you applied to a top school. Not only were you accepted, you've thrived. So forget about the odds and concentrate on you. If there was ever a time for tunnel vision, this is it. Besides, the recruiters don't know about the time you ... well, they don't know and we're certainly not going to tell them. You head into an interview with a clean slate.

This chapter will walk you through a first-round interview and will show you how to prepare properly for each step. Some firms set up two back-to-back 45-minute interviews for the first round. In these interviews, one interviewer spends more time questioning you about yourself and then gives a short case question, while the other interviewer spends less time on you and more time on the case.

FIRST-ROUND INTERVIEW

Usually two-45 minute back-to-back interviews

First person spends 25 minutes talking to you about you; why consulting? asking for examples of leadership, persuasion, failure and team experience. Next a small case, either a market-sizing or a factor case, and then ending with your questions for them.

The second person spends 10 minutes breaking the ice, and then gives you a full case, taking up 25 to 30 minutes and often including charts for analysis. The last few minutes are taken up with your questions.

+ Introduction

You get called, offer your clammy hand, then lie and say, "It's great to be here." Nothing to it, you did it the last time you had a blind date. (Let's hope this goes a little better.)

Cliché time: you never get a second chance to make a first impression. Eye contact, a pleasant smile and a firm handshake are paramount.

+ Questions About You

The first part of the interview is all about "getting to know you." McKinsey calls it a PEI, which stands for Personal Experience Interview. They will ask you to come up with several examples of times when you influenced or persuaded a group, about your relationship-building style and about goals that you set for yourself and were successful in meeting. Interviewers will ask you several questions drawn from your résumé (anything on your résumé is fair game). They may even ask, "Your life is a newspaper article. What's the headline?"

What they are looking for:

- a confident, comfortable demeanor and strong communication skills (Are you a nervous wreck?)
- leadership ability and initiative (Forget about the time you organized that keg party)
- ability to be a team player (Do you play well with others?)
- drive, aspirations, energy, morals and ethics (Do you have any?)

In this part of the interview you should be responding, not thinking. You're going to do enough thinking during the case questions to last you for a week. You need to research yourself beforehand. Look at the list of the most commonly asked questions in a consulting interview (see sidebar). You may not be asked any of these questions, but if you take the time to write out the answers or, better yet, bullet point out the answers, you will be forced to think about things you haven't thought about in years (or ever). Don't be surprised if the interviewer asks, "Tell me about a time you persuaded a group to do something they didn't want to do." You give her your answer and she replies, "Great, give me another example." It is common for interviewers to ask for two or three examples for the same question. When thinking through your answers, go three stories deep. Remember to bullet point out your answers instead of writing passages. People try to memorize passages and unless you're Gwyneth Paltrow there is no way you're going to deliver your answer and make it seem real.

COMMONLY ASKED CONSULTING INTERVIEW QUESTIONS

If you take the time to answer these questions before the interview, you will be more articulate and focused when it comes time to perform.

- Tell me about yourself.
- What are you doing here?
- Why consulting?
- Why did you pick your school?
- What do you think consultants do?
- What do you know about this job and our firm?
- Why would you choose our firm over our competitors?
- How are your quantitative skills?
- What percentage is 7 of 63?
- Tell me of a time you showed leadership skills.
- Tell me of a time you were a team player.
- Give me an example of a time you influenced or persuaded a group.
- Tell me about a recent crisis you handled.
- Have you ever failed at anything?
- Tell me about a time you took the initiative to start something.
- What type of work do you like to do best?
- With which other firms are you interviewing?
- Which other industries are you looking into?
- What accomplishments have given you the greatest satisfaction?
- What experiences/skills do you feel are particularly transferable to our organization?
- Why should I hire you?

Interviewers remember stories and accomplishments more than common answers ▶ ▶ ▶

You want to get labeled. If you tell the interviewer your captivating tale about windsurfing across the English Channel, then at the end of the day when the interviewer sees your name on her list she'll remember you as "the windsurfer." Everything you spoke about will come back to her. If she sees your name and thinks, "Which one was he?" your candidacy is over.

So dig into the old treasure chest and come up with memorable stories and accomplishments which substantiate the skills that will make you a strong candidate.

How do I answer? ▶ ▶ ▶

Three of the most problematic interview questions are:

- **Have you ever failed at anything?**
- **With which other firms are you interviewing?**
- **Which other industries are you interviewing?**

How do you answer these truthfully?

A DOZEN REASONS TO ENTER CONSULTING

Just in case you're not sure, below are 13 (a baker's dozen) of the most popular reasons students go into consulting.

1. You'll work and learn from very intelligent and articulate people.
2. You'll develop a vast array of marketable skills in a prestigious environment.
3. The learning curve never ends.
4. You'll receive exposure to the corporate elite: the way they think, act, and analyze their problems.
5. You'll be exposed to many industries.
6. You'll work as part of a team.
7. You'll solve problems.
8. You'll make organizations more efficient.
9. You'll work on multiple projects.
10. You'll travel.
11. You'll improve your chances of being accepted into a top business school.
12. It will always look great on your résumé.
13. The money's good.

Q : 1 Have you ever failed at anything?
Say yes! Everybody has failed at something. People fail all the time. That's how you learn.

• **Dos:** Do talk about a failure and what you learned from that failure. Better yet, talk about how you failed, what you learned from that mistake, then how you turned it into a success. A perfect example comes from Michael Jordan. He failed to make his high school basketball team his freshman year, persevered and became a basketball legend. Have a story to tell; make it memorable.

• **Don'ts:** Don't talk about a personal failure. Stay away from anything that is going to make the interviewer feel uncomfortable (i.e., "I never got to straighten things out with my Dad before he passed away," or, "My girlfriend dumped me ..." or, "I couldn't out run that police car when I was seventeen."). Interviewers don't want to hear it. The other thing they don't want to hear is an academic failure. I can't tell you how many Harvard students have told me in mock interviews, "I took an upper-level science class, worked like a dog, but I failed." "What did you get in the class?" I'd ask. "B minus." That's not failing. If you really did fail a course, they would know about it and ask why it happened.

Q : 2 With which other firms are you interviewing?
It's okay to tell them that you're interviewing with other consulting firms. Competition's tough; you'd be foolish to put all your energy into just one firm. However, you must be able to tell them why they're your first choice and what makes them better in your mind than the other firms.

Q : 3 Which other industries are you interviewing?
Consulting goes hand-in-hand with two other industries. While interviewing for a consulting position, it's okay to mention that you are looking at investment banking and/or strategic planning. These positions look for the same qualities in a candidate and require similar job skills. In fact, McKinsey's and BCG's biggest competitor is Goldman Sachs — not one another.

+ Why Consulting?

You know the interviewer is going to ask you why you want to be a consultant. Now this is important — not only should your answer be immediate, but you must look the interviewer right in the eye. If you look away, it indicates that you are thinking about the question and that's enough to end the interview right then and there. You should have given this answer a great deal of thought long before you walked into the interview. While I don't want you to memorize your answer, I do want you to memorize bullet points. This makes your answer focused, linear and an appropriate length. Avoid talking aimlessly. Having several good reasons why you want to be a consultant isn't enough. It's not always what you say but how you say it and most importantly what they hear. Your voice should carry sincerity and enthusiasm.

+ Possible Math Question

They may ask you about your quantitative skills. This could be followed by a small math question such as, "What's 100 divided by 7?" Or, "9 is what percentage of 72?" The questions aren't hard, but they might take you by surprise. It may be time to break out the flashcards.

* **Note:** *During the first part of the interview, you're being judged. The interviewer is asking herself whether or not she'd like to work and travel with you. Are you interesting? Engaging? Do you have a sense of humor and like to have fun? This is better known as the "airport test." The name comes from the question, "How would I feel if I were snowed in with this candidate for nine hours at the Buffalo airport? Would we have a lot to talk about, or would I have to pretend that I was in a coma so I wouldn't have to talk?"*

The interviewer is also measuring your maturity, poise and communication skills, while thinking, "Would I feel comfortable bringing this candidate in front of a client?"

An important component of the "maturity test" is to determine whether you think before you speak. I had a Harvard student, when asked what percentage is 3 of 17, he blurted out 80%. (I don't know how he got into Harvard either.) For him that interview was over. He might as well have gotten up and walked out because nothing was going to save him. Not because he got the wrong answer, but because it was clear that he didn't think before he spoke. If he does something like that in an interview, what is he going to do in front of a client? I couldn't trust him, and if I can't trust him, I am not going to hire him.

+ Case Questions

The second part of the interview is the case question. These questions carry a tremendous amount of weight. You can pass the airport test and be as poised and articulate as John F. Kennedy, but if you fumble the case, that's it. Alternatively, if you hit a home run on the case but have the social skills of Napoleon Dynamite, then you have bigger problems than getting a job. We'll cover the case questions in depth in Chapter Three.

+ Your Questions

The last part of the interview requires a good deal of research about both the industry and the company. In addition, if you can find out who will be interviewing you, you should be Googling them to see what articles they have written or issues they are involved with. You can bet that they will be Googling you. In your research, you should be looking for answers to the pre-interview questions (see sidebar, next page). Questions for which you can't locate answers become excellent questions to pose to your interviewer.

PRE-INTERVIEW QUESTIONS

1. What type of consulting does the firm do?
2. In what industries does the firm specialize?
3. How big is the firm?
   - How many domestic and international offices does the firm have?
   - How many professionals are in the firm?
4. What kinds of training programs does the firm offer?
5. What type of work does an entry-level consultant do?
6. How much client contact does an entry-level consultant have the first year?
7. Does the firm have a mentor program?
8. How often do first-years sleep in their own beds? What's their travel schedule like?
9. How many hours make up a typical work day?
10. How is a case team picked?
11. How often do you get reviewed?
12. How many consultants does the firm expect to hire this year?
13. How does that compare to last year?
14. Where do the consultants go when they leave the firm?
15. Is it possible to transfer to other offices, even international offices?

However, before you ask your first question, if there is anything critical that you didn't get a chance to bring up in the interview, now is the time. Simply state, "Before I ask my first question, I just want to make sure you understand ..." Get it out before you leave the room. If you don't, you're going to kick yourself all the way home, and even worse, you'll never know if that statement could have turned the tide.

The best ways to collect these answers are to: ▶▶▶

❑ **Attend career fairs and speak to the firm representatives.** Pull out your list of questions and ask three or four. Make sure that you try to turn this meeting into a conversation. At the end, thank the reps for their time, ask them for their business cards, and inquire whether it would be all right if you called or emailed them with further questions. At this point, no one is going to judge you on your level of company knowledge. They are there to provide information and hype the firm.

❑ **Scour the company's website.** This will let you know how the firm sees itself and the image that it's trying to project.

❑ **Talk to alumni and graduate school students who used to work for the companies that you're interviewing with.** Often, career services offices will be able to match you up with alumni who are working in a specific industry. Interviewing past employees can be very enlightening. They will tell you more about their old firm in a half an hour than you'll learn by spending two hours on the Internet. Plus, they'll tell you things that you'll never find on the Internet. They can be completely objective; they don't have to try to sell the firm.

❑ **Attend company information meetings.** Get your name and face in front of firm representatives so that they can associate your face with your résumé. While these people don't have the power to hire you, they do have the power to get you on the interview list. Top-tier firms often get 400 resumes for 100 first round interview slots. Ensure that interview slot by networking and schmoozing with firm representatives every chance you get. One of the best kept secrets of company presentations is to go early. If a company presentation is scheduled to start at 6:00 pm, show up at 5:45. Most students won't arrive until 6:00 pm or a little after, but the firm's representatives show up at around 5:30 to make sure that the room is set up correctly and the cheese table is laid out nicely. If you show up early, not only will it impress the consultants, but it will allow you to get at least five minutes of quality face time with one of them. They are more likely to remember you if you talk for five minutes at the beginning of the night than if you hang around until the end hoping for 45 seconds of their time. They are also more likely to have their business card with them. Remember to ask for their business card and send a follow-up email.

❑ **Search *The Wall Street Journal* and the Internet for articles and information on the firm.** This allows you to be current on any firm's news.

Have your list of questions with any specific facts or figures you've dug up written out when you walk into the interview. It shows that you have done your homework and have given this interview a great deal of thought. Besides, if you freeze up, it's all right there in front of you.

+ The Grand Finale: Why Should I Hire You?

This is your opportunity to shine and market yourself. But before you launch into a laundry list of skills and attributes, you may want to simply state that they should hire you because you want to be a consultant. Then, reiterate all the reasons that you brought up earlier when they asked you, "Why consulting?"

Consulting firms look for "low-risk" hires. You're a low-risk hire if you've worked in consulting, liked it and want to return, or if you've done your homework. Consulting firms' biggest fear is that they will spend a lot of time and money recruiting, hiring and training you, only to have you bail out after six months because consulting isn't what you expected it to be.

If they aren't convinced that this is what you want to do, then it doesn't matter how talented you are, it's not worth it for them to extend you an offer. Think of it this way: How would you feel if someone accepted your dinner invitation because their first choice fell through? If your heart's not in it, they don't want you.

Students who receive job offers in consulting do so for four reasons: ▶ ▶ ▶

1. They are able to convince the interviewer that they are committed to consulting and know what they're getting into (i.e., type of work, lifestyle, travel).
2. They can demonstrate success-oriented behavior.
3. They exhibit good analytical skills when answering case questions. (That's where we come in.)
4. They are able to articulate their thoughts, create a positive presence and defend themselves without being defensive.

Now that you understand the structure of the interview for the first round, the subsequent rounds are not all that different. The second round is often held at a nearby hotel and usually consists of two interviews, both 60 minutes in length, each with a heavy focus on case questions. The third round is typically held in the firm's offices where there are five interviews, 60 minutes each, again with a heavy emphasis on case questions. During all the final rounds you can expect to analyze many charts. In addition, some firms give written cases requiring you to not only analyze the information but to design charts to back up your recommendations.

There are other kinds of first round interviews. Some firms conduct phone interviews while others conduct group case interviews.

First Round Telephone Interviews

There will be times when your first round interview will be conducted over the phone. Sometimes this is a screening interview; other times you'll get a case question as well. There are several things to remember. If possible, go to a quiet and private place. Turn off the television and lock the door so your roommate doesn't barge in and interrupt you.

Most importantly, you are your voice. That is the only thing the person on the other end of the line has to go on. Your voice should be upbeat and enthusiastic; speak clearly and with confidence, but not arrogance.

Finally, lose the calculator. I know that it is tempting to have it right there, but if you get the answer too quickly, or the interviewer can hear buttons being pushed in the background, you're sunk.

First Round Group Case Interviews

McKinsey and other firms have started holding group interviews for non-MBA graduate students as part of their first round interviews. During a group interview, consultants look more at the group dynamics than how the group answers the question. Does this candidate have the ability to build relationships, empathy and teamwork? On one hand, you are a competitor to the other people in the group, but on the other hand, for this moment in time you are teammates. People who are aggressive and try to dominate the conversation are the ones that don't get called back. Remember, consultants work in teams and if you're not willing to be a team player, then you're out.

In my Harvard Business School classes, the professor rarely called on anyone who had his hand raised while someone else was speaking. This indicated to the professor that the hand-raising student wasn't listening to his classmate and had his own agenda. Like a business school case class, you are expected to build on what others have said. You are expected to move the discussion forward, not take it off on a tangent or move the discussion back because you had a point you wanted to make.

Remember, build on what other team members have said and don't interrupt a team member when she is speaking.

+ Stress Interviews

Well, they're back. Stress interviews. They usually come in one of two forms. The first type is the two-on-one (you're the one). The interviewers ask you question after question without giving you much of a chance to answer. They'll make unfavorable comments to each other about your answers, dismissing your answers as amateurish or ridiculous. They may even turn rude and snappish.

Why do the interviewers do this? They put you through this to see how you react. Can you defend yourself and your answers without getting defensive? Can you maintain your cool and your professionalism? Can you handle it if someone snaps at you or will you crumble and cry?

The second type is the silent treatment. The interviewer doesn't smile; he usually sits in silence waiting to see if you start talking. If you ask the interviewer a question, he'll usually shoot back a one word answer. He might question many of your statements, making you explain even the simplest of answers.

Why do they do this? They'll tell you that silence leads to stupid statements, where interviewees will blurt out irrelevant conversation just to fill the silence, and it's important to know how you would react in a situation like this with a client.

Sometimes during a case you'll be asked to make a decision. You will be forced to choose between A and B. If you choose A, the interviewer will look you right in the eye and say, "Let me tell you why you are wrong." If you had chosen B, he would have looked you right in the eye and said, "Let me tell you why you are wrong." It doesn't matter which one you choose, He is going to tell you why you are wrong. Again, he does this to see how you react. Do you turn red? Does your jaw tighten or do your eyebrows shoot up? Clients are going to challenge your findings and ideas all the time. He wants to make sure you can handle criticism when someone gets in your face.

While he is telling you why you are wrong, if you don't find his answer very persuasive, then simply say, "That was an interesting argument, but I didn't find it compelling enough. I'm sticking with answer A." That's what he wants you to do: stick with your answer if you think you are right. Defend your answer without getting defensive.

If in his argument he brings up something that you didn't think about and now that you're thinking about it, it changes everything, admit that you were wrong. Simply say, "That was a very persuasive argument, and to be honest, I didn't think about the inventory issue. I think you're right; I think B is the right answer." There is no shame in changing your answer if you were wrong. It shows that you are still objective and open to reason. Remember, one of the main reasons corporations hire consulting firms is because of their objectivity. If you can remain objective about your answer, then you are one step closer to being a consultant. What he doesn't want you to do is change your answer just because he said you were wrong.

+ Confidence

To add to the fun, while all this is going on, you need to sound confident even if you don't feel it. If your confidence level is too low, they're going to question everything you say. There is an old saying about Harvard professors: they're often wrong, but never uncertain. You need to carry that same mindset into your interview. Even if you are uncertain, you need to remain confident.

Rules for stress interviews

- Don't take it personally
- Try not to get flustered
- Roll with the punches
- Watch what you say; make sure that it is relevant to the interview
- Remain confident

+ Advice for International Students

Having spent 18 years at Harvard, I've advised thousands of international students pursuing a career in consulting. Most of these students wanted to work initially in the United States before returning to their home countries. While many were successful, like their American classmates, the majority were not. Consulting jobs are very competitive and highly sought after. I offer three additional pieces of advice for international students.

1. Communication skills
Be honest with yourself about your language skills. Much of the interview process is driven by communication skills. Are you truly fluent in English? Do you have an accent? How pronounced is it? A couple of years ago, I worked with a brilliant Chinese student at Harvard. He did very well in the mock case interviews I gave him; however, his language skills, particularly his presentation skills, were poor. While his understanding of English was excellent, his verbal and written skills left much to be desired. Against my advice he applied to the Boston offices of all the top firms. While he received a number of first round interviews, he didn't get a single second round interview. He found himself competing against American Harvard students and he didn't stand a chance.

2. Think long-term and play to your strengths
I met several times with a Russian student. Her English was excellent, she could articulate her thoughts and she even had a good command of "business English". While she had an Eastern European accent, she was easy to understand. Her grades, work experience and extracurricular activities were just okay, but nothing great, so she faced some pretty stiff competition from her American classmates. She wanted to work in New York. Her problem was getting the first round interview. We talked about thinking long-term. If she applied to the Moscow office of these firms, she would have a significantly better chance of getting hired than if she focused on New York. She knew the language, the culture, the economics of the region, and she had a degree from a prestigious American university. She could work in Moscow for two years then transfer back to the United States; which is exactly what she did.

3. Come back to campus in case-fighting form
Summer internships are tough to get, so don't get discouraged if you don't land one. I have pockets full of stories about students who didn't get a summer internship but landed a full-time consulting job upon graduation. There are many more full-time opportunities than summer

positions, but it is still very competitive. Don't waste your summer; use it to become a better candidate in the autumn. The first step is to secure a summer job where you will be developing some of the same skills you would if you worked in a consulting firm. The second is to practice your cases over the summer. I had a brilliant student from the Caribbean who had no business experience but plenty of great leadership experience. He received four first round summer internship interviews. He made it to the second round with two firms but didn't get an offer. He spent the summer working for a large international financial agency in Washington, DC where he wanted to settle. He spent the summer contacting alumni who worked in the DC offices of the two major consulting firms and invited them out for lunch, coffee and beer. He learned about their firms, and he made great connections within those offices. Every time he sipped a coffee or drank a beer with them, he asked them to give him a case question. This went on all summer long. When he returned to campus in September, he was in case-fighting form and had many supporters within each firm. He ended up with a full-time offer from both McKinsey and BCG.

To summarize:

- Strengthen your communication skills
- Think long term and play to your strengths
- Come back to campus in fighting form

One last note on preparation: Be familiar with business terms and trends. No firm is going to judge you on your business acumen, but if you can't define profit and loss, revenues, fixed and variable costs or cost benefit analysis, then start reading. (Please refer to the Consulting Buzzwords section, p. 216.) You should also read *The Wall Street Journal* every day to keep abreast of national and world news. In other words, climb out of that academic shell and join the rest of the world. Your familiarity with business terms and trends will make it easier for you to communicate with the interviewer and demonstrate your interest in business and consulting.

And now, at last, it's time for...

A case question is a fun, intriguing, and active interviewing tool used to evaluate the multi-dimensional aspects of a candidate.

WHAT FIRMS LOOK FOR

Consultants spend a great deal of their time on the road at the client's site. They work in small teams and are sometimes put in charge of groups of the clients' employees. Often, consultants work under great pressure in turbulent environments while dealing with seemingly unmanageable problems. It takes a certain type of personality to remain cool under pressure, to influence the client without being condescending and to be both articulate and analytical at the same time.

As we said earlier, the business of consulting is really the renting of brains, packaged and delivered with an engaging and confident personality. So as you work through the case, the interviewer is asking herself: Is the candidate...

- relaxed, confident and mature?
- a good listener?
- engaging and enthusiastic?
- exhibiting strong social and presentation skills?
- asking insightful and probing questions?
- able to determine what's truly relevant?
- organizing the information effectively and developing a logical framework for analysis?
- stating assumptions clearly?
- comfortable discussing the multifunctional aspects of the case?
- trying to quantify his response at every opportunity?
- displaying both business sense & common sense?
- thinking creatively?
- rolling with the punches?
- defending himself without being defensive?

Purpose of the Case Question

Interviewers don't ask case questions to embarrass and humiliate you. They don't ask case questions to see you sweat and squirm (although some might consider it a side perk). They do ask case questions...

- to probe your intellectual curiosity
- to test your analytical ability
- to test your ability to think logically and organize your answer
- to observe your thought process
- to probe your tolerance for ambiguity and data overload
- to assess your poise, self-confidence and communication skills under pressure
- to discover your personality
- to see if you're genuinely intrigued by problem-solving
- to determine if consulting is a good "fit" for you

Case Preparation

Case questions can be made simple through preparation and practice. I never like to equate an interview with a test, but they do have in common the fact that the more you prepare, the better you'll do. Maybe you've experienced the feeling of being so prepared for an exam that you can't wait for the professor to hand it out so you can rip right through it. Case questions are the same way. Firms look to see if you have that "rip right through it" look in your eyes. It's called confidence.

Before we look at some cases, it is best to understand The Case Commandments. Follow these rules and your case interviewing life will become much easier.

The Case Commandments

[1. Listen to the Question]

Listening is the most important skill a consultant has. The case isn't about you or the consultant; it's about the client. What are they really asking for? Pay particular attention to the last sentence — one word can change the entire case.

[2. Take Notes]

Taking notes during the case interview allows you to check back with the facts of the case. As someone once said, "The palest ink is stronger than the best memory." If you blank out, all the information is right in front of you.

[3. Summarize the Question]

After you are given the question, take a moment to summarize the highlights out loud:

- it shows the interviewer that you listened
- it allows you to hear the information a second time
- it keeps you from answering the wrong question
- it fills that otherwise awkward pause when you're trying to think of something intelligent to say

[4. Verify the Objectives]

Professional consultants always ask their clients to verify their objectives. Even if the objective seems obvious, there could be an additional, underlying objective. When the objective seems apparent, phrase the question differently: "One objective is to increase sales. Are there any other objectives I should know about?"

[5. Ask Clarifying Questions]

You ask questions for three main reasons:

- to get additional information that will help you identify and label the question
- to demonstrate to the interviewer that you are not shy about asking probing questions under difficult circumstances (something you'll be doing on a regular basis as a consultant)
- to turn the question into a conversation (nothing turns off an interviewer quicker than a five-minute monologue)

In the beginning of the case, you have more latitude in your questioning. You should ask basic questions about the company, the industry, the competition, external market factors and the product. The further you get into the case, the more your questions should switch from open-ended questions to closed-ended questions. You start to get into trouble when you ask broad, sweeping questions that are hard for the interviewer to answer. These kinds of questions give the impression that you're trying to get the interviewer to answer the case for you. You'll know that you crossed that line when the interviewer says to you, "What do you think?" When this happens, substitute assumptions for questions.

[6. Organize Your Answer]

Identify and label your case, then lay out your structure. This is the hardest part of a case, and the most crucial. It drives your case and is often the major reason behind whether you get called back. We will spend more time on this in Chapter Four.

[7. Hold that Thought for "One Alligator"]

The interviewer wants you to think out loud, but also to think before you speak. If you make a statement that is way off base in an interview, the recruiter will wonder if he can trust you in front of a client. If he thinks he can't trust you, the interview is over.

[8. Manage Your Time]

Your answer should be as linear as possible. Don't get bogged down in the details. Answer from a macro-level and move the answer forward. It's easy to lose your way by going off on a tangent. Stay focused on the original question asked. Finally, don't lose track of the question, the objective or the framework. Go back to the original question and objectives during the case to make sure you haven't lost your way.

[9. Work the Numbers]

If possible, try to work numbers into the problem. Demonstrate that you think quantitatively and that you are comfortable with numbers. When doing calculations, explain what you are thinking and how you are going to do it. Take your time. I'd rather have you get it right than make a careless mistake.

[10. Be Coachable]

Listen to the interviewer's feedback. Is she trying to guide you back on track? Pay attention to her body language. Are you boring her? Is she about to nod off? Is she enthralled?

Being coachable also means asking for help when you need it. If you run into a wall, lose your train of thought or are just in over your head, ask for help. There is no shame in asking for help; it's a sign of maturity. Look at it from the interviewer's point of view. If you were working on an actual project and got stuck, she would much rather that you ask for help than waste time spinning your wheels.

[11. Be Creative and Brainstorm]

Some of the best experiences you'll have as a consultant will be brainstorming over Chinese food at 10 o'clock at night. *Brainstorming without commitment*, as consultants call it, allows you to toss out uninhibited suggestions without being married to them. It gives you the opportunity to review all the options and eliminate the inappropriate ones. Consulting firms like liberal arts candidates with intellectual curiosity who can "think outside the box" and offer up a new and interesting perspective.

[12. Exude Enthusiasm and a Positive Attitude]

Earlier we spoke about a "rip right through it" attitude. It's not enough to do well on the case; you have to thrive on the challenge of the case. Recruiters want people who are excited by problem-solving and can carry that enthusiasm throughout the entire interview.

[13. Bring Closure and Summarize]

If you have done all of the above and you've made it through the analysis, the final action is to create a sense of closure by summarizing the case. Review your findings, restate your suggestions and make a recommendation. You don't need to sum up the whole answer; pick two or three key points and touch on those. Students are often afraid to make a recommendation, thinking that their analysis was faulty so therefore their answers will be wrong. There are no wrong answers. Just make sure your answer makes good business sense and common sense.

Types of Case Questions

Case questions generally fall into one of four major categories: brainteasers, back-of-the-envelope questions (which are often called market-sizing questions), factor questions and business case questions. It's quite common to find a market-sizing question enclosed within a larger business case question. Whether fun or frustrating, all case questions are valuable learning experiences.

Brainteasers

Brainteasers are scarce these days, but they still pop up in the occasional first round interview, so it's important to be aware of them. Brainteasers are basically the same riddles and conundrums that we've all been struggling to solve since fourth grade. Some brainteasers have a definite answer; others are more flexible in their solutions. Interviewers are looking to see not only if you can come up with a good answer, but also whether you can handle the pressure. Do you get frustrated, stressed and upset? The key is to keep your cool and try to break the problem down logically. Just give it your best shot and don't be afraid to laugh at your mistakes or be a bit self-deprecating. It makes you human and more fun to be with.

Below is an example of a brainteaser with a definite answer.

The Bags of Gold

Q : 1 ***There are three bags of gold. One of the bags contains fake gold. All the bags and all the coins look exactly alike. There is the same number of coins in each bag. The real gold coins weigh one ounce each, the fake coins weigh 1.1 oz. apiece. You have a one-pan penny scale and one penny, which means you can weigh something just once. (You load the scale, put the penny in, and the scale spits out a piece of paper with the weight.) How can you tell which bag has the fake gold?***

A : 1 *You take one coin from the first bag of gold, two coins from the second bag, and three coins from the third bag. Place them all on the scale. If the coins weigh 6.1 oz., then you know that the first bag held the fake gold. If they weighed 6.2 oz., then it was the second bag. If the coins weighed 6.3 oz., then the third bag held the fake gold.*

There are numerous puzzle and brainteaser books to be found in your local bookstore. If you are worried about these types of questions, you may want to pick up one of these books.

Market-sizing Questions

Market-sizing questions surface all the time and can be found during any round of interviews and within many larger business case questions. The back-of-the-envelope question received its name because the questions used to start with, "You're on an airplane with no books, phone, or any other resources. On the back of an envelope, figure out ..." You'll find some of these questions intriguing; some will be fun, others preposterous. However, it's important to have the "rip right through it" look in your eyes; at least pretend that you're having fun.

Oftentimes during market-sizing questions, all you have to work with are logic and assumptions. There are going to be instances when your assumptions are wrong. Sometimes the interviewer will correct you; other times he will let it go. The interviewer is more interested in your logic and thought process than whether your answer is correct. If you are still concerned, you can always say, "I'm not that familiar with this market, so if my assumptions are off, please correct me." Ninety percent of the time, the interviewer will tell you not to worry about it. Everything you say has the potential to be questioned — be ready to stand behind your assumptions. Your assumptions should be based in some sort of logic. If you just pull them out of the air, you're risking the interviewer aggressively challenging your assumptions and your credibility. Examples are:

- **How many gas stations are there in the US?**
- **How many garden hoses were sold in the US last year?**
- **How many pairs of boxers are sold in the US each year?**
- **How much does a 747 weigh?**

Although they seem similar, these are four very different questions. Here are some hints.

- First of all, there are no right answers. Even if you had just read a *Forbes* article on the number of gas stations and could recite the exact total, the consultants wouldn't care. They want to see how logically you answer the question.
- All you really have to work with are logic and assumptions. If your assumptions are too far off, the interviewer will tell you; otherwise, guesstimate.
- Use easy numbers — round up or down.

MARKET-SIZING QUESTIONS

Your answer should be based on logic and assumptions.

Structure
- Listen to the question, then determine the type of case, population-based, household, general population or preposterous.
- Ask clarifying questions, only if you don't understand the question or terminology.
- Lay out your structure first, the steps you'll need to answer the question, and then go back through it with the numbers.

Assumptions
- Don't worry if your assumptions are off, the interviewer is more interested in your thought process than whether your assumptions are correct.
- If your assumptions are way off they will tell you, otherwise they'll let it go.
- Base your assumptions on some sort of logic otherwise the interviewer might press you on how you drew that conclusion.
- You can group several assumptions into one number (i.e. The 20% takes into account X, Y, and Z.)

Math
- Estimate or round numbers off to make it easier for calculation.
- Write all numbers down.

- Write the numbers down. Half of your brain is trying to figure out how best to answer this question and the other half is trying to remember the sum you just figured. Write the numbers down so you can focus on the process, not the numbers.
- **Determine if this is a population-based question, a household question, an individual question, or a "Who thinks this stuff up?" question. To determine whether it's a population, household, or individual question, ask yourself if the item is used by a population, a household, or an individual.**

❑ **How many gas stations are there in the US? (Population question)**

I live in a town with a population of 30,000. There are six gas stations serving our town. Therefore, I'll assume that each gas station serves about 5,000 customers. If the population of the US is 300 million, I'll just divide 300 million by 5,000 and get 60,000 gas stations in the US.

If you tried to answer this question based on households or individuals you would quickly find yourself mired in numerous and unnecessary calculations.

❑ **How many garden hoses were sold in the US last year? (Household question)**

The population of the US is 300 million people. The average US household is made up of 3 people, so we are talking about 100 million households. (You always want to work with 100 million households in the US and 200 million in Europe.)

I'm going to estimate that 50 percent of the households are either suburban or rural. That makes 50 million households. I'll also assume that 20 percent of those homes are apartments or condos. That narrows us down to 40 million houses which most likely use a garden hose. Garden hoses are relatively inexpensive, so people are likely to have a hose in the front and a hose in the back yard. That makes 80 million hoses. I want to add in another 10 million hoses which can be found in nurseries, zoos, and other outdoor facilities. Most of those businesses have at least two hoses.

We are now up to 90 million garden hoses. Hoses aren't replaced every year. I'd say that they are replaced every 3 years unless they are run over by a lawn mower or run into the business end of a dog's tooth. So we take 90 million hoses, divide it by 3 and come up with 30 million garden hoses sold each year.

❑ **How many pairs of boxers are sold in the US each year? (Individual question)**

I'm going to start by stating some assumptions. I'm going to assume that the population of the US is 300 million, that the life expectancy is 80 years, and that there are the same number of people in each age group (i.e., there is the exact same number of 3 year-olds as 73 year-olds). So if you divide 300 million by 80, you get a little over 3.75 million people per age group. We'll round it off to 4 million people. I will also assume a 50/50 split between men and women.

Children ages 0 – 3 mostly wear diapers, and kids ages 4 – 9 mainly wear jockey-style. So we'll focus on the ages between 10 and 80. That's 70 years to cover. I'm going to go out on a limb here and say that only 10% of females ages 10 – 30 own a pair of boxers and, of that group, each might buy one pair a year.

So:
(2 million females x 20 years) x 10% = **4 million boxers.**

Males between the ages of 10 and 20 wear them as a fashion statement, so I'll assume that 75% wear boxers and that they buy 3 pairs a year (the economical 3-pack).

So:
(2 million males x 10 years) x 75% = 15 million boxers
15 million boxers x 3 pairs = **45 million boxers.**

Of males between the ages of 21 and 80 (round off to 60 years), 50% wear boxers and buy or receive as birthday or holiday gifts 6 pairs (2 sets of 3-packs) a year.

So:
(2 million males x 60 years) x 50% = 60 million males wearing boxers.
60 million x 6 pairs = **360 million pairs of boxers.**

Add them all together:
4 million + 45 million + 360 million = 409 million pairs of boxer shorts were sold in the US last year.

❑ **How much does a 747 weigh? ("Who thinks this stuff up?" question)**

Your guess is as good as mine. Ask questions, then break down the elements and make assumptions. Are there passengers on board? No. Any baggage? No. Are the fuel tanks full or empty? Full. Any food or beverages on board? No.

Now you just go ahead and calculate the weight of each part of the plane.

- **8 full fuel tanks:** I'll assume the plane can fly 6,000 miles and uses 10 gallons to the mile. So that's 60,000 gallons at 2 pounds a gallon equals 120,000 pounds.
- **18 tires:** I'll assume that the tires weigh 200 pounds each — that's 3,600 pounds.
- **4 engines:** I'll assume 2,500 pounds each, which adds another 10,000 pounds.
- **2 wings:** 200 feet long by 30 feet wide is 6,000 square feet, times a square foot weight of 5 pounds times 2 wings equals 60,000 pounds.
- **Interior:** 75 rows of seats times 4 feet per row equals 300 feet. Add on the cockpit, bathrooms, etc. — let's say around 400 feet long. I assume that the average weight per foot is 10 pounds, which equals 4,000 pounds.
- **The seats:** They number, say, 500 and weigh 10 pounds each, so that's 5,000 pounds.
- **Air in the cabin:** It's captured air so we need to add one ton for the air in the cabin — 2,000 pounds.
- **The aluminum exterior:** It's pretty thin and lightweight. If the plane is 400 feet long by 25 feet high, then about 10,000 exterior square feet at 1 pound per foot equals 10,000 pounds.
- **Miscellaneous materials:** The tail, overhead bins, carpet, stairs and bathroom fixtures add on, say, another 2,000 pounds.

Now you add up the pieces:
120,000 + 3,600 + 10,000 + 60,000 + 4,000 + 5,000 + 2,000 + 2,000 + 10,000 = 216,000, or round up to 220,000 pounds, or **110 tons**

❑ **How many NetFlix DVDs get lost in the mail each year? (Household problem)**

There are 300 million Americans. The average American household is made up of 3 people, thus there are 100 million American households. In order to order NetFlix, you need access to the Internet and to own a DVD player. I'll assume that 50% of American households have both access to the Internet and a DVD player. That gives us 50 million households.

Netflix was first to market, and they've been around for about eight years. They have a great marketing campaign and good customer service. However, consumers still like to go to the video store, can download movies on their iPods®, have access to video on demand, and Blockbuster recently entered the DVD by mail market as well. Considering all this, I'll assume that 10% of the households have NetFlix. That means that NetFlix has 5 million subscribers.

Netflix has different service plans where consumers can rent anywhere from one to five DVDs at a time. I'll assume that the average NetFlix household rents four movies per month. Five million subscribers renting four movies a month equals 20 million DVDs a month or 240 million DVDs a year. Taking in to account that the DVD makes a round trip from NetFlix to my house and back again, I'll assume that 1% of the DVD mailers get lost in the mail. Based on those assumptions I'd estimate that 2.4 million DVDs get lost in the mail each year.

Notes: I was conservative with my estimates. The advantage of this is that it keeps your numbers manageable. Otherwise I could be calculating in the billions.

❑ **Estimate the size of the bubble gum market in the US (Population question)**

First, I'm going to make a few assumptions. I'll assume that there are 280 million Americans and that the average life expectancy of an American is 80 years. I'm also going to assume that there is an even number of people in each age category. So, I divide 280 million by 80 and get 3.5 million people in each age group. To make things easier, I'm going to calculate assuming 50 weeks in a year.

I'd also like to think about where bubble gum is sold. As I remember, bubble gum is sold in packs of 10 pieces in convenience stores, grocery stores, bodegas, newsstands, etc. You can also find bubble gum inside baseball trading cards and gumball machines.

I'm going to break the population down into different age categories, estimate the number of people who chew bubble gum in each age group, and the number of pieces they chew each week and convert that into an annual number. Let's make a chart.

Ages	No. People	No. that Chew	Pieces per week	Pieces per year
0–5	17.5m	1m	2	100m
6–10	17.5m	12m	10	6b
11–15	17.5m	12m	20	12b
16–20	17.5m	10m	5	2.5b
21–40	70m	4m	1	200m
40–80	140m	1m	1	50m
Totals	280m	40m		20.85b

So I'm going to say that 20 billion pieces of bubble gum are sold each year. Ten pieces per pack equals 2 billion packs, at 50 cents a pack, equals $1 billion.

With a "population type" market-sizing case that you think you'll break down by generation, have certain numbers and assumptions planned out in advance. Pick a number (like 280 million Americans) that is easily divisible by four so you'll know in advance how many people per generation. You wouldn't believe the number of people who stumble through this, come up with odd numbers, and thus start off on the wrong foot.

As in the pacemaker example, (see chart at right) I'll assume that there are 280 million Americans and the average life expectancy is 80 years. I'm going to break them down by generation assuming equal numbers within each generation.

Ages	No. of people in millions	% that need pacemakers	No. of people with pacemakers
0–20	70	0	0
21–40	70	1	.7
41–60	70	2	1.4
61–80	70	5	3.5
Total	280		5.6

Also, when you are determining percentages of the generations, use easy numbers like 1%, 2%, 5%, 10%, etc. You want to make it as easy for yourself as you can.

❑ **There were 165,000 American children born with autism last year. What percentage of the babies born that year are autistic? (Population question)**

There are 300 million Americans. I'll assume that the average life expectancy of an American is 80 years. I'll also assume that there are even numbers of people in each age category; thus, there are the same number of 3 year-olds as 73 year-olds. 300 million divided by 80 years equal 3.75 million people per age group. We can assume that 3.75 million children were born last year: 165,000 divided by 3.75 million equals 0.044 or around 5 percent.

▶ Factor Questions

Factor questions usually start with "What factors influence..." or "What factors would you consider...". The factor questions are gaining popularity when time is short and interviewers can't devote significant time to walking you through an entire case but want to see how you think in broad strokes. They may also pop up in place of stand-alone market-sizing questions during the first round interviews. Think in broad terms; try not to get too detailed.

❑ **What factors would you consider when marketing a theatrical film?**

First, I'd want to know something about the film, particularly who is its target market. You would have a different marketing strategy for a Baby Boomer film then you would for a Millennial film. Since the majority of the films are geared toward Millennials, I'll use that example.

Millennials spend a lot of time online. There are digital marketing agencies that develop social media APIs called "widgets" which often feature sweepstakes or some call to action and are virally spread across MySpace, Facebook, and Mebo. Similarly a great trailer, sometimes "unauthorized" or seemingly user-generated on YouTube, is often seen by more people than the official trailer, which is placed on traditional TV and shown at theaters before current movies.

Second, I'd like to know, is this a studio film with big name stars attached or an independent film? Is it a branded title, like *American Pie,* or a new indie film without any brand recognition? This is going to determine the number of screens it is shown on. If it is a studio movie showing on 3,000 screens the first week, then most of the marketing budget will be spent in the two weeks prior to the film's release. Ads would be placed on network TV during shows like *American Idol* and *Gossip Girls*. Billboards will be displayed as well as signs on the side of a bus — the more traditional movie marketing efforts. If it is an indie film being shown on 50 screens, then the limited budget has to be allocated toward the more viral online environment. If the film does well and builds a buzz, then the distributor may kick in additional marketing funds as the number of screens increase – think *Slum Dog Millionaire* or *The Wrestler*.

Pan-media 'takeovers' are becoming more commonplace, as a film's stars and creative team will blitz multiple outlets in hopes of achieving a massive opening weekend. In one day, for example, Olivia Wilde might appear on *Good Morning America*, cut a ribbon in a ceremony in Central Park with local TV crews, attend a charity luncheon (photographed for the tabloids) and hit Letterman and Jon Stewart's *The Daily Show*, in the evening — all while the studio is running multiple display ads across Yahoo! and MSN's landing pages. The idea being that 'media ubiquity' will grab the attention of an audience whose consumption habits are becoming increasingly fragmented.

In sum, like anything, you need to analyze the market as well as your product and figure where you'll get the best ROI (return on investment). And because technology is changing so quickly, you need to constantly research new ways to get the word out.

▶ Business Case Questions

Business case questions come in all shapes and sizes, but they usually fall into two categories: (1) numbers cases and (2) business strategy and operations cases.

❑ **Number Cases:** There are pure number cases that are really just math problems you are expected to do in your head. There are also "case-like" numbers cases, which seem like strategy cases but are not. Case-like number cases are about numbers. They sound simple, but most people get them wrong because they don't listen to the question and try to turn it into a strategy case.

- **Pure number cases to do in your head**

A) The total widget market is $170 million and our sales are $30 million. What percentage of the market share do we hold?

B) Our total manufacturing costs are $20 million. With that we can make 39,379 units. What is our approximate cost per unit?

C) Our total costs are $75,000. Labor costs make up 25% of the total costs. How much are our labor costs?

D) You bought a stock for $36 a share. Today it jumped 6%. How much is your stock worth?

E) You raised $3.5 million for a start-up. Your commission is 2.5%. What's your commission in dollars?

F) What's 7 x 45?

G) In 1999, the number of current outstanding shares for Macromedia Inc. was 41,084,000. Institutional investors hold 25,171,000. What is the approximate percentage of shares held by institutions?

	Price	Change	Percentage change
H)	$27.00	$0.54	
I)	$31.00	$0.62	
J)	$40.00	$1.00	
K)	$75.00	%3.00	
L)	$10.00	$1.70	
M)	$50.00	$2.50	

N) Banana Republic makes 14% of The Gap's estimated $16 billion in sales. What are BR's sales?

O) Europe's population is approximately 480 million. By 2012, the EU population is expected to drop to 450 million. What percentage change is that?

Go figure: Try to estimate some of the percentages in your head, and then work out the others without a calculator. Round off the answers as you would during a case question. (worth noting, these are from a 5th grade math test.)

P) 60% of 70 = ___ **Q)** 25% of 124 = ___ **R)** 68% of 68 = ___ **S)** 12% of 83 = ___

T) 23% of 60 = ___ **U)** 27% of 54 = ___ **V)** 13% of 19 = ___ **W)** 65% of 80 = ___

X) 78% of 45 = ___ **Y)** 78% of 90 = ___

Answers:

A) about 18% B) about $500 C) $18,750 D) $38.16 E) $87,500 F) 315 G) 60%

H) 2% I) 2% J) 2.5% K) 4% L) 17% M) 5%

N) approximately $2.3 billion O) Europe's population around -6 percent

P) 42 Q) 31 R)46 S)10 T) 14 U) 15 V) 2 W) 52 X) 35 Y) 70

• Case-like number cases:

Every three minutes an American woman is diagnosed with breast cancer. How many American women will be diagnosed this year?

One woman every three minutes equals 20 women an hour. Twenty women diagnosed an hour times 24 hours in a day equals 480 woman a day. 480 women a day times 365 days equals 175,200 American women diagnosed with breast cancer each year.

In Brazil, each airline is allocated a certain number of landing spots: Airline A 2,000, Airline B 1,000, Airline C 500 and Airline D 100. Airline C goes out of business and its landing spots are distributed proportionally to the other airlines. How many spots does each airline get?

You find the percentage of landing spots each airline has without C. Airline A has 65% of 3,100 spots, B has 32% and Airline D has 3%. Next you figure out what percentage of the 500 spots C used to have. Thus A has 65% of 500 which equals 325; B has 32% of 500 which equals 160; and C has 3% which equals 15. Add them up and they total 500.

American Express is facing stiff competition from a host of new credit cards that have no annual fee and low interest rates. In response, American Express is considering dropping its $50 annual fee. What are the economics of dropping the $50 fee? (This is a popular case and one that has repeatedly turned up in interviews.)

Nine out of 10 students think this case is about competition. They focus their answer on strategy and alternatives to dropping the fee. The first part of this question is not relevant. The real question is **"What are the economics of dropping the $50 fee?"**

In order to answer this question, you need to ask three questions:

- How many card members does Amex have?
- What is the average amount that each card member spends annually?
- What are Amex's revenue streams?

Amex has 10 million card members. Amex card members average $2,000 a year in purchases. Amex makes 2% from each purchase.

Amex Revenues:

10 million customers paying a $50 annual fee equals $500 million. Each member spends $2,000 x 2% = $40 a year x 10 million customers = $400 million. Total revenues then = $900 million, with 55% of that figure coming from fees.

Would card members spend more money if they didn't have to pay the annual fee? Amex card members would have to more than double their purchases to make up for the loss in fee revenues. It seems unlikely that they would go from spending $2,000 a year to spending $5,000 a year because of a dropped $50 fee. Even a modest bump in new members couldn't make up the difference.

How many new customers would Amex have to secure in order to make up the $500 million difference? Amex would have to more than double its card members from 10 million to about 25 million in a short period — say, two years. Is that feasible? It took Amex 25 years to reach the 10 million customer base it currently has. So doubling it in two years seems unrealistic.

My advice to Amex is to keep its fee in place.
That's it. That's the answer. The interviewer doesn't want to hear about reducing the fee to $25 or turning Amex into a credit card. This is a straightforward question. Listen to the question.

❑ **Business Strategy and Operations Cases:** Some business strategy and operations cases should be answered in less than 15 minutes. These are referred to as mini-cases. An example:

- *GE has invented a new light bulb that never burns out. It could burn for more than 500 years and it would never blink. The director of marketing calls you into her office and asks, "How would you price this?" What do you tell her?* *(See answer on page 82.)*

A regular case question, like the DuPont case below, could take anywhere from 25 to 35 minutes to answer. It could be a market-sizing question and a strategy question all rolled into one, such as:

- *DuPont has just invented a lightweight, super-absorbent, biodegradable material that would be perfect for disposable diapers. Estimate the size of the diaper market and tell me if Dupont should enter this market and if so, how?* *(See answer on page 84.)*

Written Case Questions and Tests

Over the last couple of years, we have seen more and more firms turn to written cases, particularly in the second and third rounds. Monitor Group was the first to pioneer the written case. Since then they have added a few new twists to the process. The interview can go something like this:

You arrive for the interview and are handed a written case (usually about five pages; three pages of text and two pages of charts and graphs). You are given 20 to 30 minutes to read and take notes. When the time is up, a consultant comes in and you are expected to "present" the case, much like in a business school class. More often than not it turns into a discussion. Chances are you will be touching on all the same points as you would if given a verbal case.

Here's where it gets really interesting. Sometimes when you have finished reading the case, you are taken into a room where you'll meet two to three other candidates (you all have read the same case and are applying for the same position). Again, you are expected to "present" the case. The consultants watch closely to see how you interact with the other candidates. Are you dominating the discussion? Are you sitting back and being dominated by others? Or are you building on what the other candidates say in a positive and civil manner? The Monitor consultants look to see how you interact with your peers. Are you a team player? Do you play well with others? Can you hold your own? It all boils down to fit, communication skills, respect for others, empathy and teamwork.

This is taking the brilliance of case questions as an interviewing tool one step further.

There could be one last twist. Sometimes when you arrive, you are joined by two or three other candidates in a small conference room. You are all given the same case and asked to present it in 20 minutes. A Monitor consultant stays in the conference room with you to monitor the group's interaction and dynamics while assessing the leadership skills of all the candidates. When your team is ready to present, two other consultants join in and your "team" presents the case.

Now, one, two or all three of the candidates might be called back for the next round. While you act as part of a team during presentation of the case, you are all judged individually.

Besides the Monitor format, we have seen other firms develop their own version of a written case. The most common one is similar to Monitor case. The interviewer will give you two – three pages of written text and tell you to read it and then be prepared to present the case. They will also want you to prepare three PowerPoint® slides to go along with your presentations. Keep in mind that you have no calculator or computer, which means no PowerPoint® or Chart Wizard®.

The other type of written case is when a consultant gives you a 120-page document and tells you to read it and present it to him in 30 minutes. In a case like this, you'll want to read the executive summary upfront and then spend the rest of the time in the back of the document analyzing the exhibits. You can learn much more by studying the exhibits than by reading as far as you can in the document.

McKinsey & Company now requires that some candidates take a written test. "The test is testing problem-solving in a written format; folks will be surprised that the straight 'quant' questions are the minority. It's not like a GRE quant test," explains a senior McKinsey recruiter.

"The bulk of it involves making judgment calls/recommendations based on information available to you at that point," the recruiter explains. "The exercise is supposed to feel like a case interview, but with multiple choice responses."

Last year the McKPST contained 26 questions and you got an hour to complete it. Candidates receive a bit more information about the business, the environment and the problem with each question.

Students can't bring in calculators or scratch paper. The test was developed internally by McKinsey and validated by Applied Psychological Techniques, Inc. (APT). "It was fun, now that it's over," recounts a non-MBA Harvard graduate student. "There are some ratios and percentages, a couple formulas, but nothing too overwhelming. Also, a few charts are used to present some of the information, but again fairly basic, in my opinion."

A McKinsey recruiter states, "You need to be comfortable with calculating some percentages, basic equations, understanding relationships among data, but nothing terribly advanced."

Some international offices have a math section that one student says is more like the GMAT than the GRE. You have 18 questions and get 30 minutes to complete it. "You start with probability and it gets harder from there," recounts a Harvard graduate student.

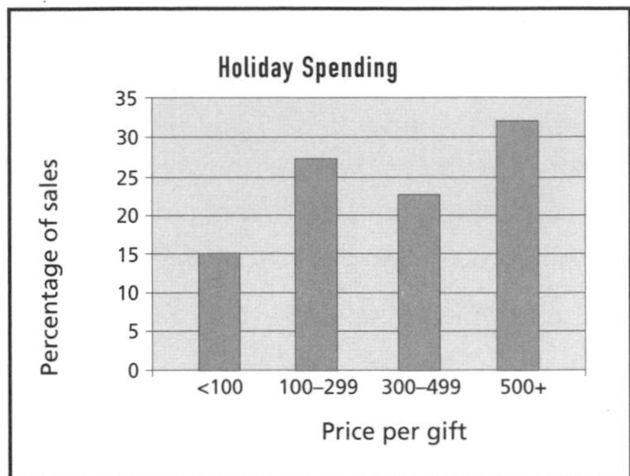

Source: The Conference Board 2005

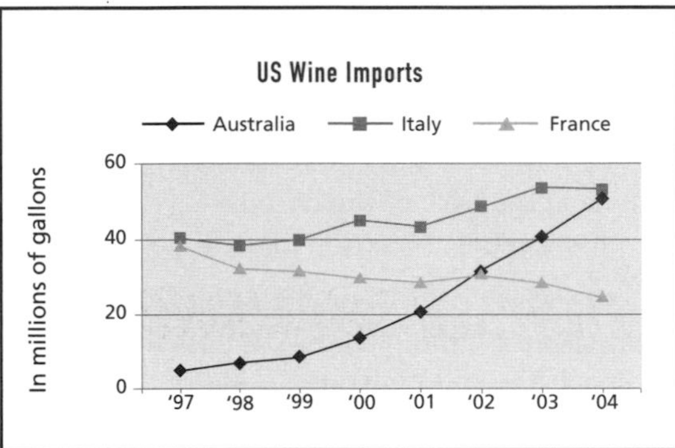

Source: US Commerce Department

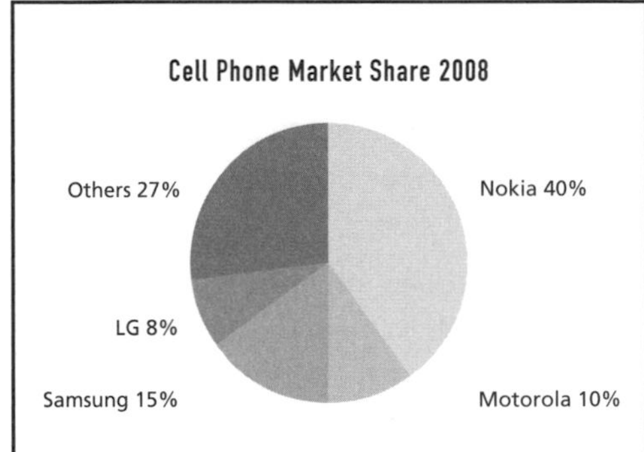

The McKinsey recruiter explains, "The resulting score is used as one more 'data point' on problem-solving for the interviewers to refer to if they have concerns or opposing reads.
There is no magic or required score, and performance in face-to-face interviews are of greater importance to us."

Reading Charts and Graphs. One of the best ways to shake the dust off your chart and graph reading is to look at the charts and graphs printed in *The Wall Street Journal* and *The Economist* and draw some conclusions. Then read the article and compare your thoughts to the main points of the article.

Making Slides and Graphs. There is another twist: making slides and graphs. The recruiter hands you a few pages of data and asks that you create (on paper) three or four PowerPoint® slides. You are then expected to present them during the case as you would during a presentation to a client.

You will be given charts, sometimes at the outset of the case. Sometimes they slip them in the middle of the case, changing the dynamics of the question. You are expected to quickly analyze the charts, extract the most important information and then apply it to your answer. It is easy to get overwhelmed. Candidates tend to get beleaguered by the pressure to perform and don't always see the elegance of the chart or the simplicity of the message.

Therefore, as you look at each chart, I recommend that you eyeball the numbers, round them off and then determine how they are related to one another, what trends do you see and what message do you derive from what you see?

As you review the charts, there are three easy steps that will help you get your bearings:

(i) identify the chart form — is it a bar graph, a line chart, or pie chart
(ii) determine what comparison each chart calls for
(iii) summarize the message

Chances are you will only need to use one of the three basic graph forms: the bar graph, the line graph or the pie chart (BCG doesn't like pie charts). Be sure to give your charts and graphs an appropriate title that explains what the data measure.

Use the bar graph when you want to show relationships between groups. The two items being compared don't need to affect each other. The top chart shows what percentage of holiday sales fall into what price category.

Trends over time are generally shown in line graphs. The line graph plots the rise and fall of one data set or multiple data sets. The line graph is needed when you want to show the effect of an independent variable on a dependent variable. The second chart follows US wine import levels from Australia, Italy and France over an eight-year period.

A pie chart is used to show how something relates to the whole. It usually deals with percentages. This last chart shows the market share of the US cell phone market in 2008.

+ Irking the Interviewer

Interviewers get easily bored and irked. Let's face it, these guys and gals spend most of their days telling the CEOs of Fortune 1,000,000 companies what to do. Now they've been yanked out of a really important assignment to interview you and a dozen of your closest friends. Yawn …"I postponed my meeting with Bill Gates for this? Dazzle me!"

The first step toward CID (Case Interview Dazzlement) is to avoid costly and obvious mistakes. Listed below are the most common mistakes that past interviewees (some still unemployed) made.

❑ **The Leno / Letterman syndrome**
A five-minute monologue will do more to hurt your career than any of the other mistakes. Remember, you ask questions not only to get additional information but to draw the interviewer into the case with you. Make the interviewer feel that he is a stakeholder in your candidacy. Turn the question into a conversation.

❑ **What was the question again?**
Listen to the question, write it down, then repeat it to the interviewer. Candidates are always answering the wrong question because they don't take the time to identify what the interviewer is really asking.

❑ **Explosion of the mouth**
I see it all the time: people can't give me the answer fast enough. Slow down. Don't jump off the mark and give the first answer that pops into your head. Take your time and analyze the information. The interviewer is there to observe the logic and thought process behind your answer.

❑ **Digression city**
You go off on a tangent because it's easy, you're on a roll and it provides you with a false sense of security. You think it hides the fact that you can't move forward in your answer, but it doesn't. Tangents take you off the path and it becomes extremely difficult to get back on the straight and narrow.

A case question is like a long corridor with numerous side doors. Suppose the question was, "How do we increase sales for the local 7-Eleven convenience store?" You start walking down the corridor and you open the first door on the right and yell, "We can raise our prices." Close the door and move on to the next door. Open that door and yell, "We need to get more people in the store." Close the door and move on.

The problem arises when you open the door and yell, "We need to get more people in the store." Then you start walking down the side hall trying to come up with creative ways to get more people in the door. You come up with all sorts of promotions involving your favorite late-night snack food. Hey, this is easy! But that's NOT the question.

❑ **The bull in the consulting china shop**
Don't use terms that you don't fully understand. Throwing out a buzzword or business term in the wrong context highlights the fact that you have a nasty habit of discussing things you know little about. You may be able to get away with that in class, but it doesn't fly in a case interview. If you do that in an interview, will the firm be able to trust you in front of a client?

❑ **Asking open-ended questions**
Open-ended questions that try to get the interviewer to answer the case for you will irk the interviewer, big time. It is far better to make assumptions than to ask the interviewer for the answer. An example would be if you were reviewing labor costs.

Right: Because the economy is strong and there are plenty of jobs, I'll assume that our labor costs have gone up.

Wrong: What has been going on with our labor costs?

❑ **Silence**
One of the questions I get asked most often is about silence. Is it ever okay to be silent? Yes and no. The simple rule to remember is that silence is okay when you are doing something like calculating, writing down your thoughts or drawing a graph or decision tree. You can get up to

40 seconds of silence before the awkward clock starts ticking and the interviewer get restless. It is not okay when you are just thinking while staring out the window or looking down at your shoes, particularly in the beginning of the case. If the interviewer gives you the case and you just sit there thinking you lost your momentum, you are sitting dead in the water. (See The First Four Steps and read Summarizing the Question on page 34.)

+ If You Get Stuck

If you get stuck during a case and the interviewer doesn't ask you a question to help you along, then there a few things you can do. First, take a moment to recap where you've been. Chances are you've either gone into too much detail and are now stuck in the mud or you went off on a tangent. Recapping pulls you out of the mud and back above the trees. Remember, for the most part, you want to view the case from a macro point of view. Many times as you recap you can see where you got off track. The second thing is to quickly run through the Five C's (see page 51) in your head to see if there is something obvious that you missed. Finally, if you are still stuck, ask for help. There is no shame in asking for help. If we were working on a project together, I would much rather have you ask me for help than have you waste a lot of time banging your head against a wall. That being said, I wouldn't ask for help more than once.

+ The Trouble with Math

Do you have trouble doing math in your head? Are you often off by a zero? When I do case interviews with students, the most common problem is basic math. It's the zeros that students have trouble with. From Ph.D.s to undergraduates, it's the zeros. Take a look at the table below, and get to know it very well.

Number Table*

	10	100	1,000	10,000	100,000
10	100	1,000	10,000	100,000	1,000,000
100	1,000	10,000	100,000	1,000,000	10,000,000
1,000	10,000	100,000	1,000,000	10,000,000	100,000,000
10,000	100,000	1,000,000	10,000,000	100,000,000	1,000,000,000
100,000	1,000,000	10,000,000	100,000,000	1,000,000,000	10,000,000,000

* Number Table produced and designed by Maria Teresa Petersen, Harvard MPP '01.

+ Notes Design

While there is no standard for notetaking, the landscape format is becoming the norm. The first page of notes is divided into two sections.

Case Notes. In this section write down all the information that the interviewer gives you. Be sure to verify the objective.	Write the objective(s) across the top of this section. Write the answers to questions that you asked about the case. Draw or lay out your structure. E (P = R - C) M

Many consulting firms favor the use of graph paper. There are several reasons why.

- Graph paper makes it easier to draw your notes.
  - Be visual with your notes. Draw boxes, graphs, arrows, decision trees, value chains, and flow charts.
  - When appropriate, turn your notes toward the interviewer to explain your thought process. It makes him feel more like a team member and less like an interviewer.
- Graph paper lines up your zeros. There is a lot of math in these questions and you can't use a calculator. It is not always easy to tell when you are off by a zero when your answer has eight zeros at the end of it.
- Graph paper organizes your notes. Well-organized notes make it easier for the interviewer to follow. When he isn't looking into your eyes, he's looking at your notes to see what you wrote down because he knows what you should be writing down. In addition, there is a good chance that the interviewer will collect your notes at the end of the interview. He uses your notes as one more data point — what did you write down? how did you write it? how did you do your math? and can he read your handwriting?

When it comes time for the case portion of your interview, rip out five pages of graph paper and number them (you can do this before the interview to save time and look well-organized). Remember to just write on one side of the page. Flipping pages back and forth can be disruptive and it makes it hard to find important data at a glance. Using bullet points will make your notes seem better organized and makes it easier to go back to find information. Star or highlight important points that you think will make the summary. This way those points will jump out at you when it comes time to summarize the case.

As you fill up the pages (while leaving plenty of white space on your notes), spread your notes out in front of you. That way you can see the whole case at a glance. You'll want to check the first page of notes from time to time. There is a lot of important information on that first page. Some of it is immediately relevant; some is smoke put there to throw you off track. Other information will become relevant as you move through the case.

Some students use a separate sheet for their math. That way your main notes stay clean and linear. If you do use a separate sheet, make sure that you label each calculation so you can tie it back into the case and are not left looking at a page full of random calculations.

Oftentimes the interviewer will hand you a chart. Always ask for permission before you write on the chart. As strange as it may seem, sometimes interviewers only show up with one copy of a chart.

✢ The Summary and The Final Slide

In most case interviews you will be asked to summarize the case. You need to jump right into this without any down time to collect your thoughts. A good summary is about a minute, minute and a half. It is not a rehash of everything you spoke about; it is a short recap of the problem and two or three main points that you want the interviewer to remember.

In some cases — particularly those that compare two or more strategies, ideas or options using the same criteria — you can create the 'final slide' right at the beginning of the case. No one ever remembers to do this, so if you can think of it, you'll score big points with the interviewer.

On a separate sheet of paper you draw a chart listing the product or markets (whatever it is that you are comparing) and below that the criteria. As you calculate the numbers, fill them in on the final slide; it keeps all relevant information in one place and it makes it easier for the interviewer to follow (think of it as a scorecard). Once all the information is filled out, the student turns the final slide towards the interviewer and walks him through it. It is the best summary. It is similar to the final slide of a deck that a consultant would present to a client. In the Partner Cases section of the book (page 169) there are two great examples of the final slide.

✢ Case Journal

I had a student that had graduated Phi Beta Kappa from an Ivy League school. She had spent her time between undergrad and graduate school working for a non-profit. While at Harvard's Kennedy School, she decided that she wanted to do consulting, but she had no business background. Her first attempt at a mock case interview with me was a disaster. That day she started a journal. She recorded structures, concepts, ideas and strategies for every live case she did with me, her classmates and alumni (she did around 30 live cases) and every case that she read (which was about 80 cases). When she had spare moments between classes or riding on the bus, she would flip through her journal. When she read articles in *The Wall Street Journal*, *Business Week* or *The McKinsey Quarterly*, she would add to her journal. It never left her side.

She ended up at a top firm and took the journal with her. With every engagement she learned something new and would add it to her journal. When she and her co-worker sat around brainstorming problems she would flip through her journal and throw out ideas which often sparked discussions and occasionally lead to a solution.

I saw her five years after she had graduated and she still had her journal. Although it was as beat up as Indiana Jones's journal, it held just as many treasures. She was headed to a new job and the journal was the first thing she packed.

Since then, I have recommended creating a journal whenever I speak at schools. Besides keeping all your notes in one place, it becomes a single source for case material that is also extremely helpful for your classes. If you are truly serious about case interviewing, then you will continue to read and practice all summer long. Recruiting events start as soon as you get back to campus, so if you take the time over the summer to practice, life is going to be easier in the fall.

Best Case Thinking

In my years of training Harvard students to answer case questions, I've realized that the major problem many of my students have is simply getting started. Sometimes they're overwhelmed, sometimes they're nervous and sometimes they just don't have a clue. So in 1996, with the help of a student, I developed the Tomensen/Cosentino Case Framework. Over the years it has been successfully tested in thousands of case interviews. After hundreds of debriefings, I have refined it, simplified it and renamed it. But the biggest change is that I turned it from a framework into a system, The Ivy Case System©.

A framework is a structure that helps you organize your thoughts and analyze the case in a logical manner. Often; however, you have to cut and paste from a number of frameworks in order to answer any single case question. As I've mentioned, the difference between a framework and a system is that a framework is really a tool, while a system is a process. Instead of memorizing seven individual frameworks and then trying to decide which one(s) to apply, you learn the system, which already has the tools built in.

The Ivy Case System© is a two-part system made up of four easy steps to get you going and 12 popular case scenarios (see sidebar), each equipped with a collection of ideas and questions that will help you structure the remainder of your response. If you follow through the outline I've given for each scenario, you can be confident that your response will be logical and cohesive. You will find that there is much overlap between the 12 scenarios, so that you're not learning 12 different ideas, you're learning maybe five. And because it is all based on business sense and common sense, you'll find that there is nothing in there that you don't already know … it is just organized a little differently.

These first four steps will provide you with a quick start (no long, awkward pause between question and answer). They'll get you five minutes into the question, give you momentum and provide you with enough information to decide which of the 12

THE TWELVE CASE SCENARIOS

Business cases have traditionally focused on either business strategy or business operations. However, with today's more complex cases, candidates are getting case questions that cover both categories and multiple scenarios.

Strategy Scenarios:

1. Entering a new market
2. Industry analysis
3. Mergers and Acquisitions
4. Developing a new product
5. Pricing strategies
6. Growth strategies
7. Starting a new business
8. Competitive response

Operations Scenarios:

9. Increasing sales
10. Reducing costs
11. Improving the bottom line
12. Turnarounds

When operations cases are really about strategy (e.g., Strategy: Should we proceed with a turnaround? vs. Operations: How do we proceed with a turnaround?) then think about using cost benefit analysis.

case scenarios (or whatever combination thereof) is most appropriate to the case question at hand. You will recognize the four steps from the "Key Guidelines" section.

You may want to read through the following explanation of the Ivy Case System© and then check out a practice case or two to see how the system can be applied. Then it will be time to revisit the system and learn it.

The interviewer has just finished giving you the case. Here's what you do!

+ The First Four Steps

[1. Summarize the Question]

It shows the interviewer that you listened. It allows you to hear the information again. It keeps you from answering the wrong question. And it fills the gap of silence between the interviewer's question and your answer. When listening to the question, try to weed out the irrelevant information to hear what the interviewer is asking; one word in the question could make a big difference in your answer.

[2. Verify the Objectives]

You can bet that when a consultant has her first meeting with a client, she always asks about objectives and goals. What are the client's expectations, and are those expectations realistic? Even if the objective to your case seems obvious, there is always a possibility of an additional, underlying objective. So ask, "One objective is to raise profits. Are there any other objectives that I should know about?" If the interviewer says, "No. Higher profits is the only objective," then we can determine that the choice of case scenario comes directly from the objective. If there are two objectives, you will probably need to break the case in half and tackle one objective at a time.

At this point you should be able to determine whether this is a numbers case and should proceed accordingly. (Look back to page 22 for more information on numbers cases.)

[3. Ask Clarifying Questions]

As we've said, you ask questions for three reasons: to get additional information, to show the interviewer that you are not shy about asking questions and to turn the case into a conversation. The key is to ask broad, open-ended questions that help you narrow the information at the start, because as the case progresses, you'll lose your "right" to ask these sweeping questions. (It may give the impression that you're trying to get the interviewer to answer the case for you.) The 12 case scenarios will guide you in asking these questions.

However, if you still don't know which scenario to use — for example, whether this case is about increasing sales or increasing profits (or entering a new market, producing a new product, growing a company...) — you can choose the appropriate case scenario by asking broad, generic questions about:

- the company: Is it public or private? How big is it? Is it growing?

- the industry: Where is the industry in its life cycle?
- competition: Both internal (Who are the major players? What is our market share?) and external market factors (i.e., substitutions, the economy, interest rates, unemployment rate, price-cutting by competitors, rising material costs).
- the product: If it's a new product, ask about both the advantages and the disadvantages. (Everyone forgets to ask about the disadvantages, but oftentimes disadvantages can drive your answer more than the advantages.)

* ***Note:*** *Keep in mind how the economy, the Internet and other new technologies affect each question.*

[4. Lay Out Your Structure]

This is by far the toughest part of the process and you may want to "take a moment" to think about structure at this point. Thirty seconds of silence now may save wasted time later in the interview. You've decided which case scenario(s) to work with, and you have asked a few broad questions that have given you the information you need to form a logical response. Because you have studied the scenarios, you can quickly go through the bullet points in your mind and decide which are most relevant to this particular question. You then just need to clue in the interviewer about how you plan to proceed.

With some cases, laying out your structure is the answer to the case itself — you tell the interviewer how you would go about fulfilling the company's objective, and voilà, you're done. With other cases, you'll actually need to walk through some of your proposed steps. It should be obvious (by the nature of the question and by the interviewer's feedback) which path a specific case calls for.

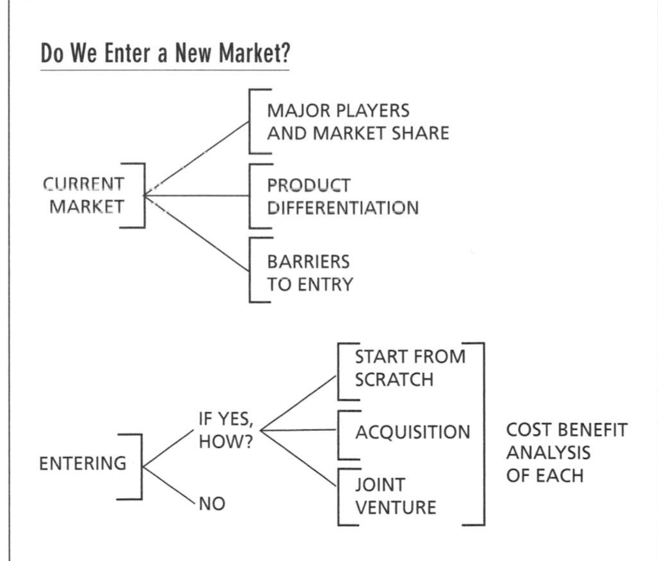

Most consultants think graphically. They communicate to clients through PowerPoint® slides, graphs and charts. Many students find that it helps to draw a decision tree. A decision tree is a map of the reasoning process — visually breaking the case down into components and laying out your structure. It allows you to review your options and investigate the possible outcomes, while weighing the risks and rewards of each course of action.

* ***Note****: The more cases you practice, the more you'll be able to draw on those practice cases during the interview. For example, if you know you're working with an entering a new market case, you can think back to that Yellow Stuff Chemical Company case (page 73) and use it as a guide.*

+ The 12 Case Scenarios

[1. Entering a New Market]

Question: Your client manufactures hair products. It's thinking about entering the sunscreen market. Is this a good idea?

Step 1: Determine why. What's our goal? What's our objective?
Does it fit into our overall strategy?

Step 2: Determine the state of the current and future market.

- What is the size of the market?
- What is the growth rate?
- Where is it in its life cycle? (Stage of development: Emerging? Mature? Declining?)
- Who are the customers and how are they segmented?
- What role does technology play in the industry and how quickly does it change?
- How will the competition respond?

Step 3: Investigate the market to determine whether entering it would make good business sense.

- Who is our competition and what size market share does each competitor have?
- How do their products and services differ from ours?
- How will we price our products or services?
- Are there substitutions available?
- Are there any barriers to entry? Examples are: capital requirements, access to distribution channels, proprietary product technology, government policy.
- Are there any barriers to exit? How do we exit if this market sours?
- What are the risks? For example, market regulation or technology.

Step 4: If we decide to enter the market, we need to figure out the best way to become a player. There are three major ways to entering a market:

- Start from scratch (see Starting a New Business).
- Acquire an existing player within the desired industry.
- Form a joint venture/strategic alliance with another player with similar interests.

Analyze the pros and cons of each. This is sometimes called a cost benefit analysis. You can use this whenever you are trying to decide whether to proceed with a decision.

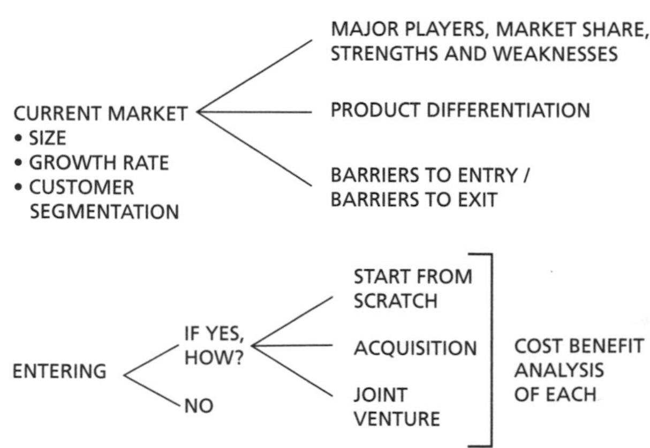

[2. Industry Analysis]

Question: Our client is thinking of acquiring a diversified company that has holdings in three different industries. One of those industries is entertainment. Our client knows nothing about the entertainment industry and has asked us to do an analysis. What do we analyze?

Step 1: Investigate the industry overall.

- Where is it in its life cycle? (Emerging? Mature? Declining?)
- How has the industry been performing (growing or declining) over the last one, two, five and 10 years?
- How have we been doing compared to the industry?
- Who are the major players and what kind of market share does each have? Who has the rest?
- Has the industry seen any major changes lately? These include new players, new technology and increased regulation.
- What drives the industry? Brand, products, size or technology?
- Profitability. What are the margins?

Step 2: Suppliers

- Have the suppliers been consistent? What is going on in their industry? Will they continue to supply us?

Industry Analysis
CURRENT MARKET
LIFE CYCLE (EMERGING? MATURE? DECLINING?)
PERFORMANCE (GROWING OR DECLINING?)
CLIENT'S POSITION WITHIN THE INDUSTRY
MAJOR PLAYERS AND THEIR MARKET SHARE
INDUSTRY CHANGES (NEW PLAYERS, TECHNOLOGY, REGULATIONS)
DRIVERS (BRAND, SIZE, TECHNOLOGY)
PROFITABILITY, MARGINS
SUPPLIERS
HOW MANY?
PRODUCT AVAILABILITY
WHAT'S GOING ON IN THEIR MARKET?
FUTURE
ARE PLAYERS ENTERING OR LEAVING THE MARKET?
MERGERS AND ACQUISITIONS?
BARRIERS TO ENTRY, TO EXIT?
SUBSTITUTES?

Step 3: What is the future outlook for the industry?
- Are players coming into or leaving the industry?
- Have there been many mergers or acquisitions lately?
- What are the barriers to entry and/or to exit?
- Will substitutes be introduced?

[3. Mergers and Acquisitions]

Question: Ben & Jerry's is buying a mid-size cream cheese manufacturer. Does this make sense? What should they be thinking about?

Step 1: Determine the goals and objectives. Why are they buying it? Does it make good business sense, or are there better alternatives? Is it a good strategic move? Other reasons could be to:
- Increase market access
- Diversify their holdings
- Pre-empt the competition
- Gain tax advantages
- Incorporate synergies: marketing, financial, operations
- Create shareholder value

Step 2: How much are they paying?
- Is the price fair?
- How are they going to pay for it?
- Can they afford it?
- If the economy sours, can they still make their debt payments?

Step 3: Due diligence. Research the company and industry.
- What kind of shape is the company in?
- How secure are its markets, customers and suppliers?
- How is the industry doing overall? And how is this company doing compared to the industry? Are they a leader in the field?
- What are the margins like? Are they high volume low margins or low volume high margins?
- How will our competitors respond to this acquisition?
- Are there any legal reasons why we can't, or shouldn't, acquire it?

Step 4: Exit strategies, looking for a way out.
- How long are they planning to keep it?
- Did they buy it to break it up and sell off parts of it?

Mergers and Acquisitions

Objectives, costs, due diligence, exit strategies

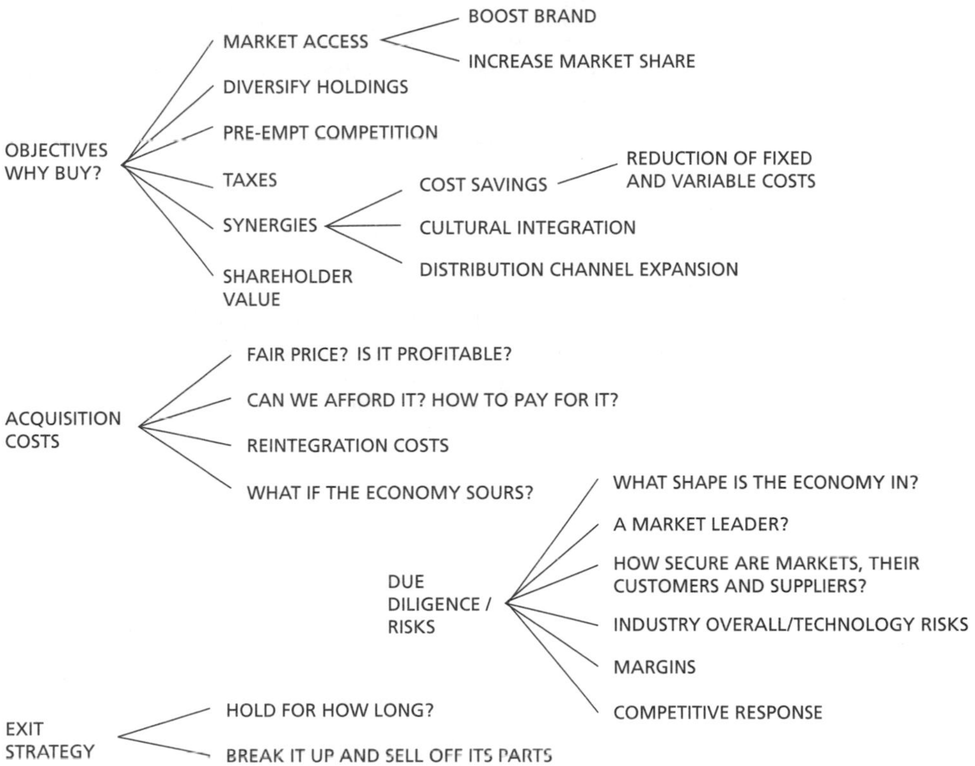

[4. Developing a New Product]

Question: Our client has developed a new biodegradable product, which is both a soft drink and a car wax. What should they be thinking about?

You can approach the next four steps in any order you like.

Step 1: Think about the product.

- What's special or proprietary about our product?
- Is the product patented?
- Are there similar products out there? Are there substitutions?
- What are the advantages and disadvantages of this new product?
- How does the new product fit in with the rest of our product line?

Step 2: Think about our market strategy.

- How does this affect our existing product line?
- Are we cannibalizing one of our existing products?

COST-DRIVEN PRICING
(The Deadly Business Sin)

Before there was Michael Porter and all the other modern day business gurus, there was Peter Drucker. The following is from Peter Drucker's ***Wall Street Journal*** article "The Five Deadly Business Sins."

The third deadly sin is cost-driven pricing. The only thing that works is price-driven costing. Most American and practically all European companies arrive at their prices by adding up costs and then putting a profit margin on top. And then as soon as they have introduced the product, they have to start cutting the price, have to redesign the product at enormous expense, have to take losses — and often, have to drop a perfectly good product because it is priced incorrectly. Their argument? "We have to recover our costs and make a profit."

This is true but irrelevant: Customers do not see it as their job to ensure manufacturers a profit. The only sound way to price is to start out with what the market is willing to pay — and thus, it must be assumed, what the competition will charge — and design to that price specification.

Cost-driven pricing is the reason there is no American consumer-electronics industry anymore. It had the technology and the products. But it operated on cost-led pricing — and the Japanese practiced price-led costing.*

- Are we replacing an existing product?
- How will this expand our customer base and increase our sales?
- What will the competitive response be?
- If it's a new market, what are the barriers to entering this market?
- Who are the major players and how much market share does each firm have?

Step 3: Think about our customers.
- Who are our customers?
- How can we best reach them?
- Can we reach them through the Internet?
- How can we ensure that we retain them?

Step 4: Think about financing.
- How is the project being funded?
- What is the best allocation of funds?
- Can we support the debt? (What if interest rates change? What if the economy sours?)

[5. Pricing Strategies]

Question: Our client has developed a new Hollywood screenwriting software package. How are we going to price it? What's our strategy and why?

Step 1: Investigate the product.
- What's special or proprietary about our product?
- Are there similar products out there, and how are they priced?
- Where are we in the growth cycle of this industry? (Growth phase? Transition phase? Maturity phase?)
- How big is the market?
- What were our R&D costs?

Step 2: Choose a pricing strategy.
Is the company in control of its own pricing strategies, or is it reacting to suppliers, the market and its competitors?

- Cost-based pricing vs. price-based costing (i.e., do you decide pricing based on how much the product costs to produce or on how much people will pay?)
- How much does it cost to make or deliver/provide?
- What does the market expect to pay?

* Peter Drucker. "The Five Deadly Business Sins." *The Wall Street Journal* (October 21, 1993).

- Is it a "must have" product?
- Do we need to spend money to educate the consumer?

Step 3: Supply and demand (you'll win big points for graphing your answer).

- What's the supply? How's the demand?
- How will pricing have an affect on the market equilibrium?
- Matching competition: What are similar products selling for?
- Are there substitutions (in this case, Microsoft Word®, typewriters, etc.)?

Basically, there are three main ways to price the product: competitive analysis, cost-based pricing and price-based costing.

Competitive Analysis: Are there similar products out there? How does our product compare to the competition? Do we know their costs? How are they priced? Are there substitutions available?

Cost-based Pricing: Take all our costs, add them up and add a profit to it. This way you'll know your breakeven point.

Price-based Costing: What are people willing to pay for this product? If they're not willing to pay more than what it costs you to make, then it might not be worth making. On the other hand, they may be willing to pay much more than what you would get by just adding a profit margin. Profit margins vary greatly by industry. Grocery stores have a very thin profit margin, while drug companies traditionally have a large profit margin.

When solving a pricing problem, you need to look at all three of these strategies and see where, or if, they intersect.

Pricing Strategies

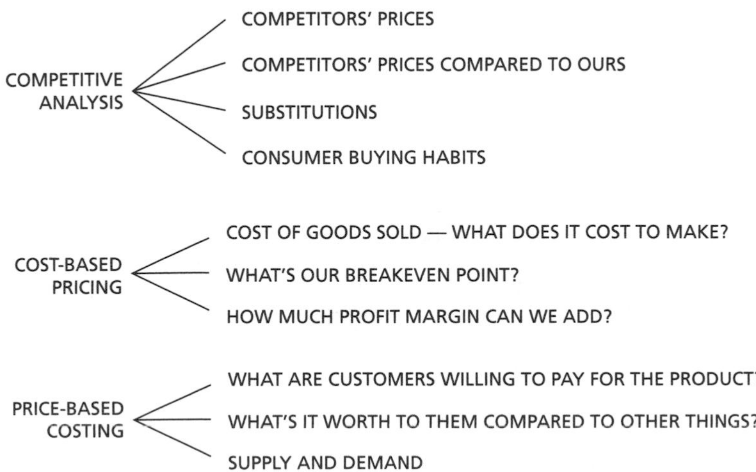
COMPETITIVE ANALYSIS
COMPETITORS' PRICES
COMPETITORS' PRICES COMPARED TO OURS
SUBSTITUTIONS
CONSUMER BUYING HABITS
COST-BASED PRICING
COST OF GOODS SOLD — WHAT DOES IT COST TO MAKE?
WHAT'S OUR BREAKEVEN POINT?
HOW MUCH PROFIT MARGIN CAN WE ADD?
PRICE-BASED COSTING
WHAT ARE CUSTOMERS WILLING TO PAY FOR THE PRODUCT?
WHAT'S IT WORTH TO THEM COMPARED TO OTHER THINGS?
SUPPLY AND DEMAND

[6. Growth Strategies]

Question: XYB Corporation has a high cash reserve (lots of cash on hand). How can we best use that money to grow the company?

Step 1: Ask your feeler questions. Growth strategies could mean focusing on a certain product, division or the company overall. This is a true strategic planning question, and you must determine the direction of questioning.

- Is the industry growing?
- How are we growing relative to the industry?
- Are our prices in line with our competitors?
- What have our competitors done in marketing and product development?
- Which segments of our business have the highest future potential?
- Do we have funding to support higher growth?

Step 2: Choose a growth strategy. Increasing sales is one of the ways you grow, though not the only one. You need to determine if all or some of the following strategies for growth fit the question.

- Increase distribution channels.
- Increase product line.
- Invest in a major marketing campaign.
- Diversify products or services offered.
- Acquire competitors or a company in a different industry.

[7. Starting a New Business]

Question: Two brothers from Ireland want to start a travel magazine. They've come to us for strategic advice and to develop a business plan for getting started. What do you tell them?

Step 1: Starting a new business encompasses entering a new market as well — the first step is the same. Investigate the market to determine whether entering the market makes good business sense.

- Who is our competition?
- What size market share does each competitor have?
- How do their products/services compare to ours?

- Are there any barriers to entry? These include: capital requirements, access to distribution channels, proprietary product technology or government policy.

Step 2: Once we determine that there are no significant barriers to entry, then we should look at the company from a venture capitalist point of view. Would you, as an outsider, invest in this start-up? Would you risk your own money? Venture capitalists don't simply buy into an idea or product, they invest in:

- Management
  - What is the management team like?
  - What are its core competencies?
  - Have they worked together before?
  - Is there an advisory board?
- Market and Strategic Plans
  - What are the barriers to entering this market?
  - Who are the major players and what kind of market share does each firm have?
  - What will the competitive response be?
- Distribution Channels
  - What are our distribution channels?
- Products
  - What is the product or technology?
  - What is the competitive edge?
  - What are the disadvantages of this product?
  - Is the technology proprietary?
- Customers
  - Who are our customers?
  - How can we best reach them? Can we reach them on the Internet?
  - How can we ensure that we retain them?
- Finance
  - How is the project being funded?
  - What is the best allocation of funds?
  - Can we support the debt? (What if interest rates change? What if the economy sours?)

[8. Competitive Response]

Question: Sperry Topsider® has developed a new non-slip sailing shoe that has been eating into the sales of our bestseller, The Commodore 2000. How can we respond?

Step 1: If a competitor introduces a new product or picks up market share, we want to first ask such questions as:

- What is the competitor's new product and how does it differ from what we offer?
- What has the competitor done differently? What's changed?
- Have any other competitors picked up market share?

Step 2: Choose one of the following response actions:

- Acquire the competitor or another player in the same market.
- Merge with a competitor to create a strategic advantage and make us more powerful.
- Copy the competitor (e.g., Amazon.com vs. BarnesandNoble.com).
- Hire the competitor's top management.
- Increase our profile with a marketing and public relations campaign.

COMPETITIVE ANALYSIS
COMPETITOR'S NEW PRODUCTS
WHAT'S CHANGED?
HAVE THEY PICKED UP MARKET SHARE?
RESPONSES
ACQUIRE THE COMPETITOR
MERGE WITH THE COMPETITOR
COPY THE COMPETITOR
HIRE THE COMPETITOR'S MANAGEMENT
INCREASE OUR OWN PROFILE WITH P.R. CAMPAIGN

[9. Increasing Sales]

Question: BBB Electronics wants to increase its sales so it can claim that it is the largest distributor of the K6 double prong lightning rod. How can BBB Electronics reach its goal?

Step 1: Increasing sales doesn't necessarily mean increasing profits. Think about the relationship. What can be done? What do we need to know?

- How are we growing relative to the industry?
- What has our market share done lately?
- Have we gone out and asked customers what they want from us?
- Are our prices in line with our competitors?
- What have our competitors done in marketing and product development?

Step 2: There are four easy ways to increase sales. Determine which action (or combination thereof) is your best strategy:

- **Increase volume**. Get more buyers, increase distribution channels, intensify marketing.
- **Increase amount of each sale.** Get each buyer to spend more.
- **Increase prices.**
- **Create seasonal balance.** Increase sales in every quarter — if you own a nursery, sell flowers in the spring, herbs in the summer, pumpkins in the fall, and trees and garlands in the winter.

INCREASING SALES
INCREASE VOLUME
INCREASE AMOUNT OF EACH SALE
INCREASE PRICES
CREATE SEASONAL BALANCE

[10. Reducing Costs]

Question a: A publishing company is having a cash flow problem and needs to reduce its costs, otherwise it will have to lay off staff. How should the company proceed?

This is a straightforward reducing costs question. In such a scenario, you need to:

Step 1: Ask for a breakdown of costs.
Step 2: If any cost seems out of line, investigate why.
Step 3: Benchmark the competitors.
Step 4: Determine whether there are any labor-saving technologies that would help reduce costs.

Question b: EEC's sales are flat and profits are taking a header. How can we fix things?

If there has been a surge in costs, you need to approach this question by focusing on the internal and external costs that could account for the rise. For example, if labor costs have skyrocketed, is it because of the good economy and because good workers are hard to find? Or is it that your workforce has unionized? Some examples of:

- Internal costs: union wages, suppliers, materials, economies of scale, increased support systems
- External costs: economy, interest rates, government regulations, transportation/shipping strikes

[11. Improving the Bottom Line: Profits]

Question: Our client manufactures high-end athletic footwear. Sales are up but profits are flat. What do we need to look at?

Whenever you hear the words "bottom line" or "profits" you should immediately think: Profits = (Revenues – Costs). However, I'm going to change this formula to E(P=R–C)M. The E represents the economy and M represents the market or industry. You always want to look at external factors first. You want to know whether this is an industry-wide problem or a company problem. Start with the economy. Spell out your take on the current economy, just the parts that would directly affect the company or industry overall. This shows the interviewer that you know what's going on outside the classroom. More importantly it allows you to define the economic environment in which this case is taking place. This is a huge advantage because it reduces the number of surprises that the interviewer can throw at you. Information about the overall market will help you decide whether the rest of the industry is having similar problems.

Going inside the parentheses is the same as going inside the company. Start by reviewing the revenue streams. Ask, "What are the major revenue streams and how have they changed over time?" And when you get to the costs: "What are the major costs, both fixed and variable, and how have they changed over time?" It is always good to know trends.

Because profits are an underlying theme in many cases, you need to make sure that profit is the main subject of the question before choosing to focus exclusively on this case scenario. (Asking feeler questions can help determine this: "How have we been doing compared to the rest of the industry? How is the overall economy performing?") Price, costs and volume are all interdependent. You need to find the best mix, because changing one isn't always the best answer. If you cut prices to drive up volume, what happens to profit? Do profits increase or decrease? There needs to be a balance. The reason behind the decision needs to make sense.

Step 1: Use the E(P=R–C)M framework. Start with the external factors first. Try to determine whether this is an industry-wide problem or just a company problem.

Step 2: Once inside the parentheses ask what are the major revenue streams and how have they changed over time?

- Always look at the revenue ("price" is sometimes substituted) side first. Until you have identified your revenue streams, you can't know where best to cut costs.
- What are the revenue streams? Where does the money come from?
- What percentage of the total revenue does each stream represent?
- Does anything seem unusual in the balance of percentages?
- Have those percentages changed lately? If so, why?

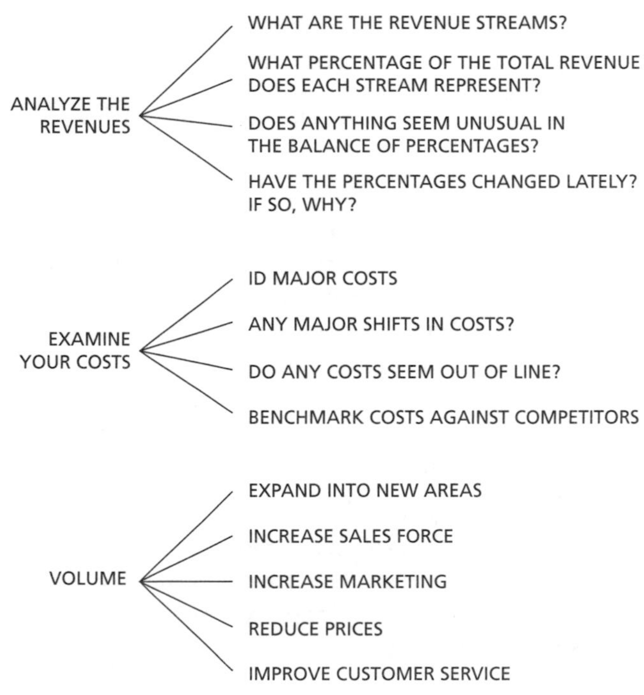
ANALYZE THE REVENUES
WHAT ARE THE REVENUE STREAMS?
WHAT PERCENTAGE OF THE TOTAL REVENUE DOES EACH STREAM REPRESENT?
DOES ANYTHING SEEM UNUSUAL IN THE BALANCE OF PERCENTAGES?
HAVE THE PERCENTAGES CHANGED LATELY? IF SO, WHY?
EXAMINE YOUR COSTS
ID MAJOR COSTS
ANY MAJOR SHIFTS IN COSTS?
DO ANY COSTS SEEM OUT OF LINE?
BENCHMARK COSTS AGAINST COMPETITORS
VOLUME
EXPAND INTO NEW AREAS
INCREASE SALES FORCE
INCREASE MARKETING
REDUCE PRICES
IMPROVE CUSTOMER SERVICE

Step 3: Examine your costs. Ask what are the major costs, both fixed and variable, and how have they changed over time.

- Identify the major variable and fixed costs.
- Have there been any major shifts in costs (e.g., labor or raw material costs)?
- Do any of these costs seem out of line?
- How can we reduce costs without damaging the revenue streams?
- Benchmark costs against our competitors.

Step 4: Determine whether you want to pump up the volume. If so, you can:

- Expand into new areas.
- Increase sales force.
- Increase marketing.
- Reduce prices.
- Improve customer service.

To learn more about a typical Profit and Loss question go to Anatomy of a Profit and Loss Case on page 62.

[12. Turnarounds]

Question: AAS Company is in trouble and you've been brought in to save it. What do you do?

Step 1: Gather information.

- Tell me about the company.
- Why is it failing? Bad products, bad management, bad economy?
- Tell me about the industry.
- Are our competitors facing the same problems?
- Do we have access to capital?
- Is it a public or privately-held company?

Step 2: Choose the appropriate actions from the following list. While this isn't a quick fix for all troubled companies, these are the main actions you should be thinking about.

- Learn as much about the business and its operations as possible.
- Review services, products and finances. (Are products out of date? Do we have a high debt load?)
- Secure sufficient financing so your plan has a chance.
- Review talent and temperament of all employees, and get rid of the deadwood.
- Determine short-term and long-term company goals.
- Devise a business plan.
- Visit clients, suppliers and distributors, and reassure them.
- Prioritize goals and get some small successes under your belt ASAP to build confidence.

✢ Ivy Case System at a Glance

Type	Approach	Elements
Entering a New Market	Market	Competition Market share Comparative products and services Barriers to entry
	Entry	Start from scratch Acquire an existing player Joint venture/strategic alliance with existing player
Industry Analysis	Current Industry Structure	Life cycle? (growth, transition, maturity) Performance, margins Major players and market share Industry changes (new players, new technology) Drivers (brand, size, technology)
	Suppliers	How many? Product availability What's going on in their market?
	Future	Expanding or shrinking? Mergers and acquisitions? Barriers to entry or exit?
Mergers & Acquisitions	Objectives	Increase market access Diversify holdings Pre-empt the competition Tax advantages Incorporate synergies Increase shareholder value
	Price	Fair? Affordable? How to pay? If the economy sours . . . ?
	Due Diligence	What shape is the company in? The industry? How secure are its markets and customers? What are the margins? Competitive response to acquisition Legal issues
	Exit Strategies	How long to keep it? Divest parts of the organization?
New Product	Product	Special or proprietary? Financing? Patented? Substitutions? Advantages and disadvantages Place in product line Cannibalizing our own products? Replacing existing product?

Ivy Case System, continued

Type	Approach	Elements
	Market Strategy	Expanding customer base Prompting competitive response Barriers to entry Major players and market share
	Customers	Who? How to reach them? Retention — how to hold them?
	Financing	How funded? Best allocation of funds? Debt viable?
Pricing Strategies	Pricing	Competitive pricing Cost-based pricing Price-based costing
Growth Strategies	Assessment	Is the industry growing? How are we growing compared to the industry? Prices relative to competitors Competitors marketing and development Which segments have the most potential? Funding for higher growth
	Strategies	Increase distribution channels Increase product line Invest in major marketing campaign Diversity of products or services offered
New Business	Market	Who is the competition and their market share? Products comparison Barriers to entry
	Cost Benefit Analysis	Management Marketing and strategic plan Distribution channels Product Customers Finance
Competitive Response	Why?	New product? Competitor's strategy changed? Other competitor's increased market share
	Strategy	Acquire a competitor Merge with competition Copy competitor Hire the competitor's management Increase profile with marketing campaign

Ivy Case System, continued

Type	Approach	Elements
Increasing Sales	Assessment (increasing sales doesn't necessarily mean increasing profits)	Growth relative to market share Changes in market share Customer polls Prices competitive? Competitor's strategies (marketing and product development)
	How?	Increase volume Increase amount of each sale Increase prices Create seasonal balance
Reducing Costs	Assessment	Get cost breakdown Investigate for irregularities Benchmark competitors Labor-saving technologies
	Cost analysis — Internal	Union wages, suppliers, materials, economies of scale, increased support system
	Cost analysis — External	Economy, interest rates, government regulations, transportation/shipping strikes
Increasing Profits	Revenue E (P = R – C) M Always look at external factors first.	Identify revenue streams Percentage of total revenue of each Unusual balance? Have percentages changed?
	Costs	ID fixed costs ID variable costs Shifts in costs Unusual costs? Benchmark competitors Reduce costs without damaging revenue streams
	Volume	Expand into new areas Increase sales (volume and force) Increase marketing Reduce prices Improve customer service
Turnaround	Strategy	Learn about company Review services, products, finances Secure funding Review talent and culture Determine short term / long term goals Business plan Reassure clients, suppliers, distributors Prioritize goals and develop some small successes for momentum

In this section, we will explore some supplements to the Ivy Case System. These include both other frameworks and additional tools so that you have an understanding of what else is out there. I've purposely limited the number of alternatives, because I've learned from experience that too many options can become a burden. Keep in mind that none of these frameworks or tools was specifically designed to answer case questions. It is far better to understand the underlying problems of the case and how to logically address those problems than to try to apply a "fix-all" framework. That being said . . .

Five C's and Four P's

These are two elementary frameworks that can do the job. You're not going to blow anyone away with these, but you won't drown either. They will allow you to touch on all the main points and appear fairly well organized.

There are two secrets to using these frameworks. First, since every case is different, the C's or the P's have to be rearranged to fit the case. If you treat these frameworks like a laundry list, your answer will seem nonlinear and possibly disorganized. Second, you need to kick up some dust to conceal the fact that you're using these frameworks. If your interviewer discovers you're using the Five C's or Four P's, you might lose some points; neither of these frameworks is particularly impressive.

[Five C's]

- **Company:** What do you know about the company? How big is it? Is it a public or private company? What kinds of products or services does it offer to its clients?
- **Costs:** What are the major costs? How have its costs changed in the past year? How do its costs compare to others in the industry? How can we reduce costs?
- **Competition:** Who are the biggest competitors? What market share does each player hold? Has market share changed in the last year? How do our services or products differ from the competition? Do we hold any strategic advantage over our competitors?
- **Consumers/clients:** Who are they? What do they want? Are we fulfilling their needs? How can we get more? Are we keeping the ones we have?
- **Channels:** Distribution channels. How do we get our product into the hands of the end users? How can we increase our distribution channels? Are there areas of our market that we are not reaching? How do we reach them?

[Four P's]

- **Product:** What are our products and services? What is the company's niche?
- **Price:** How does our price compare to the competitions'? How was our price determined? Are we priced right? If we change our price, what will that do to our sales volume?
- **Place:** How do we get our products to the end user? How can we increase our distribution channels? Do our competitors have products in places that we don't? Do they serve markets that we can't reach? If so, why? And how can we reach them?
- **Promotions:** How can we best market our products? Are we reaching the right market? What kind of marketing campaigns has the company conducted in the past? Were they effective? Can we afford to increase our marketing campaign?

+ BCG Matrix

In 1998, Wiley Press published *Perspectives on Strategy*. The book is a collection of articles and essays written by senior members of The Boston Consulting Group. One popular and useful framework is the BCG "Product Portfolio Matrix." This matrix is designed to place a product or group of products into one of four categories while taking into account a company's relative market share. BCG has been kind enough to let us reprint Chapter Three.

The Product Portfolio (*Bruce D. Henderson, 1970*)*

To be successful, a company should have a portfolio of products with different growth rates and different market shares. The portfolio composition is a function of the balance among cash flows. High-growth products require cash inputs to grow. Low-growth products should generate excess cash. Both kinds are needed simultaneously.

The Matrix

Growth \ Market Share	HIGH	LOW
HIGH	★ STAR	? QUESTION MARK
LOW	$ CASH FLOW	X PET

Four rules determine the cash flow of a product.

- Margins and cash generated are a function of market share. High margins and high market share go together. This is a matter of common observation, explained by the experience curve effect.
- Growth requires cash input to finance added assets. The added cash required to hold market share is a function of growth rates.
- High market share must be earned or bought. Buying market share requires an additional increment of investment.

* Used with permission of The Boston Consulting Group. Bruce D. Henderson, "The Product Portfolio," *Perspectives on Strategy from The Boston Consulting Group*, ed. Carl W. Stern and George Stalk, Jr. (New York: John Wiley & Sons, Inc., 1998), pp. 35–37.

• No product market can grow indefinitely. The payoff from growth must come when the growth slows, or it never will. The payoff is cash that cannot be reinvested in that product.

Products with high market share and slow growth are cash cows. Characteristically, they generate large amounts of cash, in excess of the reinvestment required to maintain share. This excess need not, and should not, be reinvested in those products. In fact, if the rate of return exceeds the growth rate, the cash cannot be reinvested indefinitely, except by depressing returns.

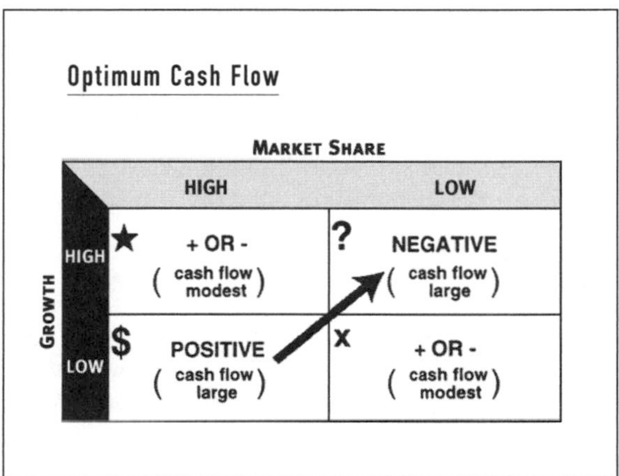

Products with low market share and low growth are pets. They may show an accounting profit, but the profit must be reinvested to maintain share, leaving no cash throw-off. The product is essentially worthless, except in liquidation.

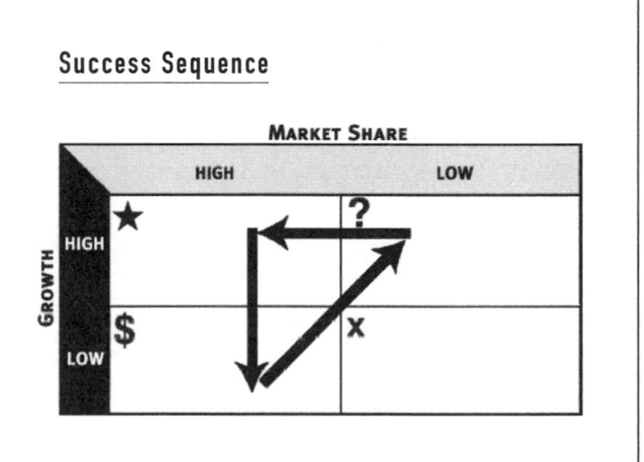

All products eventually become either cash cows or pets. The value of a product is completely dependent upon obtaining a leading share of its market before the growth slows.

Low-market-share, high-growth products are the question marks. They almost always require far more cash than they can generate. If cash is not supplied, they fall behind and die. Even when the cash is supplied, if they only hold their share, they are still pets when the growth stops. The question marks require large added cash investments for market share to be purchased. The low-market-share, high-growth product is a liability unless it becomes a leader. It requires very large cash inputs that it cannot generate itself.

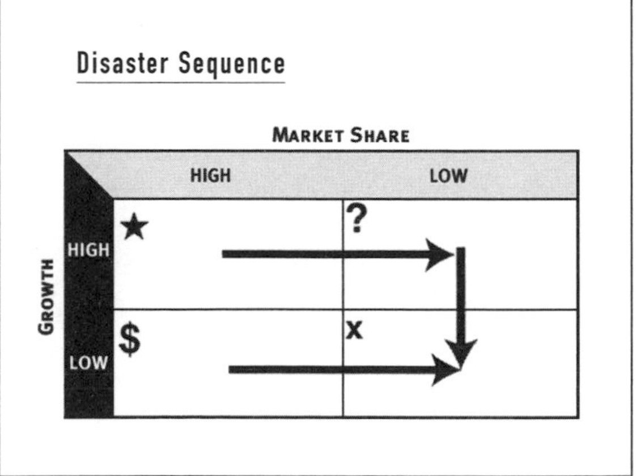

The high-share, high-growth product is the star. It nearly always shows reported profits, but it may or may not generate all of its own cash. If it stays a leader, however, it will become a large cash generator when growth slows and its reinvestment requirements diminish. The star eventually becomes the cash cow, providing high volume, high margin, high stability, security and cash throw-off for reinvestment elsewhere.

The payoff for leadership is very high indeed if it is achieved early and maintained until growth slows. Investment in market share during the growth phase can be very attractive if you have the cash. Growth in market is compounded by growth in share. Increases in share increase the margin. High margin permits higher leverage with equal safety. The resulting profitability permits higher payment of earnings after financing normal growth. The return on investment is enormous.

The need for a portfolio of businesses becomes obvious. Every company needs products in which to invest cash. Every company needs products that generate cash. And every product should eventually be a cash generator; otherwise, it is worthless.

Only a diversified company with a balanced portfolio can use its strengths to truly capitalize on its growth opportunities. The balanced portfolio has:

- stars whose high share and high growth assure the future
- cash cows that supply funds for that high growth
- question marks to be converted into stars with the added funds

Pets are not necessary. They are evidence of failure either to obtain a leadership position during the growth phase or to get out and cut the losses.

+ Michael Porter's "Five Forces" / The Structural Analysis of Industries

Michael Porter didn't develop his "Five Forces" as a case framework. However, when you are given a case dealing with developing a new product, entering a new market or starting a new business, this framework works quite well. (e.g., A regional food manufacturer is thinking of entering the gourmet toothpaste business. Should the company take the plunge?)

Please refer to Michael Porter's bestseller *Competitive Strategy* for a more in-depth explanation of his "Five Forces" model.

Porter writes that the state of competition in an industry depends on five basic competitive forces:

1. The threat of new or potential entrants. This includes new companies or acquisitions of established companies by a new player. If barriers are high or if newcomers can expect entrenchment or retaliatory measures (such as a price war) from existing competitors, then the threat of entry is low. According to Porter, barriers of entry include:

- economies of scale
- capital requirements
- government policy
- switching costs

- access to distribution channels
- product differentiation
- proprietary product technology

2. Intensity of rivalry among existing competitors.
3. Pressure from substitution products, for example, sugar vs. high-fructose corn syrup and artificial sweeteners
4. Bargaining power of buyers. Buyers compete with the industry by forcing down prices, bargaining for higher quality or more services, and playing competitors against each other — all at the expense of industry profitability.
5. Bargaining power of suppliers. Forces 4 and 5 have to do with supply and demand. When there are many suppliers but few buyers, the buyers have the upper hand. When there are many buyers, but few suppliers, the suppliers have the advantage.

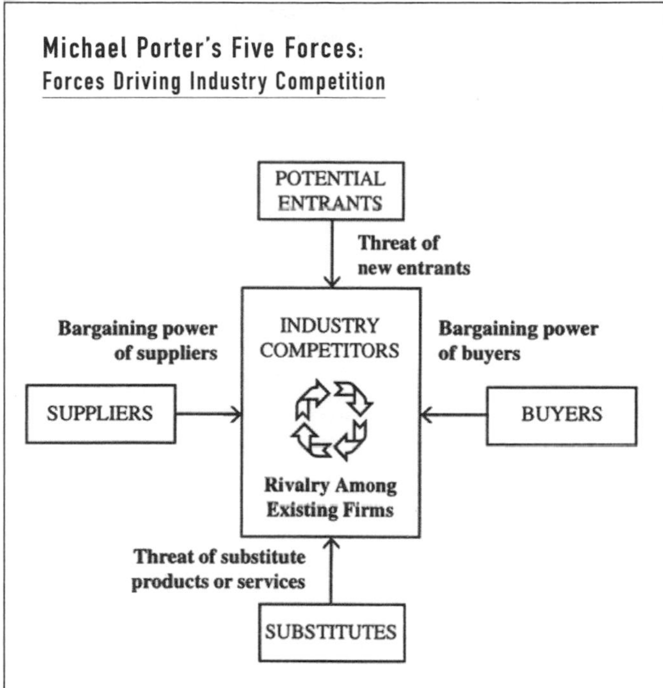

+ The Value Chain

In his 1985 book *Competitive Advantage*, Michael Porter introduced the value chain. It's a framework that follows the company's internal product processes starting with raw materials and ending with customer purchase and service. Questioning the effectiveness and efficiencies of these steps during a case question not only shows an understanding of product flow, but can lead to relevant information to help you solve the case.

Raw Materials >>> **Operations** >>> **Delivery** >>> **Marketing & Sales** >>> **Service**

Raw materials and inbound logistics: receiving materials into the warehouse, relationships with suppliers, "just in time" (JIT) delivery, etc.

Operations: processing raw materials into product through the use of capital equipment and labor.

Delivery: warehousing and distribution channels.

Marketing and Sales: marketing strategy, identification of customer base and the cost of customer acquisition, sales force issues (e.g. commission, company car, etc.).

Service: customers support, customer retention (it's cheaper to retain a customer than to go out and bring in a new one).

7-S Framework

In the early 1970s, three McKinsey consultants developed a framework called the 7-S Model. Its goal was to help managers analyze their organizations and their effectiveness. It studies seven key elements that make the organizations successful: strategy, structure, systems, style, skills, staff and shared values.

The model differentiates between the "hard" side and the "soft" side of an organization. The hard "S's" are strategy, structure and systems. The company *strategy* can be aimed toward growth, higher profits, lower costs, new product development or entering a new market. It's the action or plan the company has to make it more competitive. The *structure* refers to the organizational structure — lines of authority, chain of command and channels of communications.
The third hard S is *systems*. Systems refer to more than just information systems (which was probably the first one to come to mind). It also refers to budgeting, planning, innovation, compensation, and performance measurement. These are the systems that govern everyday business activity.

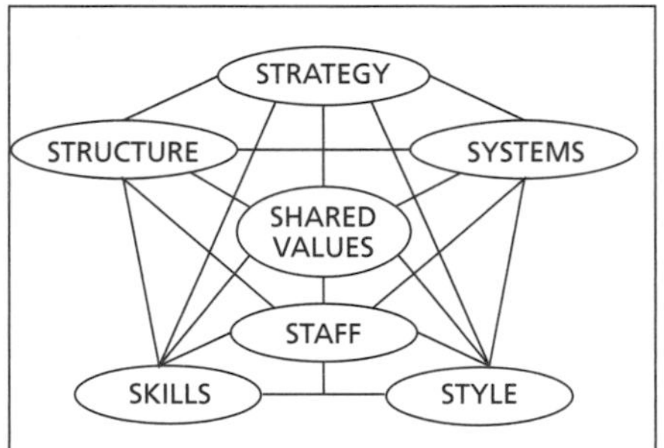

The soft "S"s are style, skills, staff and shared values. *Style*, refers to leadership style of upper management and the management style of the company — meritocracy, etc. *Skills* are the company's competencies, what it does best. The sixth "S" is *staff*. This refers to the company's people, how they are trained, managed, and motivated. The final "S" is *shared values*. Shared values are the values and principles that the company operates by and stands for — things like vision, corporate citizenship or being the best or biggest.

The key thing to remember if you plan to use the 7-S's is to look at both the hard side as well as the soft side when analyzing the internal environment of the company.

Income Statement

While you may never have to draw up an income statement, you may be handed one in an interview and be asked to analyze it. Understanding the basics of an income statement is essential for answering product and company profitability questions. How do the costs stack up? Do any numbers seem out of line or a bit high? For example, if Joe's Shoe Company's labor costs were $50,000 instead of $15,000, that should send off warning bells that something is wrong. Why are labor costs $50,000, or 50% of gross revenues?

Some of my students have found that breaking a problem down by external and internal factors helped them organize their thoughts. Here's an example of a new market case.

Should we enter a new market?

External Factors

- Market — size, growth rate, stage of development, technology changes
- Customers — who are they and how are they segmented?
- Industry — entry/exit barriers; supplier status and substitutions
- Competitors — major players and market share; strengths and weaknesses; how do their products or services differ from ours?
- Risk — market, technology and regulation risks

Internal Factors

- Strategy — does it fit our long-term strategy? Does it fit our core competencies?
- Operations
  - Marketing and Sales
  - Operations and logistics
  - Finance and control
  - Organization and culture
  - R&D — research and development

Joe's Shoe Company
Income Statement

	Gross Revenues (units x price)		**100,000**
(–)	Returns & discounts	(5,000)	
	Net Sales		**95,000**
(–)	Cost of Goods Sold		
	Direct Labor	(15,000)	
	Direct Material Costs	(10,000)	
	Overhead	(5,000)	
	Delivery Costs	(5,000)	
		(35,000)	
	Gross Margin		**60,000**
(–)	Selling, General and Admin.	(20,000)	
(–)	Depreciation	(5,000)	
		(25,000)	
	Operating Profits		**35,000**
(–)	Interest Expense	(3,000)	
	Profit Before Taxes		**32,000**

"If" Scenarios to Remember

Sales Scenarios

- If sales are flat and profits are taking a header, you need to examine both revenues and costs. Always start with the revenue side first. Until you identify and understand the revenue streams, you can't make educated decisions on the cost side.
- If sales are flat but market share remains relatively constant, that could indicate that industry sales are flat and that your competitors are experiencing similar problems.
- If your case includes a decline-in-sales problem, analyze these three things:
  - Overall declining market demand (e.g., soda sales have dropped as bottled water becomes the drink of choice).
  - The current marketplace might be mature or your product may be obsolete (e.g., vinyl records give way to CDs, which give way to digital).
  - Loss of market share due to substitutions (e.g., video rentals have declined because there are numerous substitutions vying for the leisure dollar, such as going out to dinner, going to the movies, pay-per-view, direct TV and the Internet).
- If sales and market share are increasing but profits are declining, then you need to investigate whether prices are dropping and/or costs are climbing. However, if costs aren't the issue, then investigate product mix and check to see if the margins have changed.

Profit Scenarios

- If profits are declining because of a drop in revenues, concentrate on marketing and distribution issues.
- If profits are declining because of rising expenses, concentrate on operational and financial issues — i.e., COGS (cost of goods sold), labor, rent, and marketing costs.
- If profits are declining, yet revenues went up, review:
  - changes in costs
  - any additional expenses
  - changes in prices
  - the product mix
  - changes in customers' needs

Product Scenarios

- If a product is in its emerging growth stage, concentrate on R&D, competition and pricing.
- If a product is in its growth stage, emphasize marketing and competition.
- If a product is in its mature stage, focus on manufacturing, costs and competition.
- If a product is in its declining stage, define niche market, analyze the competition's play or think exit strategy.

Pricing Scenarios

If you lower prices and volume rises, and then you are pushed beyond full capacity, your costs will shoot up as your employees work overtime, and consequently your profits will suffer.

Prices are stable only when three conditions are met:*

- Growth rate for all competitors is approximately the same.
- Prices are paralleling costs.
- Prices of all competitors are roughly of equal value.

The volume (the amount that you produce) and the costs are easier to change than the industry price levels, unless everyone changes their prices together (e.g., airline tickets or gas prices).

The perfect strategy for the high-cost producer is one that convinces competitors that market shares cannot be shifted, except over long periods of time, and therefore, that the highest practical industry prices are to everyone's advantage** — meaning that price wars are detrimental and everyone will profit more by keeping prices high.

General tips

- How the Internet affects the company should be in the back of your mind in every case.
- How the economy affects the company should be in the back of your mind in every case.
- How the competition — both internal to the industry and external (substitutions) — affects the company should be in the back of your mind in every case.

Business Case Tips

• If you ever get a case that you have already heard, as tempting as it might be to answer it, your best strategy is to tell the interviewer. Interviewers usually know when someone has heard a case. You tend to do things too quickly and your thought process is different. It is hard to reenact discovery.

• Take graph paper into the interview. It helps you organize your thoughts, keeps the numbers lined up when you multiply and add and reminds you to try to graph part of your answer.

• Ask for numbers. If the numbers aren't an important part of the case, they will more than likely tell you not to focus on them.

• Practice your math, particularly multiplication and percentages. Almost all recruiters **will not** let you take a calculator into the interview. Most students make math mistakes. They are usually off by a zero or two (see p. 30).

• Interact with the interviewer as much as possible. Remember, it should be a conversation.

A final word before you tackle the cases.

---

* Bruce D. Henderson, "The Product Portfolio," *Perspectives on Strategy from the Boston Consulting Group*, ed. Carl W. Stern and George Stalk, Jr. (New York: John Wiley & Sons, Inc., 1998), pp. 21.

** Ibid., pp.27.

Peer Advice. Here's advice from some students who had just gone through the process. They all received offers from BCG, McKinsey or both.

"As you go through the math portion of the case, think out loud. Let the interviewer know what is going through your mind. If unsure of what to say, pretend the interviewer is on the telephone and you are explaining it to her over the phone."

"For me, one of the unexpected challenges of final round interviews was their sheer length. After five hours of intense interviews, I felt like a slouching, mumbling mess with any spark of creativity long since extinguished, and I was far more likely to make simple mistakes. Before the last couple of interviews on any given day, take a few minutes, and pause to reenergize. Splash water on your face, grab another cup of coffee, take a brisk walk up and down the hallway. Do anything that keeps your brain awake and your personality alive during that final stretch."

"Motivation. Students in non-business disciplines who are looking to land a job in consulting must be able to justify their motivation for the transition. The interview process is expensive and time-consuming for firms, and interviewers are looking for clear, logical answers that will convince them of a candidate's seriousness. Additionally, candidates must be prepared to discuss how consulting fits into their long-term professional goals. Because firms recruiting outside business schools could easily fill their incoming classes entirely with business school students, the burden is greater for non-MBAs."

"Preparation. Preparing for interviews in consulting should not be limited to practicing cases. Interviews also include discussions of experiences in various environments, such as ambiguity and rancor, as well as questions related to leadership and teamwork. The candidate must be prepared not only to discuss these subjects, but also to answer subsequent questions which interviewers will ask to uncover various layers of the topic in addition to the candidate's personality. For preparation, one should practice with a group of friends. This setting, along with the resulting constructive feedback, will help one anticipate the string of questions that will inevitably be asked and improve one's communication skills. Sound preparation will give one the confidence needed during the actual interview — confidence that will create a positive impression with the interviewer. After all, while the interviewer is there to assess whether the candidate is able to structure a problem well, he or she is also judging whether or not the candidate can be put before a client."

"In preparing stories for various settings, candidates must identify and select the most appropriate anecdotes. It is unnecessary for every story to portray the candidate as a hero. A failure through which one learned about one's weaknesses can be just as effective, if not more. Conversely, an experience through which one strengthened a skill or developed a new skill through perseverance will score well. Fabricating an event, however, will result in certain doom as interviewers are adept at digging deeper into an issue and determining gaps or untruths. Therefore, a successful candidate must select and prepare honest stories that provide insight into one's personality."

"The Ivy Case System was like a roadmap. As soon as I got a question, I was immediately able to identify what type of question it was and what types of questions to ask to tease further information out of the interviewer. This is the advantage the Ivy Case System gives you. Then, having Porter's Five Forces and the Five Cs is also useful in your toolkit."

With regards to interviewing abroad: "Make sure you know what types of projects the country office is involved in. For example, offices in China are doing many 'market entry' projects. So it is important to understand the varieties and complexities surrounding 'entering a new market' and to practice those types of cases."

"Go through the interview process without second guessing how you're doing. It only handicaps your performance. Prepare and then let the cards fall. Be confident. It's impossible to know what the interviewer is thinking. They may do things intentionally to throw you off. Don't let the little things, like screwing up a math problem, upset you."

Practice, practice, practice!

Practice online interactive cases at:

www.apd.mckinsey.com: click on "Interview Prep".
www.bcg.com/careers/careers_splash.jsp: click on "Interview Prep".
www.bain.com/bainweb/join_bain/join_bain_overview.asp: click on "Case Interview".

An Aristotelian Framework

Aristotle's book *Rhethoric and Poetics* was really the first case question interview prep book. His book is about persuasion and, after all, that's what we're trying to do — persuade the interviewer that we have what it takes. Aristotle lays out a tripod (a framework) and argues that persuasion relies on the relationship between logos, ethos and pathos. As you probably remember from Philosophy 101, logos is a logical, well-reasoned argument based on facts and figures, charts and graphs. Ethos deals with the speaker's (that's you) personal voice and character. How likeable and believable are you? In other words, fit. How would I feel if we were snowed in for nine hours at the Macedonian Chariot Station? Would you be an interesting companion? Finally there is pathos, your audience's frame of mind. This is often tough to determine or control, but it can be massaged by incorporating logos and ethos into your answer. The point is that you need the tripod, the combination of logos, ethos and pathos to do well in a case interview. Too much logic and not enough personality results in a tipped tripod. As you prepare for your interviews, remember to concentrate on all three. It is as much about the presentation as it is about the logic.

✢ Anatomy of a Profit and Loss Case

As with all case questions, we assume facts not in evidence, as well as generous assumptions. Familiar companies are used for examples because of the power of their brand and their familiarity to the general public. Information concerning Harley-Davidson below may not be accurate and should not be used as reliable up-to-date data.

This is a transcript of a profit and loss interview along with my analysis throughout the case.

✢ Harley-Davidson®

Interviewer: Our client is Harley-Davidson. Their stock fell from $54 a share to $49 a share on news of declining profits. What's going on and how can we turn this around?

Student: Our client is Harley-Davidson. Their stock fell from $54 to $49 a share on news of declining profits. We need to figure out what's going on and how to fix it. Are there any other objectives I should be aware of?

Interviewer: Yes, maintaining market share.

Analysis: The student was right to summarize the case; however, she would have made a better impression if she had tried to quantify the case. Instead of saying the stock price dropped from $54 to $49 a share; she should have said that the stock dropped about 10%. Remember, so much of this is how you think — what goes through your mind when you hear some numbers.

She was also right to verify the objective and to ask if there were any other objectives she should be concerned with. Without asking, she would have never known that maintaining market share was an issue.

Student: I just want to take a moment to jot down some notes.

Interviewer: That's fine.

The student writes on her paper E(P=R–C)M.

Analysis: This is the framework you want to use for a P&L case. Inside the parentheses is the classic "profits equal revenues minus costs". That tells us what's going on inside the company. But you want to look at external factors first. Is this a Harley problem or an industry-wide problem? She starts with the E.

Student: I'd like to start with external factors first. Can you tell me what's going on with the economy?

Analysis: The student would have made a much greater impression if she had told the interviewer about the economy. If you are applying for a job in business, you should know what's going on outside the classroom, particularly with the economy. The other reason to tell the interviewer what's happening with the economy is because it gives you more control over the interview. It allows you to frame the economic environment in which this case takes place. So many of these cases take place in a vacuum and you don't know what the economy is like. When you frame it yourself, there are fewer surprises. When you talk about the economy, pick out the main factors that will affect Harley's business. Let's try it again...

Student: I'd like to start with some external factors first. I'd like to start with the economy. I know that the US is in a recession; it is in the middle of a mortgage crisis and unemployment is rising, so people have less disposable income. Gas prices had topped $4 a gallon and then quickly dropped down below $2 a gallon, but they are slowly rising again. I know that the US dollar has been gaining strength against the euro and pound, but is still fairly weak against Asian currencies, particularly the yen. And I know that interest rates have fallen dramatically and are now close to a 30-year low.

Analysis: Much better. Do you need to go into this much detail? Yes. You'll see how everything she brought up will tie into her answer later on. Make sure that you write everything down; it will give you some place to go if you get stuck.

Interviewer: Good. What's next?

Student: I'd like to know about the motorcycle industry. Can you tell me what's been going on?

Analysis: No one expects you to know what is going on in the motorcycle industry. The interviewer has a lot of information that he wants to give the student. Sometimes it takes a series of questions from the student to extract the information. Sometimes it only takes one and the interviewer does a data dump. It is then up to the student to sort through what's relevant now, what's smoke and what might become relevant later.

In this case the interviewer is going to do a data dump.

Interviewer: I have some industry information. Last year the industry grew by 5%; Harley grew by 2%; the small less expensive motorcycles and scooters grew by 8%. Female riders were up 12% and now make up 10% of all motorcycle riders, but they only make up 2% of Harley riders.

I have some market share for you, but I want you to assume that each of these companies only makes one model. For Harley it is the big Harley Hog.

Student: Okay.

Interviewer: The market leader is Honda with 27%, Harley with 24%, Yamaha 17%, Suzuki 10%, Kawasaki 8%, BMW 6%. The remaining 9% is made up of two other bikes, Scout and Indian, and two scooter companies, Vespa and Scooter Do. What else do you want to know about the industry?

Student: It looks as though Harley is not growing as fast as the industry overall. That might be because it has few female riders. The trend seems to be headed towards smaller, lighter, more gas efficient bikes. If Harley—

Interviewer: I know where you are headed. We'll talk about strategies in a minute. Do you have any other industry questions?

Student: No.

Interviewer: Do think that this is a Harley problem or an industry problem?

Student: At this point I think it is a Harley problem.

Analysis: Whenever they give you a number like the industry grew by 5%, don't be happy with it. It doesn't tell you nearly enough. You always want to ask for trends. If the industry grew by 10% the year before and 5% this year then the 5% looks very different to me than if the industry went from 2% to 5%. Very few students ever ask for trends. Ask for them and you'll stand out from your peers. Again, they are trying to learn how you think, and if you don't ask for trends, you're not thinking like a consultant.

Interviewer: What's next?

Student: I'd like to look inside the parentheses to see what's going on inside the company. I'd like to start with the revenues first. What are the major revenue streams and how have they changed over time?

Interviewer: Okay. I'm going to give the four major revenue streams for Y1 and Y2. The four major revenue streams are domestic motorcycles sales, international motorcycle sales, replacement parts and garb.

Student: 'Garb' being merchandise?

Analysis: If you ever get a phrase, industry jargon or a string of initials that you don't understand, ask for clarification. You don't lose any points for clarification questions up front.

Interviewer: Yes, garb is merchandise. For Year 1, domestic motorcycles made up 45%, international 40%, replacement parts 10% and garb 5%. For Year 2, domestic motorcycles made up 35%, international 40%, replacement parts 15% and garb 10%. I'd like you to look at those numbers and how they changed over the last year, and in four sentences or less tell me what's going on with Harley customers.

While the interviewer was stating those numbers the student was making a chart. The student wrote down the following chart.

Revenue Streams	Y1	Y2
Domestic	45%	35%
International	40%	40%
Replacement parts	10%	15%
Garb	5%	10%

Student: It looks as if Harley customers are buying fewer new bikes, fixing up their old bikes and buying some garb to make themselves feel good and look bad.

Interviewer: (smiles)

Analysis: She did a great job. She kept it to one sentence and added a little humor to the interview as well.

Interviewer: Okay, good. Let's talk about costs.

Student: Before we do, can I ask about volume? Do we have any numbers on volume of bikes sold?

Interviewer: I do. In Year 1 Harley sold 350,000 bikes and in Year 2 they sold 330,000 bikes.

Students: Thanks.

Analysis: Good move on the student's part. Volume is part of revenue so asking for that number was appropriate and she scored some points.

Student: What are the major costs, both fixed and variable, and how have they changed over time?

Interviewer: The only cost you need to worry about is the cost of steel. We are in the middle of a steel contract that expires in 24 months. We currently have a good deal, but we are concerned about getting slammed with high steel costs in 24 months as the economy improves. I just want you to keep that in the back of your mind.

What I'd like you to do now is to come up with some short-term strategies that will help turn Harley around. By 'short term', I mean 18 months or less.

Student: Okay. The first thing they should do is market to women.

Interviewer: What would they market?

Student: They could design a new bike…

Interviewer: It is going to take more than 18 months to design, manufacture and distribute a new bike. Leave that for the long-term.

Student: They could market the Hog to women.

Interviewer: They'd have to be pretty big women. The Hog is a hard bike to handle. That's why only 2% of Harley owners are women.

Student: Then they could market the garb. Women like to look—

Interviewer: What else?

Student: They could raise the price of garb and the price of replacement parts. We know that people are going to continue to buy those items.

Interviewer: What else?

Student: I'm not sure. They could lay people off?

Interviewer: Are you asking me or telling me?

Analysis: Whenever you are answering a P&L case and they ask you for strategies, you want to do two things: (i) write revenue-based strategies and cost-based strategies on your paper, and (ii) ask for a moment to jot down some ideas.

By writing revenue-based strategies on your paper, you are showing the interviewer that you are well-organized and thinking two steps ahead. It is easier to think of some ideas if you are looking at a heading on a piece of paper instead of a blank page. It also keeps you from ping-ponging back and forth between revenue-based and cost-based ideas. You want to present all the revenue-based ideas first, then the cost-based ideas.

The reason to ask for a moment to jot down some ideas is that it allows you to think of ideas in any order, but present them in the right order. It also gives you some place to go. Keep in mind that the interviewer has probably given this case ten times. He knows every answer that you can think of and he's heard them all before. There is a good chance that he will cut you off as soon as he knows where your answer is headed. It is very difficult for a person to drop their secondary thought and then come up with a new thought right away. When cut off in mid-thought, people tend to panic, scramble and then shut down. They can't think of another idea to save their lives.

If you take the time to jot down some ideas and he cuts you off, then you can just look at your notes and give him another idea. It takes a lot of stress out of the process and these interviews can be stressful enough.

Also, if you hit a wall and can't think of anything, try looking at your first page of notes. Remember the student told us a couple of great things about the economy: interest rates are way down and the dollar is still down against the yen.

Let's take it from the top.

Interviewer: Come up with some short-term strategies.

Student: Can I take a moment to jot down some ideas?

Interviewer: Absolutely.

The student writes revenue-based and cost-based strategies on her paper, then jots down some ideas.

Student: Okay. I'd like to break them down by revenue-based and cost-based. I'll start with revenue-based. Harley can raise the prices of their garb and replacement parts because we know people will buy them anyway. We can increase international distribution channels.

Interviewer: Where?

Student: In Asia where the dollar is still weak.

Interviewer: Okay, what else?

Student: Because interest rates are so low, we can offer low financing packages and give high trade-in values to encourage customers to buy a new bike.

Interviewer: What else?

Student: On the cost side, because interest rates are so low we can refinance our corporate debt.

Interviewer: Okay, good.

Student: And we can look at laying people off. You said the volume dropped from 350,000 bikes to 330,000. That's a about a 5% drop.

Interviewer: We are thinking about changing the price. I have some data. I want you to run the numbers and then tell me what you want to do, and more importantly why you want to do it.

If we leave the price the same, Harley will sell 330,000 motorcycles and make a net profit of $10,000 each. If we discount the price, Harley will sell 440,000 motorcycles and net $7,000 each. And if they raise the price, they will sell only 275,000 motorcycles and will net $12,000 each.

Analysis: The student should take some time to run the numbers. You are better off taking a little extra time and getting the right answer than rushing through and getting the wrong answer. Before you give your answer, ask yourself if the number makes sense. If it doesn't, go back and figure it out. You can't un-ring the bell. I'd hate to see you lose a great opportunity over a silly math mistake.

Remember silence is okay as long as you are doing calculations, writing notes or drawing a chart.

Student: If we keep the price the same, then our net profit will be $3.3 billion. If we lower the price, our net profits will be $3.08 billion, and If we raise the price, our net profit will also be $3.3 billion.

Interviewer: So if we raise the price or leave it alone, we'll make the same net profit. What do you want to do and why?

Student: I'd like to keep the price the same. You said market share was a key objective, and if we raise the price, we are going to sell 55,000 fewer bikes. That's about a 5% drop, which will probably lower our market share. If we sell more bikes, we'll sell more garb and evidentially more replacement parts. And even if we cut production, we will still probably have a lot of Year 2 inventory left over. What do we do with it when the Year 3 models come out? If we sell it at a discount, we'll probably cannibalize our Year 3 sales.

Interviewer: That's all very interesting, but let me tell you why you're wrong. If we raise the price we'll have lower labor costs because we'll be able to lay more people off. In addition, the higher price will enhance the brand. As far as your other concerns go, you told me that you plan to increase international distribution channels where the dollar is still weak. If we do that, any extra inventory can be shipped overseas and sold at the new higher price. Garb sales tend to be higher when you enter a new territory. So market share shouldn't be an issue. Besides, how do you measure market share? Is it number of units sold or total revenues?

Analysis: Ouch. The interviewer got right in her face even though she gave a well thought out answer. Luckily she knows that this "let me tell you why you're wrong" business is just a test. She keeps her emotions in check and does what the interviewer wants her to do, stick with and defend her answer.

Student: You make an interesting argument; however, I don't find it compelling enough. I can't believe that you can do all that within an 18-month period. Therefore, I think the best option in these economic conditions would be to keep the price the same.

Interviewer: Okay, good. Give me two long-term revenue-based ideas and two long-term cost-based ideas.

Student: Can I take a moment to jot some ideas down?

Interviewer: Certainly.

Student: Okay. On the revenue-based side, the first thing I'd do is come up with a new bike that is geared not only towards women but to younger men as well. This will give us something to market to women besides garb. I'd also look to see if we can acquire a scooter company. We couldn't put the Harley name on it, but we can take advantage of the fastest growing segments of the market, women and scooters. Besides, there will be a number of synergies we would be able to take advantage of. On the cost side, we were concerned about the price of steel. We can buy some steel futures to hedge against a steel increase. We could stockpile some steel at the current price, and because we are developing a new bike, we can make more parts out of composites instead of steel. We could modernize the plant with new technologies and maybe have some parts made overseas.

Interviewer: Good. Why don't you take a moment and summarize the case for me.

Student: Our client is Harley-Davidson. Their stock dropped around 10% on news of declining profits. We looked at external factors first and determined that it was more of a Harley problem than an industry problem. They are out of step with the two fast growing segments of the industry, women and scooters. So we came up with some short-term and long-term strategies both on the revenue and cost side. An example of a short-term revenue-based strategy is offering low financing to customers. On the cost side, we could refinance our debt. In the long-term we would produce a new bike geared towards women and younger men and acquire a scooter maker. On the cost side, we could hedge steel prices and have certain new parts made out of composite instead of steel. If Harley followed these strategies as well as some of the others we talked about, they should be on their way to higher profits in 24 to 36 months.

Analysis: She came on very strong at the end. The turning point was when she defended her decision to keep the price the same. That gave her additional confidence and it showed through the rest of the interview.

Case Index

+ Mexican Bank

Case 1: Our client is a major commercial bank in Mexico. Despite the fact that the bank has experienced increased revenue growth, for the past two years its profits have declined and even become negative. You have a meeting with the CEO of the bank in a week and you have to come up with answers to two questions: what is the main cause of this decline in profits, and what can we do to restore the bank's profitability?

Besides finding out why our client is experiencing declining profits and determining a strategy out of trouble, are there any other objectives I should be concerned about?

– No.

I would like to approach this case in two parts. First, I will try to diagnose the cause of the decline in profits, despite the growth in revenues. Then, based on the findings in the first part, I will try to come up with solutions to our problems and put the bank on a path to profitability.

Let's start with the first issue: the diagnosis of the problem. Here, I would like to look at three main aspects: the overall banking industry in Mexico, our bank's revenues and finally, the costs.

– Sounds like a good plan. What would you like to know?

The student writes down E(P=R–C)M? (see page 45).

First, I would like to look at the banking industry in Mexico. Is this an industry-wide problem or does it primarily affect our client? Also, can you tell me more about our client's competitive positioning within this industry?

– It's actually just our client that's experiencing the severe decline in profits. While the other banks have also experienced declines, they have been more moderate. Our client is a major player in the industry, owning 20% of the market share. There are three other major national competitors with similar market shares and many smaller, regional competitors. Anything else?

It looks like it is mainly an internal problem rather than an industry-wide problem. Before analyzing the bank's costs, both fixed and variable, I'd first like to look at the bank's revenues in more detail. I'm assuming that banks make their money from interest income and from fees. Also, on the cost side, I would like to analyze both the fixed costs and the variable costs.

– That's right. The bank makes money in two main ways: interest income and fee income. Our client has about 70% of its revenues coming from interest and the remaining 30% coming from fees. However, I would like you to look at the following graph and analyze it for me. Our client currently has 8 million customers.

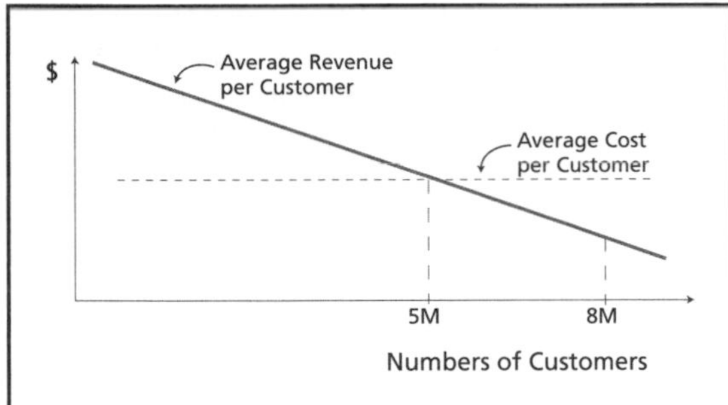

That's a very interesting graph. If our client has 8 million customers, the average cost per customer is higher than the average revenue per customer, thus resulting in a loss. Let's take them one by one.

Our client is experiencing declining average revenues per customer. There are several hypotheses why this might be happening. As the bank was growing, it was acquiring new customers that are not as profitable as the initial customers. For example, instead of signing up more doctors, lawyers or consultants, it is now signing up students or blue collar workers that don't produce as much revenue, thus resulting in the observed decline in average revenues per customer.

On the cost side, the average cost per customer is staying constant, instead of declining. We can see that there are little or no economies of scale. Potential reasons behind this would imply that as the bank was adding new customers, the costs were also increasing proportionally.

– That's great – and accurate. Due to the incentive structure which rewarded new customer acquisition, branch managers have added customers that were not as profitable as the initial ones. In addition, the bank has aggressively expanded its branch structure and has increased the number of tellers to accommodate the increased number of customers. What should the bank do?

Well, now that we have diagnosed the main reason for the decline in profits as a combination of newer, less profitable customers and the proportional increase in costs, we can propose a solution. A simple but not ideal solution would be to eliminate the additional, less profitable customers while simultaneously reducing the number of branches and tellers to bring us to the initial profitability.

A second, better solution would include two concurrent approaches. First, we should try to increase average revenues per customer, and second, we should decrease average costs per customer. In increasing the revenues, we would come up with new products that would result in increased interest income. We can also increase the fees we charge our customers. In decreasing costs, we could attempt to close off our least profitable branches and reduce our teller personnel.

My proposed solution, however, will produce even better results. I propose segmenting our current customers in several customer tiers and adjusting the service level and implicitly the costs according to the customer tier. For example, high net worth individuals would have unrestricted access to personal bankers and new services would be tailored to their specific needs.

At the other end of the spectrum, our client should educate the students about the benefits of using cheaper delivery systems like ATMs or online services. They would still have access to the tellers; however, we would limit their free access to two free teller visits per month. After those visits, we could start charging 30 pesos per visit or around $3US. In effect, we would adjust our service delivery model based on the customer's value to the bank. This would achieve both our goals of increasing revenues, by better addressing the needs of each customer segment, and reducing costs by redirecting the lower value customers to the cheaper servicing channels.

– Okay, good.

Type of case: Profit and loss, marketing, customer segmentation

Comments: What started out as a profit and loss case quickly changed into a marketing / customer segmentation case. The student did a good job analyzing the chart and came up with a number of good possible solutions for the client.

+ Yellow Stuff Chemical Company

Case 2: Our client is a manufacturer that makes industrial cleaning solvents and pesticides. Recently, sales have been declining, mostly due to new EPA guidelines. The company has been "dumping" its old products overseas into countries that have less stringent environmental laws as well as re-engineering its products to fit the new EPA guidelines. Further evaluation of sales, both past and future, indicates that the chemical industry has, and will, continue to grow slowly over the next five to seven years, with 3% annual growth.

Management has decided to diversify. While Yellow Stuff wants to keep its chemical business intact, it also wants to enter an industry that has long-term, high-growth potential. Yellow Stuff has hired us to help determine what industry or industries it should enter.

While I don't want you to come up with a list of industries, I do want you to tell me what sort of things you should be researching to determine what industry our client should diversify into.

So as I understand it, our client is a chemical manufacturer who wants to diversify outside the chemical industry into a high-growth industry.

– That's right.

And you want me to come up with a strategy on how to find the best possible match.

– Yes.

Besides diversification and profit, are there any other objectives that I should know about?

– No.

What does the company define as high-growth?

– 10% a year.

Well, the first thing I'd do is obtain a list of all the industries and eliminate the ones that are growing less than 15% or that have a potential in the next year of growing less than 15%. How much risk is Yellow Stuff willing to take?

– Medium.

Then, I'd also eliminate any high-risk or volatile industries. Next, I'd study the list to see if there are any synergies that we can share.

– Such as?

One example might be to look to see if there is a sister industry where our customer list is the same. If we sell cleaning solvents to Pepsi and then we get into manufacturing aluminum, maybe we can sell Pepsi soda cans. We also have a history of marketing and selling

business-to-business, so we might want to stay away from consumer products. We could look at other commonalities, such as distribution channels and sales force.

Once we narrow the list, we need to analyze the market to find out who the major players are and what, if any, the barriers to entering the market are.

– Okay, what else?

There are three ways to enter a new market: start from scratch, acquire an existing player, or do a joint venture. Depending on the industry and the barriers...

– What sort of barriers are you talking about?

Could be government regulations. If you try to start a business and your products have to get approved by the FDA or the EPA, then that could take years. In a case like that, you might want to acquire an existing player. A barrier might be a stranglehold on the market: if, for example, two companies hold an extraordinarily large market share and have a habit of destroying new entries. If raw materials or supplies would be hard to come by, that would be another barrier.

– Okay.

Did I mention substitutions as a barrier?

– What's next?

I'd look very carefully at the future of the industry. It may be growing currently over 10%, but is that going to last and for how long? Is the market growing or shrinking? Are the number of players growing or shrinking? Have there been many mergers or acquisitions lately? And I'd take some time to think about exit strategies as well.

– Summarize for me.

I'd identify all the relevant industries, analyze their markets, and determine the best way to enter that market. I'd also conduct an analysis to see if the company might not be better off just investing the money into the stock market. It may make a better return and its investment would be a lot more liquid.

- **Type of case: Entering a new market**

- **Comments: Ninety percent of this question is irrelevant fluff. It's not about the chemical industry, it's about entering a new market. The candidate took the time to ask for the company's definition of high-growth. From there, it was straight logic. Now, some of you might argue that this was really a growth strategies question, but the question tells us that the client really wants to diversify, which narrows the growth strategies to one: diversification. The question then becomes one of identifying the new industry.**

✛ Eastern Training Network

Case 3: Our client is a mid-size training company that serves New England and the Atlantic Seaboard regions. It offers a variety of computer training and consulting services. Eastern just found out that IBM is going to enter into its segment of the market. What does it do?

Eastern Training Network just found out that IBM is entering its segment of the market and wants to know what to do. I'm assuming that the objectives are to either keep IBM out of our market or to maintain as much market share as we can. Is that a fair set of assumptions?

– Yes.

Are there any other objectives that I should be aware of?

– No.

Are there other firms in our area that we currently compete with?

– Yes. Including us, there are three major players that do what we do and maybe three smaller firms that serve one or two clients exclusively.

Do we know what Eastern's market share is?

– Eastern's market share within the region is 24%.

Do we know what our two other competitors are doing to keep IBM out?

– No. Good question but not relevant.

Since one of my major objectives is to maintain market share, I'd break my strategy down into three prongs. First, I'd try to keep IBM out. Second, I'd try to protect what's mine. And third, I'd go after new customers.

RAISE BARRIERS TO ENTRY
KEEP IBM OUT
RAISE SWITCHING COSTS
STRATEGY
PROTECT MARKET SHARE
VISIT CUSTOMERS / CREATE LOYALTY PROGRAM
LONG-TERM CONTRACTS
GET NEW CUSTOMERS
INCREASE MARKETING EFFORTS / INCREASE SALES COMMISSION
STEAL SALES STAFF AND CUSTOMERS AWAY FROM COMPETITION
GROW THROUGH ACQUISITION

– Explain.

I would try to figure out what I can do to raise the barriers of entry and keep IBM out. Since they have almost unlimited resources and because this is an unregulated industry, I think the chances of that are pretty nil.

Second, I'd try to protect what's mine. It is much cheaper to keep your current customers than it is to go out and get new ones. So I'd do three things. I'd raise switching costs, make it so that it wouldn't make sense to leave us for IBM.

– Give me an example.

Since I don't know the industry that well, I'd like to give another example. AOL makes it hard for customers to leave because they have what are called "sticky" features. Customers have their email address with AOL; they have their address book with AOL; and their customers have access to certain web information and additional benefits. So to switch over to another Internet provider becomes a hassle.

– Point taken. What's next?

I'd protect what's mine. I'd visit with my customers and find out what is important to them. Maybe increase my promotional efforts. Maybe come up with customer loyalty programs. Make them feel wanted and special. Everyone likes to feel appreciated. And second, I would do everything I could to establish long-term contracts to lock customers in. To go along with that, I'd build in incentives or give commissions to our sales staff to re-sign a client.

– Third?

Bring in new customers. I'd increase my marketing efforts, place ads, go to conventions, lobby for state contracts. I'd try to steal sales staff and customers away from my competition. And finally, I would grow through acquisition. You mentioned that there were a number of smaller players that had one or two big accounts. I'd see if they would like to sell their businesses.

– Don't you think that's risky? To lay out capital to buy up small firms when IBM is coming to town. What's to guarantee that the small firm's clients won't jump to IBM?

There are no guarantees. However, being IBM is a double-edged sword. On the one hand, IBM is big, has an incredible amount of resources and the potential to do great things. On the other hand, it is because it is so big that things might very well fall through the cracks. Am I wrong in thinking that the training we offer is similar to what IBM offers? I think the things that will differentiate us are our people and our customer service. We're going to fight and do everything we can to hold on to our customer base while we prospect for new business. Being the biggest isn't always an advantage.

– What if IBM comes in and offers the same services you do, but offers a steep discount for clients to sign up? Do you lower your prices?

No. I wouldn't engage in a price war with IBM. There is no way to win. I believe that Eastern offers great products at competitive prices. If customers like us, they're not going to go to IBM to save a little money. This is not like shopping around for the best deal on a new refrigerator. We're in the services business; it's all about the service. That doesn't mean I wouldn't be flexible in cutting existing customers a favorable deal to sign a long-term contract.

– I think I almost believe you. Summarize for me.

My strategy would be three-pronged. One, keep IBM out by raising the barriers to entry. Two, do whatever it takes to keep our current customers. We talked about raising switching costs, increasing promotional efforts — things like customer loyalty programs and establishing long-term contracts. And finally, grow through acquisition and a major marketing effort.

– That was good.

Type of Case: Competitive response

Comments: The three-pronged approach served the student well. He was able to lay out his strategy in a clear and logical manner that was simple and easy to follow. The student stood his ground when pushed about a price war. Whether you agree with him or not, he articulated his point and stuck with it.

+ Coke®

Case 4: Coca-Cola is trying to boost profitability domestically by raising its prices. It's focusing on the grocery store market where the volume is high but the margin is low. What are the economics of raising the prices and is this a good idea?

So, Coke plans to increase profitability by raising prices. They want to know if that's a good idea.

– That's right.

I know that raising profitability is their main objective. Are there other objectives that I should be aware of?

– They don't want to lose market share.

Are we just focusing on Coke and not any of their other brands?

– You can think of all Coke products as one product, Coke.

What's Coke's current market share?

– Not relevant to the question.

How much does it cost to make a can of Coke?

– Not relevant to the question.

How many cans does Coke sell to US grocery stores and at what price?

– Coke sold 100 million cans at 23 cents each to grocery stores last year. If prices remain stable, they expect volume growth of 6%. They want to raise the price to 27 cents per can and they forecast volume growth of only 1%.

Let's see. First I can multiply and then find the difference:

100,000,000 cans x .27 x 1.01 = $27,270,000
100,000,000 cans x .23 x 1.06 = $24,380,000
$ 2,890,000

So even though they would be selling 5 million less cans of Coke, they'd be making more of a profit, about 3 million dollars more.

– Profitability would be boosted by what percent?

I can take 27 minus 24 equals 3 divided by 24 equals approximately 12%.
By raising prices and selling less, Coke can boost its sales by approximately 12%.

– To maintain market share, Coke needs to stir up consumer demand with a major marketing campaign to raise brand awareness and focus on lifestyle issues. Knowing that, and if you were Pepsi, what would you do?

Pepsi has three choices. It can follow Coke's lead and raise its prices to match Coke's: it can leave prices the way they are; or it can take advantage of the price change and lower its price.

If Coke spends a fortune marketing its product and it does its job and gets people into the stores, Pepsi can snatch sales away at the last minute with a lower price. We are talking grocery stores here. Women do most of the buying in grocery stores and are often price conscious. If they saw two brand name colas, Pepsi and Coke, and if Coke sold for $2.99 a 12-pack compared to $2.59 for a 12-pack of Pepsi, then most shoppers would choose the one on sale or the one with the lower price.

Pepsi might even want to lower its price so it can increase its market share.

In sailing, if you are behind, you're not going to catch up with or beat the opponent by sailing the same course. You have to take a different tact. If Pepsi lowers its prices and cuts marketing costs, it can steal customers away from Coke through in-store promotions and point-of-contact displays.

– So, if you were Pepsi, what would you do?

Let's run some numbers. How many cans does Pepsi sell to grocery stores.

– Pepsi sells 80 million cans at 23 cents a piece.
If Pepsi follows Coke and raises its prices, its volume will drop from 6 to 3%.
If Pepsi keeps its price the same, its volume will increase from 6 to 12%.
If Pepsi lowers its prices to 21 cents, Pepsi's volume will increase from 6 to 20%.

80,000,000 x 1.03 = 82,400,000 x .27 = 22,248,000
80,000,000 x 1.12 = 89,600,000 x .23 = 20,608,000
80,000,000 x 1.20 = 96,000,000 x .21 = 20,160,000

I'd follow Coke's lead.

– Even if you knew that Coke's volume would rise from 1% to 3%?

Yes.

– Interesting. Thanks.

- **Type of case: Strategy based on numbers**
- **Comments: It's a straightforward case once you have the numbers.**

+ Road to Ruin

Case 5: A chemical company recently developed a road-surfacing compound designed to extend the life of major highways. Currently, the federal and state governments must completely dig up and replace their highways every five years. If highways are treated with this chemical, their effective life span increases to 20 years. Currently, the government spends $1,000 per mile to replace its roads. The total cost of the chemical (production and application) amounts to $50 per mile. The management of the chemical company would like to know the following:

- **Estimate the number of miles of state and federal highways in the US.**
- **How should management price the product?**
- **What other issues should the company be aware of?**

Let me make sure I understand. A chemical company has developed a compound that extends the life of highways from five to 20 years. Currently, it costs the government $1,000 a mile to rip up a road and replace it. We can apply the compound for $50 a mile, and this $50 covers all development and application costs. Now the client wants us to estimate the number of government highway miles, price the product on a per mile basis and determine what other issues we should be taking into consideration.

– Yes.

Besides those three items, are there any other objectives or goals I should be aware of?

– No.

How big is this chemical company?

– It's a venture-backed start-up. This is their first and only product.

Are there any other competitors or substitutions? And do we have a patent?

– No and yes, respectively.

We know the advantages of this product, but are there any disadvantages to this product like environmental concerns?

– Excellent question, but the answer is no.

Okay, let's start with the first request. To estimate the number of government highway miles, I'm going to make some assumptions. First, I'm going to assume that the distance between the east and west coasts is 3,000 miles and that the distance between the northern and southern borders of the US is 2,000 miles. I'm also going to assume that if you straighten out all the highways, you'll have 10 roads running east to west and another ten running north to south. So 10 times 3,000 is 30,000 and 10 times 2,000 equals 20,000 miles. Add them together and you get approximately 50,000 miles of government highways.

– Okay, I'll buy that. What's next?

We need to determine a price. There are several pricing methods that we can look at as a base and then make a determination. There is competitive pricing, but since we have no competitor, this is impossible. We can look at substitutions, which is what the government is currently doing — ripping up the roads at a cost of $1,000 a mile every five years. Since this process lasts for 20 years, we should use 20 years as a common denominator. I'll get back to that in a minute. We can use cost-based pricing and stick a margin on top. Our cost is $50 per mile. If we double that to a 100% markup, we'd come up with a price of $100 a mile. Finally, we can look at price-based costing. This is what the government would be willing to pay.

I mentioned the 20-year common denominator. So if you take 50,000 miles and multiply it by four, you get 200,000 miles. Under the current plan, it costs the government 200,000 times $1,000 a mile, which equals — $200 million. Our break-even point is 50,000 times $50, which equals $2.5 million. So, our price range is $2.5 million to $200 million.

– That's quite a range.

I think it is time to look at some of the other factors. If the government does this, it will have the construction lobby on its back, not to mention the labor unions. People will be laid off and the government will be facing unemployment issues and payments. Even though I'm assuming that this is a Department of Transportation decision, you can bet that Congress will weigh in on the subject. So the secret is to price it so that the savings are substantial and Congress can't stop it without looking fiscally irresponsible. What if we charged them $100 million? We would be in good shape and that's half of what they pay now. They can divert the $100 million in savings to other infrastructure projects so no one gets laid off.

– So what does that breakdown to per mile?

Fifty thousand miles divided into $100 million equals — $20,000 a mile — no that's wrong, it's $2,000 a mile.

– Are you sure?

Yes, $2,000 a mile. In addition, as far as cash layout goes, the government currently pays $50 million a year. Our total is $100 million. We can spread that over the length of the project, which I assumed would be two or three years.

– Okay. Thanks for coming by.

Type of Case: Estimate the market size, new product and pricing

Additional Comments: This is an interesting case because it touches on so many different aspects and scenarios. The student first asked about the product, then she estimated the market size. She was smart enough not to answer the pricing question until she took the outside factors into account.

✛ Longest-lasting Light Bulb

Case 6: GE, they bring good things to life, has invented a new light bulb that never burns out. It could burn for more than 500 years and it would never blink. The director of marketing calls you into her office and asks, "How would you price this?" What do you tell her?

Let me make sure I understand. GE has invented a light bulb that never burns out, and the marketing director wants us to help her decide on a price.

– That's correct.

Is coming up with a price the only objective? Or is there something else I should be concerned about?

– Pricing is the only objective.

Is there any competition for this product, and do we have a patent?

– We have a patent pending, and there is no other competition.

We know that the advantage is that this bulb never burns out. Are there any disadvantages to this product? Does it use the same amount of electricity?

– There are no disadvantages, except maybe price. And that's why you're here.

What did you spend on R&D?

– It cost $20 million to develop this product.

What are the costs associated with a conventional light bulb?

– It costs us five cents to manufacture. We sell it to the distributor for a quarter, the distributor sells it to the store for 50 cents, and the store sells it to the consumer for 75 cents.

And what does it cost us to manufacture the new light bulb?

– Five dollars.

So if we use the conventional bulb-pricing model, that would mean that the consumer would have to pay $75 for this light bulb. If we use another simple model and say that a light bulb lasts one year and that people will have this new bulb for 50 years, that's an argument for a retail price of $37.50 (50 years x $0.75). Then we need to ask ourselves whether a consumer would pay $37.50 for a light bulb that never wears out. Now we're looking at price-based costing. What are people willing to pay? And is it enough to cover our costs and give us a nice profit?

The other main issue is that the more successful we are, the less successful we'll be in the future. For every eternal light bulb we sell, that's 50 or 75 conventional bulbs we won't sell in the future. In a sense, we're cannibalizing our future markets. So, we have to make sure that there is enough of a margin or profit to cover us way into the future.

– Good point.

I'll tell you, I have reservations about selling to the consumer market. I just don't think the opportunity for pricing is there.

– So, what do we do, scrap the project? We've already spent over $20 million in R&D.

Not at all. We turn to the industrial market. For example, the City of Cambridge probably has 2,000 street lamps. Those bulbs cost maybe $20 and have to be changed twice a year. The real expense there isn't the cost of the bulb; it's the labor. It might take two union workers. In addition, you have to send out a truck. It probably costs the city $150 in labor costs just to change the light bulb. Now, if we were to sell them this ever-lasting bulb for $400, they would make that money back in less than two years and we would make a handsome profit.

– Not bad.

Type of case: Pricing

Comments: First, the candidate looked at cost-based pricing and realized that the price was too high and that the typical consumer would not shell out $75 for a light bulb. Then he looked at price-based costing and concluded there wasn't enough of a margin built in to make it profitable. Thinking outside the outline given in the pricing case scenario, the student also realized that he would be cannibalizing his future markets. Thus, he decided that neither pricing strategy made sense for the retail market. So, instead of suggesting that GE just cut its losses and walk away from the project, he went looking for alternative markets and concluded that there was great potential in the industrial market.

Because this product has yet to be released, and is without competition, the supply and demand theory doesn't work in this case.

✛ Getting into Diapers

Case 7: DuPont has just invented a lightweight, super-absorbent, biodegradable material that would be perfect for disposable diapers. What should they do with it?

DuPont has developed a new material that would be great for disposable diapers and they want to know how best to take advantage of this product.

– Yes.

One objective is to figure out what to do with this material. Any other objectives?

– Yes, make a handsome profit. But first, I'd like you to figure out the size of the disposable diaper market.

Okay. I'm going to make some assumptions. I'll assume that the population of the US is 280 million and that the life expectancy of an average American is 80 years. I'm also going to assume that there are even numbers of people in each age group. So, that means that there are the exact same number of three year-olds as 73 year-olds. So you divide 280 million by 80 and you get 3.5 million people per age group. Children wear diapers from age zero to three, so that's 10.5 million children. Let's round it down to 10 million children. I'm going to assume that 80% of the children wear disposable diapers, so that's 8 million kids times five diapers a day equaling 40 million diapers a day. Multiply that by 365 days and you get 14.6 billion diapers times, I don't know, say, $1 a diaper. So the market is $14.6 billion a year.

– So, now we know the market size. What's next?

We look at the market and see who the major players are, what kind of market share each has, and what the pricing differentials are. I know P&G has a large part of that market and I know that there are a number of generic brands as well. The competition is tough, but I can't think of any barriers that would really stop us.

– So, you think we should get into the diaper business?

Yes, but we need to figure what part of the business. When I asked you if there were any other objectives or goals, you said profit. What you didn't say was to become a major player in the consumer diapers market. That means that there are several ways we can enter. I'd like to list them, then look at the advantages and disadvantages of each.

We can start up our own diaper company, form a joint venture, buy a smaller player and substitute our product for theirs or manufacture the diapers and license them to a number of companies.

First, let's look at starting our own company. We have name recognition, but not in that industry. We would have to set up a manufacturing plant, hire a management team, marketing team and sales force and establish distribution channels. Time consuming and expensive, but doable.

Second, we can form a joint venture with an established diaper company. The advantages there are that the company would already have everything in place as far as name recognition, management team, sales force and distribution channels. But we might find this limiting. Depending on the deal, we might only be able to manufacture for them.

Third, we can buy a diaper company and substitute our product for theirs. This has merit for all the same reasons the joint venture has. We need to ask ourselves if we really want to manufacture and market diapers or just manufacture them.

The fourth option is to license our product to a variety of companies. If our technology is superior to the existing product, then let's get multiple companies on board and let their marketing experts fight it out.

– Good. So which one would you choose?

With just the information I have so far, I'd venture to say the last option: manufacture and license the rights, become a supplier and do what DuPont does best — manufacture.

We could even go to the different diaper companies and get pre-orders to ensure that the market is there and our pricing is in line.

- **Type of case: Market-sizing and entering a new market**

- **Comments: At first, some might think this to be a developing a new product question, and they could probably make a decent case out of it. But the question really asks, "What should they do with it?" That implies that the product has already been developed and the company is searching for the best way to exploit this new technology; thus, this is an entering a new market case.**

What impressed the interviewer here was the fact that he picked up on what the interviewer didn't say and built on that. That's an extraordinary example of great listening — the best skill a consultant can have.

✛ New York Opera

Case 8: Our client is the New York City Opera. They want to develop a growth strategy for the next five years. What would you advise them to look at, and what are your recommendations for growth?

The New York City Opera wants us to develop a growth strategy for the next five years.

– That's right.

Besides developing this five-year strategy, are there any other objectives?

– No.

So I don't need to look at increasing sales, reducing costs or increasing profits?

– Those are all key ingredients to growth, are they not?

Yes, I guess they are. I was just trying to determine the direction of the question. I'd like to ask a few questions. Is the industry growing?

– No, down 7% last year.

How are we faring compared to the industry?

– Better, but not much. Our growth rate last year was 2%.

Who are our competitors and how much market share does each one have?

– Who do you think our competition is?

It's anyone or anything that competes for the leisure dollar. It could be as widespread as a restaurant, a hockey game, events at Lincoln Center, or a trip to the Hamptons. But it is also other opera companies in New York. I'm not sure how many opera companies there are in New York.

– There are about four. The biggest is the Metropolitan Opera. Can you name any operas?

Sure. There's *Tommy* and *Figaro*. Oh, and *The Barber of Seville*.

– Okay. That helps me put your answer in perspective. So what do you do?

The first thing I would do is a competitive analysis. I would not only look at the other four New York opera companies, but those in other major US cities and maybe London and Paris as well.

– What would you analyze?

Everything. Revenues and revenue streams, ticket distribution outlets, fixed costs, marginal costs, production costs, season schedule, ticket prices, the names and types of operas produced, marquee names in each production, marketing campaigns and other uses for the venue.

– That's quite a list. After you did the analysis, what would you do?

I'd take the best practices and see if it makes sense to incorporate any of those practices at the New York City Opera.

– You mentioned revenue streams. What do you think the revenue streams are currently?

Ticket sales, sales of programs, drinks during intermission, and merchandise like CDs, t-shirts — that sort of thing. And I think fundraising is an important revenue stream as well.

– How would you increase revenues?

Three ways. We can look at increasing ticket prices; we can increase our marketing campaign to get more people to come to the opera; and once they're there, get them to spend more money.

– Can you think of additional revenue streams?

Maybe holding lectures and panels or possibly giving lessons?

– We're not offering singing lessons. What else?

I'll assume that an opera does not perform 365 days a year and that there are often stretches of time when the venue is open or in preproduction. Every night that the opera house sits empty, we're losing money. So, why not hold other events in the venue, specifically musical events. I mean, the acoustics have to be unbelievable, don't you think?

– I would imagine. Okay, good. You also mentioned ticket distribution.

Yes. I'd check to see if you can buy tickets over the web and at other ticket outlets. See if we can come up with a few additional and maybe untraditional outlets or distribution channels. I'll assume that they have discounts for season ticket holders, large groups, students and senior citizens.

– That's correct.

I think schools are a good place to educate future opera fans. We have to rebuild the audience. Get the next generation interested in opera.

– The next area you mentioned was costs. I don't want to spend too much time on this, but I'll assume that you'll work hard to reduce all our costs.

Yes.

– To be honest with you, your answer isn't going where I want it to go. I feel like we're getting too bogged down in details. The question was about growth strategy. Unless you have more to say about growth strategies, we'll end this interview right now.

Well, we've talked about increasing sales by bringing in a big name singer, adding new distribution channels for tickets and merchandise sales, as well as possible new revenue streams. We talked about increasing the product line and the diversity of that product line. That could

mean new merchandise or more operas, but I think it means different shows, concerts or maybe stand-up comic revues — anything that fills the opera house on nights when there is no performance. A third strategy — that doesn't apply, but I thought I would mention — is acquiring the competition, maybe buying one of the smaller opera companies. But it doesn't sound like we have a lot of extra cash on hand, and what we do have can be better allocated toward driving more people in our door.

– That was a nice summation, but there was nothing new there.

One last thing. This summer I worked for a mutual fund company and what we discovered is that 95% of the business came from 5% of the customer base. This company wasn't fully taking advantage of the opportunities to grow through its existing customer base. Up until this summer, they never differentiated between customers who represented real profits and customers that only represented costs.

– This is good. Continue.

They found that over one-third of the money spent on marketing and customer service was wasted on efforts to acquire new customers who cost us more than we made. In some cases, we were marketing toward our established customers when that money could have been better spent.

– So what are you telling me?

We should focus the company on bringing in new and profitable customers. That may mean changing the way we currently and traditionally market. It means developing better relationships with our profitable customers. And finally, it means abandoning those customers that cause us to lose money.

– I think that theory applies to a mutual fund company better than an opera company, but I'll give you points for trying.

Type of Case: Growth strategies

Comments: Her answer was all over the place. Parts of it were very strong; other parts weren't. She went off on a tangent and got herself into trouble. The other thing is that she never really came up with anything extraordinary. Everything she mentioned had been tried before. The last bit about growing through existing customers and weeding out the dogs was interesting if not totally relevant.

N.B. Many firms have a version of this question. They could ask about a music school, a museum or a symphony.

✛ The Discount Brokerage Race

Case 9: Look at this chart. Your client is a discount brokerage. The majority of its revenue comes from online trading. It achieved a 10% growth rate last year (Y1) and was ranked number six in the industry. In Y2 it fell to seventh. The company wants to get back its sixth place ranking. How much will it have to grow to maintain that 6th place ranking in Y3, given the rate of growth of its competitors?

Company	Industry Ranking	Current Size in Year 1 (Revenue)	Growth Rate	Year 2	Industry Ranking
A	1	$1000m	1%	1010	1
B	2	$900m	2%	918	2
C	3	$800m	0%	800	4
D	4	$800m	5%	840	3
E	5	$700m	5%	735	5
F	6	$600m	10%	660	7
G	7	$600m	20%	720	6
H	8	$500m	20%	600	8
I	9	$500m	10%	550	9
J	10	$400m	30%	520	10
K	11	$300m	20%	360	11
L	12	$300m	30%	390	12

Our client is Company F, a discount brokerage. In Y1 we were ranked sixth with a growth rate of 10% and sales of 600 million. In Y2 we dropped to seventh place with a growth rate of 10% and revenues of $660 million. You want me to figure out how much we will have to grow by in order to get our sixth place ranking back in Y3.

– Yes, that's right.

Is it fair to assume that the growth rates of all the other firms will remain the same?

– Yes.

Do you mind if I write on the chart you gave me?

– No, go ahead.

I'm going to do part of this through a process of elimination. Everyone below Company F growing at a smaller or equal rate or whose revenues are significantly below ours can be eliminated. So that's easily the bottom four — I through L.

We also know that A and B will remain the top two. So I need to concentrate on C through H, including us — F. So, first, I'm going to do the calculations for each of those and see where they stand.

Company	Industry Ranking	Current Size in Year 1 (Revenue)	Growth Rate	Year 2	Industry Ranking	Year 3	Industry Ranking
A	1	1000	1%	1010	1		1
B	2	900	2%	918	2		2
C	3	800	0%	800	4	800	5
D	4	800	5%	840	3	882	3
E	5	700	5%	735	5	772	6
F	6	600	10%	660	7	726	7
G	7	600	20%	720	6	864	4
H	8	500	20%	600	8	720	
I	9	500	10%	550	9		
J	10	400	30%	520	10		
K	11	300	20%	360	11		
L	12	300	30%	390	12		

If we stayed at a 10% growth rate we'd have revenues of $726 million, which would put us in seventh place. So, how fast do we need to grow? If we round Company E's sales off to $772 then that's our target number. We need to beat 772. So we need an increase of over $46 million (772 – 726). So 660X = 772. Divide each side by 660 and we get X equals ... about 1.17 or 17%. A minimum 17% growth in Y3 would put us in sixth place.

Company	Year 3	Industry Ranking
A		1
B		2
C	800	5
D	882	3
E	771.75	7
F	772	6
G	864	4
H	720	8

– Okay, good. Which company would you invest in and why?

I'd invest in G, provided they can continue their 20% growth rate.

- **Type of case: Numbers**
- **Comments: This case was a pure numbers case. The student did well by eliminating what was obvious and using her time efficiently.**

+ Cow Brothers Premium Ice Cream

◗ Case 10: Cow Brothers is a maker of super premium ice cream, low-fat ice cream, low-fat yogurt, and sorbet. Its products are high quality and the company uses only natural ingredients. Cow Brothers products are distributed nationwide through supermarkets, grocery stores, convenience stores, franchises and company-owned ice cream shops and restaurants.

Cow Brothers has 30 flavors and sells its products in one-pint containers. It also has single servings on a stick.

Cow Brothers has strong brand recognition. Its "Have a Cow" marketing campaign met with great success. Last year sales were $200 million ($177 million came from supermarket and grocery store sales), which put the company third in the industry behind Haagen-Dazs and Ben & Jerry's. These top three competitors hold 62% of the market.

The president, Winston Cow, is still not satisfied. He wants to increase company sales to $250 million by next year. How do you do it?

Let me make sure I understand. Cow Brothers, the number three maker of premium ice cream, wants to increase its sales from $200 million to $250 million next year. That would be an increase of around 25%. How much did Cow Brothers' sales increase last year?

– 10%.

And that was mainly due to the "Have a Cow" marketing campaign?

– Yes.

One objective is to increase company sales. Are there any other objectives or goals that I should be aware of?

– No.

Is the company privately held?

– Yes.

What was the overall industry growth last year?

– 12%.

So Haggen-Daz and Ben & Jerry's only grew by 12% last year?

– No. Ben & Jerry's grew by 20%; Haagen-Dazs by less.

First, we should analyze what Ben & Jerry's did to increase its sales and compare it not only to what we did but to what Haagen-Dazs did as well.

– Fine. What else?

Student draws the decision tree as she speaks.

We need not only to increase sales but also to grow the company. The three major ways to increase sales are to raise prices to get customers to buy more when they purchase Cow Brothers and to expand our market base. Are we priced competitively?

– Our prices exactly match our competitors.

So that's a no for raising prices. You mentioned that Cow Brothers only produces ice cream in the one-pint containers. Have they thought about a two-pint container? That way customers would buy more per transaction.

– That's a possibility.

The third way is to expand our market base. I'd like to talk growth strategies. I know of five main growth strategies: increase distribution channels, increase product line, launch a major marketing campaign, diversify and acquire a competitor. I'd like to look at the advantages and disadvantages of each of these and see which makes sense.

It seems as if we are tied into all the major distribution channels for our products. But there must be areas of the country where distribution is weak. I'd analyze those markets and see if we can't increase the number of outlets that carry our products.

Next, we need to increase our product line: You said we have 30 flavors. How many flavors do the supermarkets and ice cream shops carry?

– The supermarkets carry five at a time; the ice cream shops carry 15.

We don't want to increase the number of flavors because no one can carry them as is. We need to add new sizes, not new flavors. You said that the "Have a Cow" marketing campaign went well. We should look at increasing our marketing budget.

The next idea is somewhat radical, but bear with me. Diversification. Cow Brothers has great brand recognition. It's well-known and stands for quality. In marketing class we read Ted Levitt's article "Marketing Myopia," in which he uses an example of the buggy whip company. When the car came along, the demand for buggy whips dropped significantly. If the buggy whip company saw itself as being in the transportation business instead of the buggy whip industry, it would still be in business today. Likewise, if Cow Brothers pictures itself in the dairy business or gourmet foods business, it can take better advantage of its brand name.

Cow Brothers might want to try a line of gourmet cheeses and cream cheeses. The cream cheeses could be distributed through all the regular distribution channels, but we could also create new distribution channels through various chains of bagel shops, which may also want to sell our single-serve ice cream products.

– That's food for thought.

Now, acquisition might be a possibility if we can get the idea funded without loading ourselves up with debt. We might look to buy one of our lesser, regional competitors, particularly in an area of the country where our distribution channels and name recognition are weak.

– Okay, good. So what are your recommendations?

First, I'd continue and probably step up our marketing campaign. Second, I would increase our product line by offering a two-pint container size as well as the original one-pint size. I'd also diversify our product line into other dairy products, like gourmet cream cheeses, to take advantage of our brand name and our established distribution channels. Third, I'd analyze the possible acquisition of a regional competitor, particularly in a region of the country where our sales are weak. That way we can take advantage of their established distribution channels.

Type of case: Increasing sales and growing the company

Comments: First, she was quick to realize that this was a two-scenario case: increasing sales and growing the company. She also quickly figured out the client's expectations. Winston Cow wanted to increase company sales to $250 million. What kind of percentage did that represent? And was it feasible? Realizing that ice cream sales alone couldn't reach the client's goal, she looked at the company overall, assessing and changing its strategy. Finally, her ability to look outside the existing business led to a great idea — Cow Brothers Gourmet Cream Cheese.

✢ Hair-raising

◗ Case 11: Our client is a large pharmaceutical company that has developed a cure for baldness. It's a pill that will rapidly (within three months) re-grow your hair to the thickness it was when you were fifteen years old. The pill, called IPP2, needs to be taken every day to maintain that thickness. Please estimate the size of the US market and tell me how you would price the drug.

So, our client is a large drug company that has developed a pill that will re-grow your hair to the thickness it was when you were a teenager. The pill is called IPP2 and needs to be taken daily. You want me to estimate the size of the domestic market and develop a pricing strategy.

– Yes, that's right.

Besides estimating the market size and coming up with a pricing strategy, are there any other objectives I should be concerned about?

– Profits. We want to make sizable profits.

How about market share?

– We're more concerned about profits than market share. You price it right, the market share will come.

Before I tackle the market size, I'd like to ask a few questions.

– Shoot.

Can this be used by both men and women?

– Yes.

Is it covered by health insurance?

– No.

Is it a prescription drug or sold over-the-counter?

– Prescription.

Is this for thinning hair or just for male pattern baldness?

– Can be used for thinning hair as well.

Are there any side effects?

– Yes. It causes sexual dysfunction in 2% of men, and women thinking of having children shouldn't take it because it could cause birth defects.

I don't think that's enough to deter men. However, we need to eliminate all women 40 years old and younger, although I realize that there is a small population of women who give birth after 40. So, let's figure this out.

I'm going to assume that there are 280 million Americans and that their life expectancy is 80 years. And I'm going to assume that there are even numbers of people in each age group, and that there is a 50/50 spilt between men and women. I'll break it down by generation and by sex. So 280 divided by four generations equals 70 million per generation, and each generation has 35 million men and 35 million women. I'll also assume that as men get older, actually as people get older, there will be a greater percentage of them losing their hair.

Age	Men	% w/ thin hair		Women	% w/ thin hair		Totals
1-20	35m	0%	0	35m	0%	0	0m
21-40	35m	20%	7m	35m	0%	0	7m
41-60	35m	40%	14m	35m	1%	.35	14.35m
61-80+	35m	60%	21m	35m	10%	3.5	24.5m
							45.85m

With men ages 1–20, I'll assume that no one or no significant number falls into that category. Same with women. For those 21–40, I'll estimate that 20% of men and again zero% of women fall into that category. The 41–60 group has a higher percent, I'd say 40% of men and 1% of women. And, finally, in the age range of 60–80, I'd guess 60% of men and 10% of women.

That totals around 45 million. From that number, I'm going to subtract 5 million. The reasons are that some men shave their heads, some don't care about going bald and others can't afford it, although we don't know what the price tag is yet.

So I'll estimate the market size of 40 million American customers.

– Okay, what's next?

We need to price our product. I'd like to look at it three different ways. First, who is our competition and what do they charge? Second, we'll look at cost-based pricing. And third, we'll consider price-based costing. I just want to a take a moment to draw a diagram ...

PRICING STRATEGIES

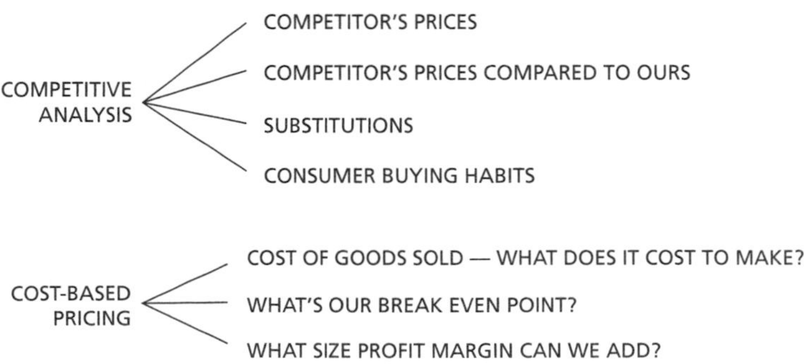
COMPETITIVE ANALYSIS
COMPETITOR'S PRICES
COMPETITOR'S PRICES COMPARED TO OURS
SUBSTITUTIONS
CONSUMER BUYING HABITS
COST-BASED PRICING
COST OF GOODS SOLD — WHAT DOES IT COST TO MAKE?
WHAT'S OUR BREAK EVEN POINT?
WHAT SIZE PROFIT MARGIN CAN WE ADD?

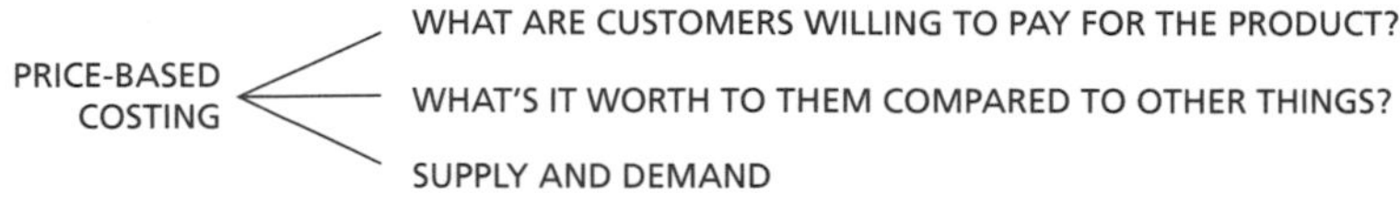
PRICE-BASED COSTING
WHAT ARE CUSTOMERS WILLING TO PAY FOR THE PRODUCT?
WHAT'S IT WORTH TO THEM COMPARED TO OTHER THINGS?
SUPPLY AND DEMAND

Who is our competition and what do they charge?

– There are two major competitors. One is a topical solution that sells for $60 for a month's supply. The second is a pill that sells for $50 for a month's supply.

How does our product compare to the competition?

– We are three times more effective. Thicker hair, faster.

Are there any credible substitutions?

– Assume no.

What about customer loyalty?

– Assume that both the competitors produce the same results and it comes down to application preference.

Let's talk about cost-based pricing. What does it cost us to make, package and market a one month supply? Were there heavy R&D costs?

– R&D costs were minimal because this was discovered by accident while we were testing a similar drug for a different illness. So the cost of the entire package, everything you need to worry about, is $1 for a month's supply.

One dollar? That's it? That's great. So with production costs of one dollar and no heavy R&D costs, we can dismiss cost-based pricing. If we look at price-based costing, we need to figure out what the market will bear. How much will people be willing to pay for a full head of hair? Currently, they are paying between $50 and $60 a month for products that aren't as good as ours. So that means that they might pay as much as $150 to $180 a month. So now we have parameters of between $2, which represents a 100% markup, and $180, which represents 18,000% markup.

– An 18,000% markup; are you comfortable with that?

I'm comfortable with the markup percentage if that's what people will pay. This isn't a life and death drug, like an AIDS drug. This is purely cosmetic. I'm not convinced that people would pay $180 a month. You're growing a little thin on top, sir. What would you pay?

– Rule number one: never insult the interviewer.

Sorry, but it looks good on you.

– And you were doing so well. What else do you have regarding pricing?

You need to look at what it is worth to them compared to other things in their life. People pay $3 a day for a cup of Starbucks coffee. Is a full head of hair worth a cup of coffee? I'd say yes.

– So $90 a month?

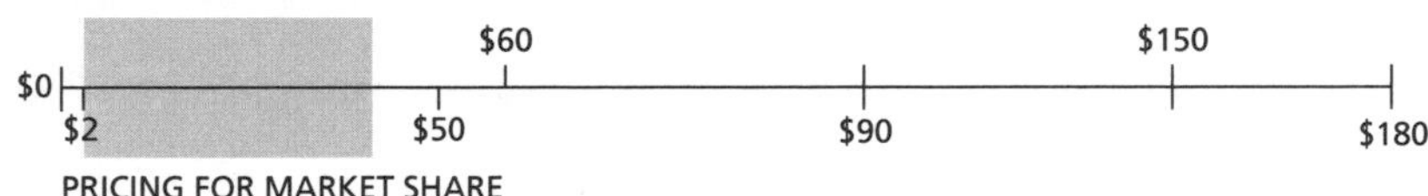

The objective of this case was profits, not market share. If it were market share, then I'd go in at $40 in order to under-price our competition, gain tremendous market share and then crank the price once we have them as loyal customers — kind of like the pricing strategies of Standard Oil in the 1930s. But I don't think we'll need to do that. If the product is that effective, we'll get heavy press coverage and soon drive the competition out of the market.

One small point as far as market share is concerned. If a large share of the market currently uses a topical solution because they like the application process, then we will have to try harder to get them to switch to a pill, realizing that a percentage of them will never switch.

Type of Case : Market-sizing, pricing

Comments: Our candidate was lucky that the interviewer had more humor than hair. He did a good job breaking down the market-sizing aspect of the case. He used a chart that kept information organized. He also looked at three pricing strategies, quickly dismissing one as irrelevant. I also liked that he took a moment to diagram his pricing strategy. Overall, a nice job.

+ Lawrence of Arabia Oriental Rugs

Case 12: Our client is a retailer of fine and expensive oriental rugs in Manhattan. They are experiencing declining profits. Why and what can they do about it?

Besides identifying why our clients profits have been shrinking, are there any other objectives I need to think about?

– No.

I'd like to lay out my structure then ask some questions.

The student writes E(P=R–C)M at the top of his sheet. (See page 45 for explanation.)

Because this is a declining profits case, I'd like to first look at the industry and markets to determine if this is just our problem or an industry problem. I'd like to know if there are any new competitors on the block and the state of the economy. Is there anything happening that is affecting our store that we can't control?

Next, I'd analyze the company, starting with the revenue streams. What are the revenue streams? What percentage of total revenues does each stream represent? And have there been any major changes or fluctuations with the revenues?

Next, I'd examine the costs, both variable and fixed costs. Have the costs changed in the last year? Do any costs seem high or out of line?

Finally, I'd like to see if there are ways to increase the volume of our sales.

– Okay, that seems like a sound plan.

I have a few questions.

– Shoot.

Is this an industry-wide problem?

– Yes.

How are we growing compared to the industry? And are there any new direct competitors?

– Our sales were down by 50% and yet our market share remained the same. There are no new direct competitors.

Can you tell me a little about the rugs?

– These are fine and expensive rugs. Our rugs sell for $50,000 each. Our profit is $20,000. In the past we sold an average of five rugs a month for annual sales of $3 million. Volume is down to two rugs a month for $1.2 million in sales.

How's the economy?

– The economy has little effect on our corporate clients.

Who are our clients?

– Hotels, corporations and wealthy individuals.

Have customer preferences changed?

– Good question. Yes, they have changed. More corporations are going casual so their décor has changed and oriental rugs are out.

What about our costs? Do you have a list of costs?

– Yes. These are all annual costs.

Rent and utilities	$72,000
Labor	$240,000
Marketing	$100,000
Debt on inventory	$360,000
Delivery costs	$10,000

Okay. Are these our only costs?

– The only ones you need to care about.

So our total costs are $782,000. Our revenues went from $3 to $1.2 million. They are still earning a profit of $418,000.

– That's right.

Have the costs changed from last year?

– Assume no. Is there anything there that concerns you?

Two things. First, if we are selling less than half the rugs as we did last year, then maybe we should lower our labor costs by laying off a few of the sales staff.

– If you pay fifty grand for a rug, you want customer service. We have always made our customers feel like a million dollars. Besides, the sales staff has been with us a long time. They know the product and they have repeat customers.

With labor costs that high, it doesn't seem like they are on commission. Can we switch them to a small base and a commission?

– No. If we did that we'd lose them. Our best sales people would go to the competition.

Okay. What about the debt on inventory? It seems high.

– It is high.

It's hurting us. Can we lower it?

– Yeah, by selling some rugs.

We need to increase the volume. Have we discounted our rugs?

– If we lower the price of our rugs to $40,000, we'll sell three rugs a month. If we lower our price to $30,000, we'll sell five rugs a month.

If we sell three rugs a month at $40,000 each, that equals 36 times 40,000 or $1.44 million — which is $196,000 more in revenues. It would also lower the debt on inventory by 12 rugs. However, while we bring more in in revenues, our profits would further decline.

– How?

If we sell 24 rugs making a profit of $20,000 on each rug, that's a profit of $480,000. If we sell 36 rugs making a profit of $10,000 on each rug, that's a profit of $360,000. So unless the savings on the inventory debt is greater than or equal to $120,000, we're better off leaving prices the way they are.

If we lower the prices to $30,000, we're just selling rugs at cost. We'd reduce our inventory debt but we wouldn't be making any kind of profit.

– Can you think of any other ways to increase volume and revenue?

Yes. When I can't afford something I really want, I try to lease it.

– Leasing the rugs?

Yes.

– Give me the pros and cons of leasing the rugs.

The student takes a minute to draw up a chart.

PROS	CONS
Larger market	Lowers value
Relieve inventory debt	Won't cover costs
Reduce inventory	
Leads to acquisition	
Service contract – new revenue stream	

On the pro side, it will lead to a larger market, relieve the inventory debt, reduce inventory and could lead to acquisition. We can also draw up a service plan where we would have to go clean the rug every four months. On the con side it will lower the value of the rug and the rental won't cover the cost of the rug.

– Okay, good. Say we can lease a $50,000 rug for $9,000 a year for two years. If we do this, say we can lease five rugs a month.

In addition to the two were selling?

– Yes. Is this a good deal for us?

How much in interest are we paying on each rug?

– It works out to $3,000 each.

That means we have 120 rugs in inventory.

– That's right.

Five rugs a month equals 60 rugs a year. Sixty times $9.000 is an additional $540.000. However, we'd still owe $3,000 on 60 rugs — or $180,000.

– So?

How much would we be able to sell these rugs for when we get them back in two years?

– $40,000.

Let me just recap. Each rug costs $30,000. But we haven't laid out the money for the rug; we just pay interest of $3,000 per rug. Over two years we'll pay $6,000 in interest per rug. If we lease the rug, we'll receive $9,000 a year or $18,000 over two years. So we're taking in 18 and only paying out six. That means we're up $12,000. If we can then sell the same rug for $40,000, we'll make an additional $10,000. So if we lease a rug for two years, then sell it, our total profit would be $22,000 per rug.

– How'd you get that?

If the rug is new and we sell it, that's 50 miinus 30 equals $20,000.

– Right.

If we lease it for $9,000 a year, that means you have $18,000 minus the $6,000 for the interest ($12,000) plus the $40,000 for the resale ($52,000) minus $30,000 which is the cost of the rug ($22,000).

I think leasing is a viable alternative to selling. It increases our cash flow which allows us to pay the interest on the loan for the rug. We still make a profit on the rug when we sell it two years later.

– All costs being equal, what would be our new profit for next year?

If our costs remain the same, our P&L would look like this.

Revenues	
Sales	**$1,200,000**
Rental	**$540,000**
Total Revenues	**$1,740,000**
Costs	
Rent and utilities	**$72,000**
Labor	**$240,000**
Marketing	**$100,000**
Debt on inventory	**$360,000**
Delivery costs	**$10,000**
Total Costs	**$782,000**
Total Profits	**$958,000**

Thus, we went from a profit of $418,000 to $958,000. Still short of the old days, but this number will increase by another $600,000 in two years if we are successful at selling all the leased rugs for $40,000.

– What kind of profit percentage increase is that? Do it out loud.

958,000 minus 418,000 equals540,000. 540,000 divided by 418 equals 1.29 or a 129% increase.

- **Type of case: Profit and loss and increasing the bottom line.**

- **Comments: The student did a good job of laying out her structure, taking time to look at outside factors first. She asked some good questions. But what put her over the top was the leasing idea. You could tell that was what the interviewer was looking for because he had all the numbers ready. The student's math was solid and she took the time to recap to make sure that she and the interviewer were on the same page.**

+ Wireless Worries

Case 13: In Q4, the number three US wireless carrier slipped further behind its rivals in the number of customers, even as profits rose 35%. What do you think is going on?

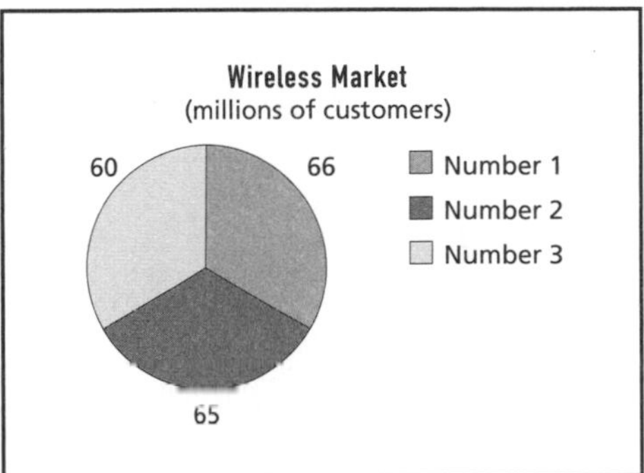

Profits are up, but the number of customers is down. We need to figure out why this is happening.

– That's right.

How many customers did Number 3 lose in Q4?

– As you can see, we closed the year with 60 million customers. That takes into account a loss of 2.5% or 1.5 million customers lost in Q4.

Annually, that's 10% of our customer base for the year.

– That's right.

Besides figuring out why we're losing so many customers, are there any other objectives I need to be concerned about?

– Not at the moment.

The student writes E(P = R –C)M.

I'd like to start by looking at the industry. Are the other two major wireless companies losing customers as well?

– Yes, but not in such large numbers. Traditionally, wireless companies lose about 1% of their customer base each quarter. However, they gain much more than they lose.

Did we gain more than we lost?

– Yes. We gained 2 million new customers that quarter.

Next, I'd like to know why we are losing so many customers?

– Why do you think?

It could be any number of reasons: the other companies might have a better and more reliable network, more effective advertising, better pricing, cooler phones or better customer service.

– Assume all that is true, but it only makes up a small portion of our losses. Why else?

Did we have a satellite problem and our network went down for a while?

– No.

The student struggles to come up with other reasons so the interviewer tosses her a bone.

– What if we wanted to lose those customers?

I'm not sure I understand.

– One of our major concerns is bad debt. We spend a lot of time, effort and money on bill collection. It's a runaway cost. We spend so much time trying to get new accounts, that we don't do a proper job vetting our customers' credit. Here's a chart for you to study. What's it say to you?

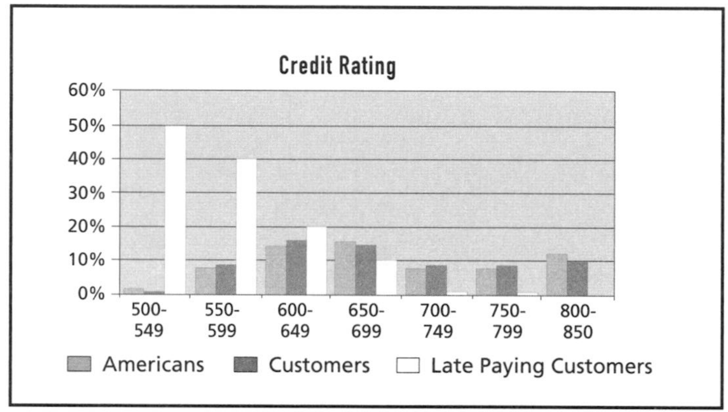

It tells me that people with credit ratings between 500 and 600 are a problem. Is it worth keeping them as customers? Let's figure out how many customers we're talking about. According to the first pie chart, we have 60 million customers. It looks as if 1% of our customers fall into the 500–549 range. They pay late 50% of the time. Is it the same 50% who pay late every month?

– Not necessarily. You can assume that everyone in that group has been late paying the bill at some point, some more than others.

If we eliminate them as customers, that's 600,000 customers. The next group isn't much better. We can see that 40% of them pay late. This is a bigger pool. We're looking at 9% of the customer base or around 5.4 million customers. If we dropped those two groups from our customer lists, that sets us back 6 million customers and puts us at 54 million. That would put us 10 million customers behind the number 2 wireless company.

– So?

How much does it cost us to collect late payments from each customer?

– $50.

How much is the average bill?

– Overall it's $40; however, in those categories, it's $75.

So we're paying $50 to collect $75. Are our margins so great that we're still making money off of those customers?

– No. Profit margins are 25%.

Do we charge a late fee?

– No.

What percentage of those customers abandon their accounts altogether, leaving us holding the bag?

– Good question, but I don't have the figure for that. Run some numbers for me. How much will we be saving if we drop all 6 million customers?

We have 6 million late-paying customers with average bills of $75. That's revenues of ... $450 million. Our margins are 25%, which brings the number down to a little less than $115 million. We need to add the cost of collection. Some customers pay late 50% of the time, other 40% of the time. Let's average it and call it 45%. So 45% of 6 million customers is 2.7. We have 2.7 million customers who pay late. We spend $50 trying to recover the money; that's $135 million. So we're losing $20 million a month going after those customers.

– So what do you suggest?

We can do a couple of things. Shed the high risk-late payers. Vet new customers better. Require them to have a 600 credit rating or better. Start charging a late fee and go after the customer collections every two months instead of every month. If we do that, we're spending $50 to go after $150.

– That's right.

- **Type of case: Reducing costs**

- **Comments: She just did alright. The student's math was solid. She got stuck and the interviewer came to the rescue, but she didn't pick up on the hint. She came up with a decent list of suggestions which showed she listened. Also, she did a good job analyzing the second chart. It's a hard chart. It is not well-designed and it has a lot of information on it. Oftentimes, they'll give you badly-designed charts to test your analytical skills.**

College Mail

Case 14: Our client is a company named Imagitas. They have a contract with the US Postal Service to print the change of address forms that you find in your local post office. Ten years ago, the change of address form was a simple green card. Now, the mover receives a booklet with helpful hints on how to move and coupons to stores and services that the mover will need when moving. This booklet is called "The Mover's Guide." Imagitas also sends a "Welcome Kit" to the mover's new address with coupons and information that she might find helpful in her new neighborhood. Imagitas saves the US Postal Service over $12 million dollars a year while making over $50 million in ad revenues.

One of the most active, yet hardest to reach, markets is the college student. Imagitas seeks ways to segment and reach the college market. Lay out a strategic plan for Imagitas to follow, keeping in mind their objectives are to:

- **Reach students sooner**
- **Provide appropriate and attractive coupons**
- **Drive student/movers to the website**
- **Retain mover information online**
- **Make a profit**

So, basically, our client is a company that handles the change of address forms for the US Postal Service. They want us to help them segment the college market, while meeting the objectives of reaching students sooner, providing appropriate coupons, getting students to use the website and retain information online while making a profit.

– Basically.

Can people currently do a change of address online?

– Yes.

The coupons that Imagitas sends out to movers, are they from local merchants or national chains?

– National chains, although we hope to distribute local merchants soon.

I can think of five segments to this market: Heading to school for the first time, heading back to school, moving back home with their parents for the summer, moving to a new city for a summer internship and moving to a new city for their first job. The three that I'd like to focus on first are heading to school for the first time, heading back to school each year and moving to a new city for their first job.

– Go on.

Heading to school for the first time is a great opportunity for a very strong Mover's Guide package if sent early enough before the parents go shopping. Coupons for Linens & Things and The Gap might be good additions to the Mover's Guide.

When the student arrives on campus, the Welcome Kit can be unique with a strong mix of national and local coupons, if segmented by school or city. Coupons should be for "room stash," batteries, pizza, dry cleaners, that sort of thing.

With the group that is heading back to school, I'd focus mostly on the Welcome Kit. If Imagitas can segment by school or city, then they can get a large number of local merchants as well as national chains.

Finally, there is the group that is moving to a new city for the first job. Again, this gives us a great opportunity to weigh heavy on the Welcome Kit. This group will need everything and now has a paycheck to pay for it. National retailers like Create & Barrel and Linens & Things should jump on it.

– What you're saying is good, but how can Imagitas reach students and get them to use the website?

College students can be reached through a variety of channels, such as strategic partnerships with universities, advertising through trade-outs and word of mouth. Preferably, we would like to capture student data before they get on campus. The best possible solution would be to work with university admissions and housing offices to place the USPS web address in their acceptance and housing letters.

– Why would schools do this?

This would save the schools a lot of work and money in the long run. First, we should build an alliance with university mail centers. Every summer, university mail centers across the country receive tons of mail for recent graduates, students away for the summer and students who have transferred or dropped out. It's an expensive and time-consuming effort to return or, worse yet, forward their mail.

In the spring, University Mail Services (UMS) usually places a postcard in the mailbox of all on-campus students urging them to notify both the USPS and the University mail services of their new address. I know that my school UMS keeps a database for students who have notified them, although I'd imagine the percentage of students that comply is probably pretty low. I know I get those notices every year and never remember to fill them out.

In return, University mail centers should be willing to place a Mover's Guide into every on-campus mailbox to try to eliminate or curtail this burden. First, it would save them the expense of printing the postcards. Second, the online switching through the USPS site would greatly curtail their excess mail.

Through the university mail services, admissions, and housing offices, we could capture a significant percentage of the college population and retain them as they move through their different life stages. In addition, by-school segmentation makes us more attractive to local vendors.

– How else can students get the word?

Word of mouth. One cannot over-emphasize "word of mouth." Word gets around fast, and now, with such a large percentage of this group using email, it has amplified the message and multiplied the listeners. If it is "quick and cool", it can be done.

– Can you summarize for me?

USPS and Imagitas should capture college students early — ideally before they go to college. They can do this by working in conjunction with colleges and universities by helping them reduce their excess mail load. USPS can collect the student's information in a database and have the individual update it over the Internet a month before each move. USPS can even send out an automatic email a month before the student moves, prompting him to make the change online.

Once they sign up, the students can reinitiate their moves over the Internet using a PIN number, not only in college, but for the rest of their lives. USPS will promptly mail them a confirmation notice and Imagitas would mail out the Mover's Guide to their current address. The Mover's Guide will continue to have coupons for products and services to help them move. Finally, a Welcome Kit. will be sent to the new address.

There is one more thing I'd like to add that we didn't talk about and that's the website. Besides changing my address, it would be very helpful if I could order my phone and cable service at the same time. So, maybe the website should have links to the appropriate companies in my new area. That way, by the time I move in, I'll be all set. Also, maybe there could be online coupons as well. I mention this because, when you're moving, your room's a mess and things tend to get lost. The last thing I unhook is my computer, so I'll have access to the webpage.

– Excellent. I'll have to remember that for my next meeting with Imagitas.

Type of Case: Strategy / marketing

Comments: Although this is a strategy case, it didn't fit neatly into one of the six strategy scenarios described in the Ivy Case Method. The student was asked about how to reach a segment of which she is a part — thus she put herself in the mix and tried to figure out how to reach students like her. Her answer went into more detail than most case questions require; however, when you have a question that asks how you reach a specific market, a little more detail is required.

✣ House of Pizza

Case 15: A major video store chain is considering the acquisition of a national chain of pizza restaurants. What factors are important in making this decision?

So you have a major video store chain, I'm assuming like Blockbuster, that is considering purchasing a national chain of pizza restaurants. They want to know what they should be looking at in order to make this decision. Why are they doing this? What are their main objectives?

– Why do you think?

Could be a number of things. Profit, increased market access, to pre-empt the competition from buying into the pizza market and to create financial, operational and marketing synergies.

– Say all of the above.

May I take a moment to jot down some notes?

– Certainly.

Student takes several minutes to draw out the M&A decision tree, or a variation of this tree.

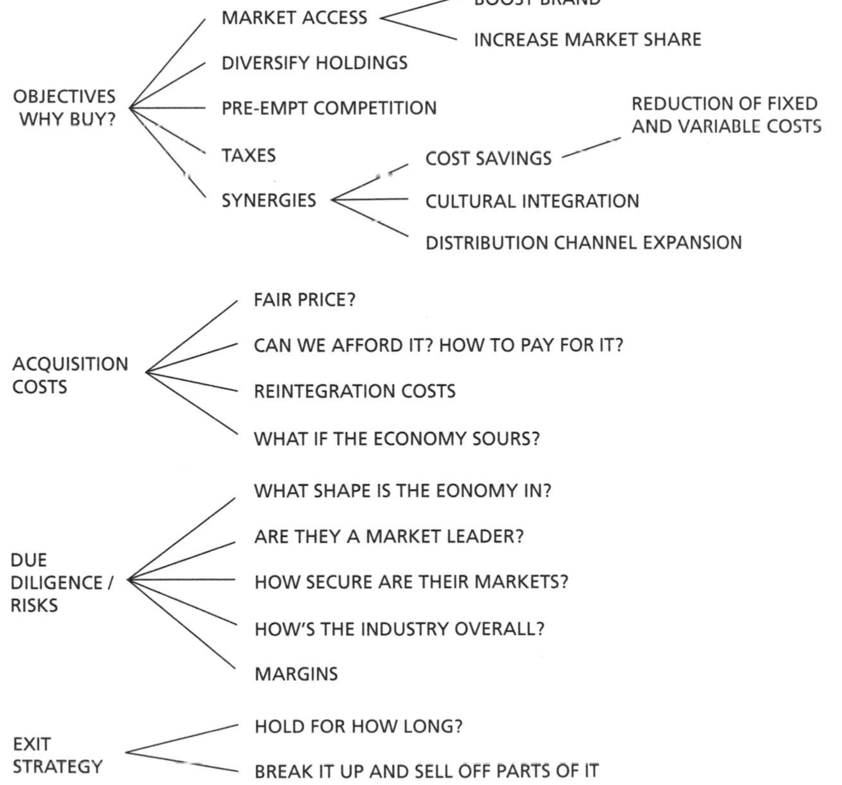

How many restaurants are there in the chain?

– Six hundred.

Where are they located?

– Mostly in and around the major cities.

Does the pizza chain currently own all its stores, or do they franchise?

– They own all their stores.

Who are the major players and what size market share does each have? What size market share do we have?

– Pizza Hut has 46% of the market, Domino's 21%, Little Caesar's 13%, Papa John's has 5% and we have 3%. All the others — the little guys — make up the remaining 12%.

Is there anything else you can tell me about the pizza market?

– Sure, what do you want to know? I can tell you that Americans eat 350 slices of pizza per second. That pizza is a $33 billion per year industry. That pizzerias represent approximately 20%% of all restaurants in the United States and that 93% of Americans eat at least one slice of pizza per month. And, oh, pizza restaurant growth continues to outpace overall restaurant growth. You find any of that helpful?

Well, yes, particularly the last part about its growth.

– Why? What does that tell you?

That it is, and continues to be, a very competitive market. You asked me about major factors. The first factor is the market. If the company that we want to buy has 3% of a $33 billion industry, that means our sales must be about $100 million.

– What? Three percent of 33 billion is 100 million? Try again.

I mean a billion. I was off by a zero. So, if we are serious about entering the pizza industry, then I think buying our way in is the only way to go. With all the competition, it would be very difficult to differentiate ourselves. It would take a long time to build brand, find great locations, build-out the restaurants and put together a management and sales team.

– And that's why we're buying our way in. Tell me something new.

We have been running a retail business, so this isn't something entirely new. We're going after the same market. I think that there could be a lot of synergies, a lot of crossover promotions. We might even combine some of the stores. Build ones that sell pizzas and rent DVDs. People could order their pizza, pick out a DVD, and by the time they are ready to leave, the pizza would be ready.

– Good. Anything else?

Do we have the cash or would we have to finance this acquisition?

– We are financing about half. What makes you think we can do a better job at running the pizza chain?

We might be able to look at the business more objectively. We can visit the idea of franchising. We can visit the idea of spinning this division off in an IPO once the market rebounds. Is this chain profitable? If so, what were the profits over the last five years?

– After tax profits have been falling over the last five years. Five years ago the company made $100 million on $500 million in sales. This year we made $30 million on $1 billion in sales.

So they've gone from a 20% return to a 3% return. Have you done an analysis on why the sales are dropping?

– I didn't say the sales are dropping. I said that after tax profits were dropping.

Sorry, that's what I meant.

– What do you think is happening?

I'll assume that the reason our sales have doubled over the last five years is because we are opening up new stores. We have invested heavily in this growth. It's time to take a close look at all the stores and find out which ones are profitable and which ones aren't. I'd analyze the ones that aren't, try to fix them, and if they can't be turned around in six months, we might want to consider closing them.

– What else?

Next, I'd ask for a breakdown of our costs. How fast have they been climbing? I'd look to see if there are any costs that are out of line. Maybe we're paying too much for space? Maybe our labor costs have skyrocketed? Are there any labor-saving technologies that would reduce costs? I'd see where we could cut back without jeopardizing the quality of the product. I'd also benchmark our costs against our competitors.

– All right. I'm feeling a little better about you, but I have to tell you your answer was all over the place. If you give me a great summary, I might call you back.

Pizza is a growth industry. It's a very large and extremely competitive market. It makes sense to enter it, if we are convinced that we can increase the company's profits. First, we need to look at revenue streams. What can we be doing that we're not? How can we increase sales? What percentage does each of the revenue streams represent? Does anything seem unusual in the balance of percentages? Have percentages changed lately? If so, why?

We also need to take a close look at costs. What's out of line? What can be reduced through technology? Have there been any major shifts in costs — like labor or raw materials? And how can we streamline work processes to reduce costs?

Next, I'd do a store analysis. Get rid of the dogs, while looking for new locations. The other component in the profit formula is volume. How do we jack up volume? One way is to open more stores; another is to increase our marketing efforts; and a third is to reduce prices to drive in traffic. And, finally, improve customer service so the customers that do come in, come back.

– So getting back to the original question.

What factors are important in making this decision? Is the price of the company reasonable? Can we afford it and service the debt when the economy is down? Is the brand strong? Can we reasonably expect to build on that brand? Do we have the expertise to increase sales while reducing costs? Are there synergies that would benefit both companies? And, finally, we need to consider the post-acquisition integration issues — things like cultural implications, strategic fit and possible exit strategies.

– That's it? That's the best you can do?

Given the time we have, yes. Give me more time and access to resources and I can do better.

– Thanks.

Type of Case: Combination of acquisition, entering a new market and improving the bottom line

Comments: The student was strong in the beginning, and then he lost his way. He seemed to get pushed around by the interviewer. However, he did come on strong at the end with an articulate summary.

Bull Moose Financial Services

Case 16: Bull Moose is a large financial services company with $98 billion under management. It has 20 different mutual funds and a brokerage company. Customers receive a statement for each individual mutual fund as well as one for their brokerage activities. So, if you own four mutual funds and a brokerage account, you get five separate statements and often multiple duplicate mailings for cross products.

Another problem Bull Moose has is that its customer service phone reps can't tell what the client's total investment is in Bull Moose products. The client may have $1 million in one fund and only $2,500 in another. So a million-dollar customer may get treated like a $2,500 customer. How do we ensure that the heavy hitters (big investors) get treated like royalty when they call into Bull Moose Investments?

So Bull Moose, a large financial services company, wants to improve customer service to its large investors.

– Yes.

Besides treating its customers like royalty, are there any other objectives I should know about?

– Well, we want to keep costs down as well.

Are our competitors having the same problems?

– We can benchmark our competitors, but I want you to come up with solutions — not just copy our competitors.

Is Bull Moose a public company?

– No, it's privately held.

Okay, so we need to come up with a way to increase efficiency while making our customers feel like royalty.

– Yes.

The first thing I would do is make an investment in technology. Bull Moose is a privately held company so we can take a hit to the bottom line and Wall Street won't freak out. I would consolidate all those accounts under one account number, maybe a master account number for both monthly statements and customer service reps. That way, the customers can see all their assets on one statement. We would mail only one statement instead of five, and we would also eliminate the duplicate mailings.

How many customers does Bull Moose have, and what is the average number of accounts?

– One million customers with an average of two accounts each.

So, that is a savings of at least one million mailings, times four for quarterly statements, times the price of a stamp, not to mention all the savings on cross-mailing. I also think it's important that the phone reps have that same information — not only so they can treat a million dollar customer like a million dollars, but also so they can service all customers better.

– Anything else?

Yes. You might want to code your customers. Break them down into groups such as platinum, gold, silver, bronze and charcoal. Give the platinum customers an 800 number that takes priority over all calls and is picked up on one ring by a customer service rep dedicated to platinum customers. How big would this platinum group be?

– It depends on the criteria. But it's safe to say that 5% of the customers do 95% of the business.

So, 5% of one million is 50,000 customers. I'm going to assume that customers call in for three major reasons — to place a trade, complain or get account information. Does the same rep handle all these functions?

– Yes.

You may want to break it up and have two separate lines, with one dedicated solely to trading. You're probably spending too much money paying traders to handle customer complaints when they should be trading. You could hire recent college grads to handle the complaints. I'd also allow the customers to view all their accounts online. This could reduce the number of overall service calls. And if Bull Moose doesn't already do online trading, they may want to look into it. I think I read that an online transaction is about one-tenth the cost of a phone call. You could even have an option where statements could be emailed to the client instead of going through the US mail.

– All right, anything else?

Well, to summarize, I'd recommend an investment in technology that would allow customers to see a consolidated statement and phone reps to view all of the accounts that a customer has with Bull Moose. I would code those customers so that the 5% get fast service with separate phone lines. You could print the new numbers right on the statements. As far as reducing costs, we'd save money on the mailing of statements and cross-marketing pieces. We'd also save money by hiring recent college grads to handle the customer complaint calls and letting our traders focus on trading. I would also try to get our customers to use the Internet to handle a lot of their needs. This would reduce our costs overall and allow us to give better service to all our customers.

– Great.

Type of Case: Reducing costs

Comments: In this case, it wasn't so much that costs have been out of control; the problem really stemmed from a customer service problem. Here, we were able to kill two birds with one stone: improve service and reduce costs.

+ PEPSICO

Case 17: This information was taken from the PepsiCo® 2004 Annual Report. PepsiCo is broken down into four divisions: Frito-Lay North America (FLNA), PepsiCo Beverages North America (PBNA), PepsiCo International (PI) and Quaker Foods North America (QFNA). I'd like you to look it over and let me know the highlights. Think out loud; I'd like to know how you approach this. And do all the numbers in your head.

	2004	2003	2002	2004	2003	2002
		Net Revenue			Operating Profit	
FLNA	9,560	9,091	8,565	2,389	2,242	2,081
PBNA	8,313	7,733	7,200	1,911	1,690	1,485
PI	9,062	0,670	7,749	1,323	1,061	910
QFNA	1.526	1.467	1.464	475	470	458
Total Division	29,261	26,969	24,978	6,098	5,463	4,934
Divested Businesses		2	134		26	23
Corporate				-689	-502	-438
	29,261	26,971	25,112	5,409	4,987	4,519
Restructuring Charges				-150	-147	
Merger-related Costs					-59	-224
	29,261	26,971	25,112	5,259	4,781	4,295

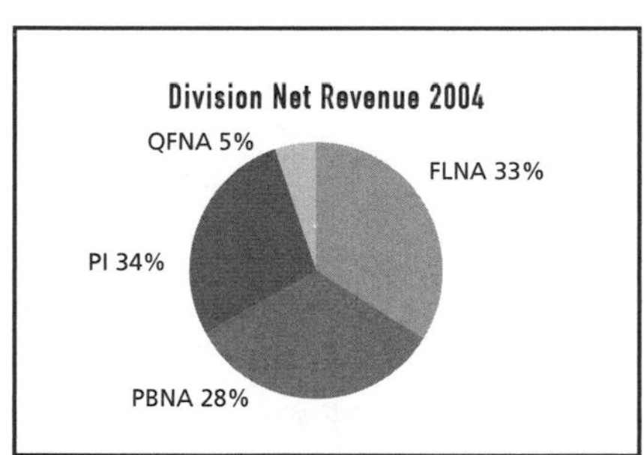

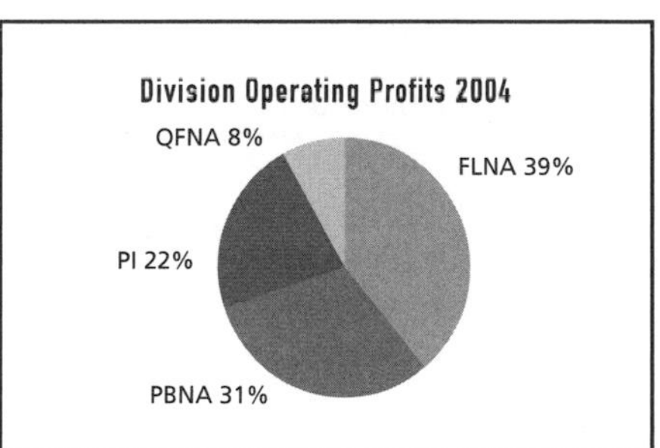

You'd like me to scan the numbers and the pie charts and let you know what has been going on inside Pepsi over the last year. Besides my summary, is there anything else you'd like to see?

– No.

Well, the pie charts help a great deal. I'm going to break it down much like Pepsi did. We

know by looking at the chart that Frito-Lay division net revenue for 2004 was 33% of total revenues. In 2003, if we divide 9,000 by 27,000, we get 33%. And if we divide 8,500 by 25,000, we get about ... 33% as well. So we know that the net revenue of Frito-Lay as a percent of Pepsi's overall sales has remained constant. I'll do the same for Pepsi North America. According to the pie chart, PBNA net revenue was 28% in 2004. For 2003, I'll divide 7,700 by 27,000, which gives me a little less than 30%, probably 28 or 29%. Then, 7,200 divided by 25,000 will give us around 29% for 2003. So, I'd state that Pepsi North America remained relatively constant as well.

I'm going to jump to Quaker Oats. I see that Quaker made up 5% of the revenues in 2004. In 2003, 10% would be 2,700 and Quaker's total is about half of that, so I'd say they remain constant as well at 5%. In 2003, they were around 6% — maybe in the high fives, if we ran the numbers instead of estimating.

So, if the three that I calculated remained the same, the fourth, Pepsi International, will remain the same as well. I'll go out on a limb here and say that as a percent of revenues, all divisions held steady.

– Who had the biggest jump in sales from 2003 to 2004? Can you eyeball that as well?

Sure. Frito-Lay grew to 9,600 from 9,100, so that equals 500. Ten percent growth would be around 910, so 500 is about 5 or 6%. PBNA grew to 8,300 from 7,700, which equals 600. So, I'm guessing that Pepsi North America grew by 7%. Pepsi International grew almost 1,100 from an 8,700 starting point. So that's ... 12%. And, finally, Quaker grew by about 60 from a 2003 base of 1,500 so that equals ... a little less than 5%. It's probably closer to 4 percent.

Pepsi International grew by about 12%, which makes it the leader among the four divisions.

– Good. Last one. Eyeball the operating profit as a percentage of revenues for 2004.

You have 6,100 divided by 30,000, which equals around 20%.

Type of case: Numbers / Company Analysis

Comments: It is becoming more common for interviewers to hand you charts and graphs and ask you not only to interpret them, but to run the numbers in your head. They are testing not only for your analytical skills, but to see if you show grace under pressure. Generally, the tripartite interest will be in your (i) analysis, (ii) innovation and (iii) calculations. This student did well. He rounded all the numbers off to make his calculations simpler. Instead of doing the actual calculations, he looked at things as percentages i.e., Quaker was 5%. And most importantly, he didn't get flustered by the numbers.

✛ Batter Up!

Case 18: You're a baseball fan and the owner of a private batting club in lower Manhattan which has six multi-use batting tunnels or cages. One tunnel also has an auto-feed Iron Mike Pitching Machine®. Members can reserve "cage time" each week. Your director of sales comes to you and wants to know what the new member target is — how many new members she needs to sign up. You know that last year the sales team signed on 200 new members. The company's revenues grew by 10%, and your (net) membership was roughly 10%, from 1,000 members to 1,100. If you wanted to meet your new target growth rate of about 15%, how many new members would you need to recruit? Is this number feasible?

Okay, we need to figure out how many new members we need to sign up in order to reach our target of 15%. Are there any other objectives of which I should be aware?

– No.

Okay. A 15% increase from 1,100 is 1,100 x 1.15 equals 1,265. You said last year that we signed up 200 new members, but the membership only went from 1,000 to 1,100. That means we lost about 100 members or about 10% of our membership. I'll assume that every year we lose 10% of our membership base. That means we are going to lose 110 members this year (1100 x .10).

If that's true, we are starting at 1,100 minus 110, which equals 990 members, and we need to reach 1265. We calculate 1,265 minus 990 equals 275 new members. That's about a 20, no — 28% increase. Is it feasible? It's double what we did last year. I'd have to explore our marketing plan: what we've done in the past and what we've got planned in the future. Tell me —

– I'd like you to focus on something else. What would you estimate our revenues are a year? Use the 1,265 member number.

What are the fees and the pricing structure?

– Members pay $1,000 a year membership fee. Non-members pay $50 for a half an hour of batting cage time and $100 for an hour.

Do we know the percentage breakdown between half-hour renters compared to those who rent for the full hour?

– Does it matter?

No, I guess not. Not if the hourly fee is the same whether you rent by the hour or half-hour. Let me ask, what are your hours of operation?

– Eighteen hours a day, seven days a week.

Well, first we have the membership fee. We start with 1,265 people paying $1,000 a year in membership fees. So that equals $1,256,000.

– I was glad to see that you could do the math in your head.

Next we have 18 hours a day times 30 days equals ... 540 hours a month of available batting cage time. I'll assume that on Fridays, Saturdays and Sundays the cages are in use 90% of the time. And since there is no difference between the hourly rates — they both equal out to $100 an hour — I'll figure this on an hourly basis. So, 90% of three times 18 times $100.

Three times 18 equals 54 hours. 90% of 54 equals around 49 hours if I round up.

Say 50 hours times $100 equals $5,000. Then I multiple it by four weekends in a month and I'll get $20,000 a month.

– Really?

You think that's too high?

– I think it's too low.

Too low? A 90% occupancy rate is too low?

– The 90% is fine, the total is too low.

Checks his notes on the page.

Ah, you must be referring to the fact that there are six cages and so far my numbers are just for one cage. I was getting to that.

– Strike one.

Okay, $30,000 (5,000 x 6 cages) times four weekends equals $120,000 a month or $120,000 times 12 months equals $1,440,000.

Now let's look at Monday through Thursday. I'll say it's full from 6 am to 9 am — people going before work. It's full from 11 to 2, a lunch time break — that's another three hours. And it's full from 6 to midnight — that's six more hours. I'll estimate that it is busy 12 hours a day times $100 equals $1,200 a day times four days a week $4,800 times four weeks equals ... $19,200 a month.

– Really?

Times six cages. $19,200 times six is ... 115,200. We'll take that number and multiply it by 12 and get ...

– Can you do it in your head?

Well, $115,200 times 10 is $1,152,000. Add two more months — $230,400 — and that equals $1,382,400.

– Good.

What other revenues streams do they have?

– What do you think?

I think that they have food and beverages. In the mornings they have coffee and egg sandwiches, maybe a fruit cup — anyway, I've estimated that people will spend $5 for breakfast. We'd probably serve lunch as well. I'll estimate $10 for lunch. For dinner time maybe $15; this includes a sandwich and a beer.

There are a lot of different ways to figure this out, but what I'm going to do is average out the food price, which would be $10, and multiply it by the number of people who use the batting cages and take a percentage of that.

So if we add up the totals of the visitor dollars and divide by 100 ($1,440,000 plus $1,382,400 divided by 100), that equals 28,224 hour-long visitors. Let's say there is a 50/50 split between full hour batters and half-an-hour batters. That means there are 14,112 hour-long batters and 28,224 half an hour batters. That total is around 42,000. And let's say that 50% of the people buy food. Fifty percent would be 21,000 meals times $10 equals $210,000. It seems low compared to the other numbers, but I think it's a good number.

– Not bad. What's next?

Merchandise. T-shirts, gloves and bats. I'll assume that half the members buy something and that the average purchase price is $50. The total number of members is 1,265 divided by two, which is around 630 times $50 equals (63,000/2) or around $32,000.

– Any other revenue streams?

Lessons. Because we booked out the revenue on the cages already, I'm just going to add an extra $100 to 20% of the batting cage revenues.

– I'm not sure what you mean.

I'm assuming 20% of the batting cage time is taken up by lessons and that the lessons cost an extra $100 per hour. So, I'll take 42,000 batters and multiply that by 20% which is ... 8,400 and multiply that by $100 for the lesson. So we make $840,000 on lessons.

Let me total it all up. The annual revenues for Batter Up! are $5,169,400.

Revenues

	Weekly	Monthly	Yearly
Membership			$1,265,000
Friday – Sunday	$30,000	$120,000	$1,440,000
Monday – Thursday	$48,000	4115,200	$1,382,400
Food and Beverages			$210,000
Merchandise			$32,000
Lessons			$840,000
Total			$ 5,169,400

– If someone offered you $12 million for the business, would you take it?

Do I own or rent the building?

– You rent it with a 25-year lease. You've got 20 years left on your lease.

Well, that's about three years worth of revenues. Not knowing what my costs are, I'd have to assume that labor costs are pretty low; there is a big margin in food and particularly beverages. The merchandise is probably marked up 50 – 75%. My biggest costs are rent, utilities and insurance. Let's say my costs are 30% of my revenues. So my costs are about $1.6 million, which leaves a profit of … ($5.2 – 1.6 million) $3.6 million.

How many more members can I handle?

– About 300. Total membership can't go past 1,500 members.

So that's an extra $300,000. Although I doubt that my occupancy rate will grow that much more. The answer is no. The price is too low. And if I'm a baseball fanatic, what else am I going to do?

Type of Case: Numbers

Comments: This is simple and straightforward. The only tricky part was picking up on the fact that the club loses 10% of its membership every year. Working out the revenues is just a function of plowing through the numbers and keeping them straight. The student made a nice chart to track the numbers.

⊹ Red Rocket Sports

Case 19: The Red Rocket Sports Company designs and markets apparel and footwear products under many brand names. All products are generally produced using similar manufacturing processes. Additionally, these products share similar distribution channels and are marketed and sold to a similar type of customer.

Take a look at the numbers below and tell me what's going on with Red Rocket Sports and where they should be concentrating their efforts. I'll be back in 30 minutes for your analysis.

Net Sales	2004	2003	2002
Footwear	$2,430,300	$2,226,700	$2,050,000
Apparel	$1,355,000	$1,258,600	$1,050,000
Total	$3,785,300	$3,485,300	$3,100,000

Net Sales	2004	2003	2002
US	$2,070,060	$2,020,000	$1,807,650
UK	$ 474,700	$ 444,700	$ 415,800
Europe	$ 810,400	$ 695,500	$ 607,400
Other	$ 430,140	$ 325,100	$ 269,150
Total	$3,785,300	$3,485,300	$3,100,000

(TAKE 30 MINUTES TO DO YOUR ANALYSIS THEN READ ON)

Red Rocket Sports Answer:

After 30 minutes the interviewer comes back into the room and the candidate presents his findings to the interviewer.

– Take me through your analysis.

The first thing we need to look at is the yearly percentage changes by type of product and by area. *Pulls out hand-made chart.* **These numbers are eyeballed but should be pretty accurate.**

		2003/2004	2002/2003
PRODUCT	Footwear	10%	10%
	Apparel	10%	20%
MARKET	US	2%	12%
	UK	7%	7%
	Europe	15%	15%
	Other	30%	20%

There are a number of things we can infer from this chart.

- Footwear has grown consistently by about 10% over the last two years.
- Apparel growth has slowed, from 20% in 2002/2003 to just under 10% in 2003/2004.
- The US market has had dramatic declining growth — from 12 to 2%, although it is still, by far, our biggest market.
- The UK growth has remained steady at approximately 7%.
- Same is true for the European market with a consistent growth rate of 15%.
- The most promising markets are the "other" markets, which I'll assume are Asia and Latin America. They grew by around 20% in 2003 and by just over 30% in 2004. At this rate, they will bypass the UK in total sales by next year. I believe that the "other" markets represents the highest area of potential growth.
- The action is in apparel, despite the slowdown in 2003/2004.

Next, I looked at what part of the business each product line and market represents.

		2004	2003	2002
PRODUCT	Footwear	65%	65%	65%
	Apparel	35%	35%	35%
MARKET	US	55%	60%	60%
	UK	12%	12%	15%
	Europe	20%	20%	20%
	Other	11%	8%	8%

What this chart tells us is:

- Footwear represents 2/3rds of our sales and has remained as such over the last few years.
- The US is, by far, our biggest market, making up more than half of our sales, but that number is inching down
- The UK has inched down as well — going from 15% to 12%
- Europe has hung in at 20%.
- The "other" markets have inched up, now representing 11% of sales

Our traditional markets in the US and UK are mature while the "other" markets have the highest growth rate. However, the traditional markets still represent the bulk of our business — over two-thirds of sales. And apparel sales have driven the growth rates over the last two years despite the slowdown in 2004.

– How can you say that? Why do you have so much confidence in apparel?

You need to look past the percentages and concentrate on the numbers themselves. Sales went from $3,100,000 in 2002 to $3,785,300 in 2004. That's an increase of $685,300. Of that number, apparel accounted for almost half, despite only representing 35% of sales.

– Okay, so what should Red Rocket do about this?

Action 1: Concentrate efforts on growth areas, particularly in "other" markets:

- **Increase product line, particularly in apparel.**
- **Increase distribution channels.**
- **Reinforce sales force.**
- **Launch a major marketing campaign.**

Action 2: Secure our traditional markets to maintain business:

- **Launch marketing campaigns to boost sales in mature markets.**
- **Focus on best performing distribution points and best performing stores.**

Action 3: Investigate market trends to anticipate future changes:

- **Talk to industry analysts and get their opinion of trends.**
- **Elaborate strategy of product/market effort based on info from experts.**

It's easy to graph these recommendations in a 2x2 matrix.

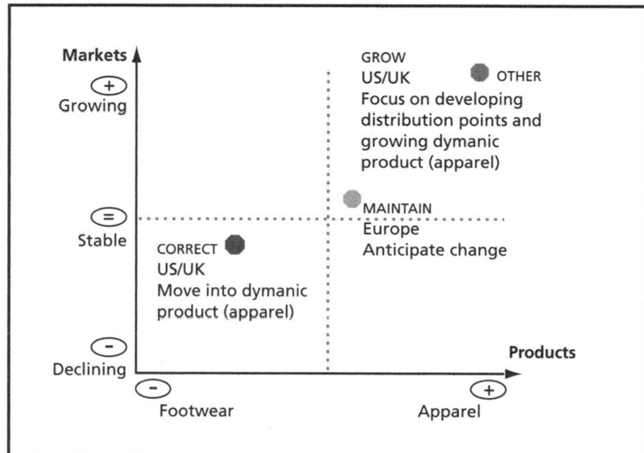

Type of Case: Company analysis

Comments: The student used charts and bullet points to make her presentation. She eyeballed the numbers because of the time constraint and the absence of a calculator. Remember, consultants use charts, graphs and PowerPoint® slides to get their point across with clients — you need to do to the same.

✣ World Spacelines

Case 20: World Spacelines has developed a rocket-boosted Spaceplane® that can take off and land like a conventional airplane but can also fly through the atmosphere and orbit the earth. World Spacelines wants to take passengers on a three-hour tour of space. They have built a prototype, which cost them $500 million. Each additional Spaceplane will cost $100 million to manufacture.

- **Estimate the size of the domestic market.**
- **Determine what price they should charge for a ticket.**
- **How many Spaceplanes should they build in the future?**
- **Should they manufacture Spaceplanes for the competition?**

So let me make sure I understand. World Spacelines has developed a Spaceplane that can take off and land like a conventional plane, and it's designed to take tourists on a three-hour tour of space.

– Yes.

You'd like me to estimate the size of the US market, determine what to charge customers, decide how many of these Spaceplanes to build and whether or not they should manufacture them for our competitors.

– That's right.

I'll assume one objective is to build a successful business. Any other objectives I should be aware of?

– Yes. They want to be the first organization to build a space hotel.

Are there any competitors?

– No.

Do we have a patent on our technology?

– Yes.

How long before someone weasels around the patent and starts to compete with us?

– Three years.

How big is the plane? How many passengers does it hold?

– One hundred.

The trip takes three hours. How many trips per day are you planning?

– Two trips a day, 360 days a year.

Well, before I can estimate the market size, I need to know the price we are going to charge. Because, if it's one dollar, then the market is just about the whole country. But if we charge $1 million, then the market is much, much smaller.

And before I can figure out the price, I need to know what it's going to cost us per passenger. So I'm going to make some assumptions about costs. How long is the life of the plane?

– Twenty years. And yes, you can allocate the costs over twenty years without interest. What do you think the major costs are?

I figure the major costs are the cost of the plane, labor (both on-board and administrative), maintenance, fuel, airport fees, insurance and marketing.

– Good. I'll give you most of the costs; however, I want you to figure out the fuel costs. The plane burns 10 gallons of fuel for every mile and the fuel costs $10 a gallon.

How far is our trip? How high is the sky?

– The Earth's atmosphere is about 300 miles thick, but most of the atmosphere (about 80%) is within 10 miles of the surface of the Earth. There is no exact place where the atmosphere ends; it just gets thinner and thinner, until it merges with outer space. In addition, we use very little fuel when we are orbiting and descending. So we'll estimate our trip goes 500 miles.

So 10 gallons per mile times 500 miles equals 5,000 gallons, times $10 a gallon is $50,000 per trip. You said two trips per day, 360 days a year. Okay, $100,000 per day times 360 days equals $36 million a year in fuel costs.

Major annual costs are:	
Cost of the plane (prototype)	**$25,000,000**
Labor (on-board & admin)	**$2,000,000**
Maintenance	**$4,000,000**
Fuel	**$36,000,000**
Gate & Airport	**$1,000,000**
Insurance	**$2,000,000**
Marketing	**$2,000,000**
TOTAL COSTS	**$72,000,000**

Our costs are $72 million. We need to divide that by the number of passengers. You said 720 flights per year and 100 passengers per flight, which equals 72,000 passengers a year. Divide 72,000 passengers into $72 million in costs and you get $1,000 per passenger.

– Good. So what are you going to charge per trip?

Well, there are three main pricing strategies: competitive analysis, cost-based pricing and price-based costing. There is no competition so we have nothing to compare it to, except

maybe exotic vacations, but that's a far reach. As far as cost-based pricing goes, our costs are $1,000, so if we double that to $2,000, that's a pretty good margin. However, this is really a special trip. To go where no tourist has gone before, to a place that has been accessible to only a few elite astronauts. To a place that everyone has wondered about, not to mention all the trekkies. I think price-based costing is the way to go.

– So, what are you going to charge?

I'd like to figure out what the market is for $10,000 a ticket. Let's start with 250 million Americans. I'll assume that 2% of the population make over $100,000 a year and can afford a $10,000 vacation. So 2% of 250 million is 5 million people. Out of that 5 million, maybe 20% would want to do it. So that's a base of a million customers.

How long does it take to build another Spaceplane?

– Each Spaceplane takes six months to build.

We have one plane now that we estimate that we can fill for the next 14 years. So I would build as many planes as I could for at least the next three years, until we see what the competition is like, then reevaluate at that point.

– Really? I think your assumptions are a little too broad. Lay it out for me.

			YEARS 1-5		
PLANES	Y1	Y2	Y3	Y4	Y5
Plane 1	72K	72K	72K	72K	72K
Plane 2	36K	72K	72K	72K	72K
Plane 3	0	72K	72K	72K	72K
Plane 4	0	36K	72K	72K	72K
Plane 5	0	0	72K	72K	72K
Plane 6	0	0	36K	72K	72K
Passengers	108K	252K	396K	432K	432K
Total	108K	108K	360K	756K	1188K
Running Total		360K	756K	1188K	1620K

By the end of Year 3, we will have six planes up and running and we would have carried a total of 756,000 passengers, well below the 1 million market estimate. However, by the end of Year 4, even without any additional planes, our running total climbs to almost 1.2 million passengers. That's 1.6 million passengers the following year. Two things can happen. First, we can lower the ticket price to $5,000 a ticket, which would spike demand. Second, our other objective is to build a space hotel, so we will need Spaceplanes to shuttle people back and forth, provided the space hotel has been built by then. Even if it hasn't been built, the new demand will continue to fill our planes. Third, even though we haven't spoken about this, I think that there will be large international demand as well.

You also said that competition might show up around this time.

– That's right. The last question I asked was whether you'd sell Spaceplanes to the competition?

Our revenues off the prototype would be $10,000 times 72,000 customers, which equals $720 million minus our costs of $72 million, which equals $648 million for the first year. If each additional plane costs $100 million, that's going to drop our costs by at least $20 million if not more, depending on shared costs. But let's reduce our costs by $20 million. So now we have revenues of $720 million minus costs of $52 million equals $668 million. For us to sell our Spaceplanes to the competition wouldn't be practical. If we're making $668 million a year off of each plane, we'd have to sell them for like $2 billion. I doubt that the competition would pay that kind of money.

To answer your questions, the market size is 1 million passengers at $10,000 a ticket. If we drop it to $5,000, we'll see a huge spike in potential customers. I'd build as many planes as I could for the next three years and then reevaluate our situation once we see what the competition is doing and how far along the construction is on our space hotel. And I wouldn't manufacture Spaceplanes for anyone but us.

- **Type of Case:** Market-sizing, entering a new market and pricing

- **Comments:** Big points for realizing that she couldn't estimate the market size without first knowing the price of the ticket, and she couldn't estimate the price without first knowing the costs.

✣ Japanese Electronics Manufacturer

Case 21: Our client is a Japanese electronics manufacturer that makes car stereo sound systems, a satellite navigation system, DVD recorders, computer hard drives, as well as mid-to-high-end home stereos. It has recently entered the plasma TV market. They are now one of five major players in the field, although the smallest player. However, they are the leader in plasma TVs over 40 inches, usually used for home theater systems.

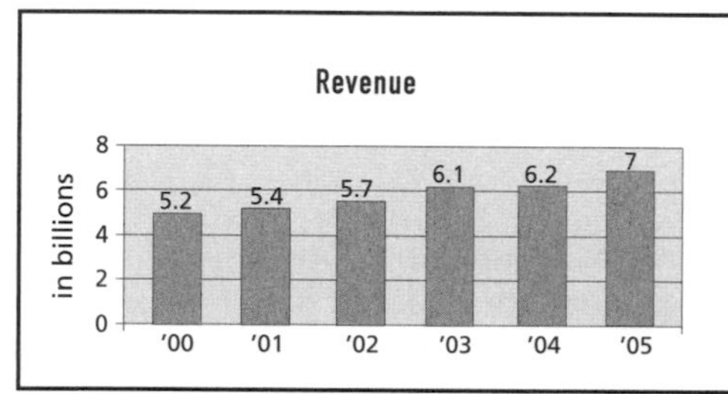

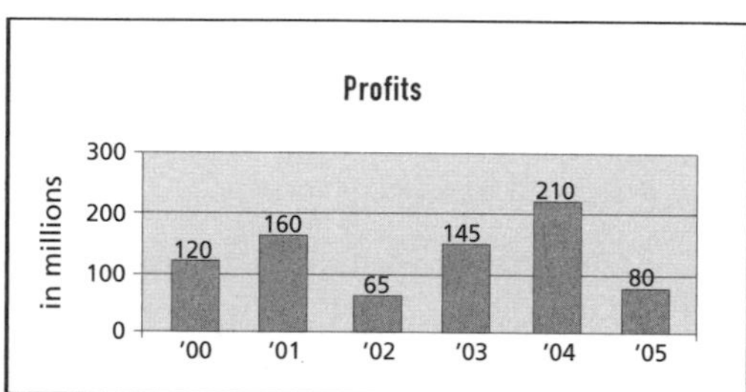

Look at these charts and tell me what's going on.

Our client is an electronic manufacturer that has seen its revenues climb steadily over the last five years from $5.2 billion to $7 billion. It looks as if revenues are growing between 4 to 7% a year, until you reach 2005 when revenues jump 10, no, almost 13%. They are doing nicely on the revenue side; however, on the profit side, they are all over the place. In 2000 they made $120 million on sales of $5.2 billion. That's a ... 2% return where the figures for 2005 indicate about a % return.

I'd like to ask a few questions about the company. Would it be fair to break the products down by auto products and home products?

– Yes.

Can you tell me how the sales are divided?

– Auto related products make up 42%of the company's sales, while home electronics make up 40%.

What makes up the other 18%?

– Not relevant.

How have the two divisions been doing?

– Sales rose in both those areas; however, profits dropped significantly. As you can see by the chart, profits were just 80 million on sales of $7 billion. What's going on?

Are their competitors facing similar problems?

– No.

So this isn't an industry problem?

– Not to this extent.

What does that mean? Does that mean other electronic manufacturers are seeing similar trends only not as exaggerated?

– It means that while some of their competitors posted bigger-than-expected profits, others just met Wall Street's expectations and profits stayed steady. To give you an example, Samsung had profits of $10 billion on sales of $53 billion — that's an 18 or 19% return on investment.

When did we enter the plasma TV market and how did we enter that market?

– The company entered it in early 2004, January or February. They bought a division of another company that wanted to narrow its focus to computers.

Profits jumped in 2004. I'll assume that's because of the increased sales of the plasma TVs and because of the fact that was an Olympic year.

– That played a part of it, yes. But that doesn't explain the huge drop in profits the following year, because sales continued to rise.

A couple of things could be going on. First, maybe some of the other players are getting into the large plasma TV market. Increased competition will drive the prices down. There could also be strong competition from a China-based competitor and from a China-based knock-off. They say that many of the manufacturers find it hard to tell the difference between the knock-offs and their own item. Is our market share down?

– Maybe a little. What else?

There could be substitutions to plasma. I read that liquid-crystal TVs are cheaper and the technology is getting much better. The third thing could be that their costs, possibly both labor and manufacturing, are rising.

– Assume everything you said could be true. What do we do?

If a competitor picks up market share or if there's a new entry into our market, we need to take a close look at the competition. How does their product differ from ours? Do they have more features, better technology? Are they priced cheaper? If so, why? Are they manufactured in China? Do their raw materials cost less? I'd want to look into all that. If we can't figure it out on our own, we may want to hire the competition's management.

Next, I'd like to see if we can increase sales. You've stated that sales are okay, but not good, that we didn't meet Wall Street's expectation. I'll assume that we are growing less than

the industry. Have we gone out and asked our customers what they want from us? Is price the only factor here or can better technology or more features differentiate us from the competition? Is it a marketing problem? Where and how are the competitors marketing their plasma TVs?

We know there are several ways to increase sales: increase volume, increase price and increase the amount of the purchase by coming up with additional products that might complement the plasma TV experience. So, I'd spend some time trying to increase our sales team, our distribution channels and our technology because it looks as though prices are headed in the opposite direction.

Once we have looked at and understood our revenue streams, we can then take a hard look at a breakdown of our costs. In this problem, revenues have climbed slowly but they have climbed every year. So while we can work on improving sales, we really need to take a hard look at lowering costs.

– Talk to me about costs.

I'd like to first look at this by breaking my costs down by internal and external costs.

Internal costs are things like labor costs, raw materials, and cost of manufacturing technology. If any cost seems out of line, I'd investigate why and put a stop to it. And, of course, I'd try to benchmark the competitors. I'd also look to see if the plasma technology can be improved, maybe made from fewer parts. Anyway, I'd look for cost savings through technical innovations.

External costs are things like the economy, interest rates and transportation costs. A good economy can not only increase our sales, but it can also increase our costs if we have to pay more for labor. The economy is doing okay and interest rates are still pretty low. So we can take a closer look at shipping costs.

Finally, I'll assume that our plants are currently in Japan. If that's true, I'd move them to China. Labor is cheaper and the technology is world class. Some of the Japanese car companies have huge plants in China, so why shouldn't we? We need to compete on price.

– Okay, good. Summarize in ten words or less.

I can do it in one word — China.

- **Type of Case: Increasing the bottom line**

- **Comments: The student did well. He was able to calculate returns in his head as he summarized the question. He had no problem identifying the problems and offered what the consulting industry calls MECE analysis: Mutually Exclusive, Collectively Exhausted. In this case, his was a fairly complete, yet general analysis of the charts and the problems the company faces. And he asked good questions. The student wasn't afraid to make the interviewer clarify an answer.**

+ Snow Job

Case 22: Snow Shovels Inc. (SSI) imports and distributes snow shovels. The snow shovel market is relatively stable. As expected, sales depend on demand and demand depends on weather. SSI has to order its shovels four months in advance. How many shovels should they order?

SSI imports and distributes snow shovels. They have to order their product four months in advance. They want to know how many shovels they should order.

– Yes.

Besides deciding how many shovels to order, are there any other objectives I should be concerned about?

– Yes. The goal is to maximize profits with the lowest amount of risk and the least amount of inventory on hand.

What areas of the country do they cover?

– Just Wellesley, Massachusetts.

I'd look at expanding into other areas.

– No. They just want to focus on their little corner of the world.

Then maybe we can increase their distribution channels. How many distribution channels do they have?

– Good question, but not relevant to what I'm looking for in this question.

How many did they order last year?

– Two thousand.

What was the weather like last year?

– Cold with lots of snow.

Did they have any inventory leftover from the year before?

– Yes, 500 shovels.

Is it fair to assume that they sold all 2,500 shovels this past year?

– Yes.

So there is no leftover inventory?

– That's right. SSI hates to carry over inventory.

Could we have sold more? Were there orders left unfilled?

– Yes. It's fair to say that if it's a cold winter, they will sell 3,000 shovels. If it's a mild winter, they will only sell 1,000.

Do we know what the forecast is for the coming winter?

– There is a 40% chance that it will be a cold winter, and a 60% chance that the winter will be mild.

Okay, let me get this straight. There is a 40% chance of a cold winter in which we could sell 3,000 shovels. There's a 60% chance of a mild winter in which we would sell 1,000 shovels. And SSI hates to carry over inventory. How much do we pay for the shovels and what do we charge?

– We buy them for $10 and sell them for $20.

So we make $10 a shovel. Let's figure that 40% of 3,000 equals 1,200 and 60% of 1,000 equals 600. If you add them together it equals 1,800 shovels.

– That's it? That's your answer? Why does everyone come up with 1,800 shovels? I've given this case five times today, and everyone has come up with 1,800 shovels. Think about the information I gave you. Think about the objective.

I'd like to look at the estimated value. If we order 1,000 shovels and assume that no matter what kind of winter we had we would still sell 1,000 shovels, then the estimated value would be:

# Ordered	# Sold	Income	Costs	Net	Times %	Expected Profit
1,000	1,000	1,000 x 20	1,000 x 10	10,000	100%	$10,000
						$10,000

If we order 2,000 shovels and there is a 60 percent chance of a mild winter in which we will only sell 1,000 shovels, and a 40 percent chance of a cold winter in which we would sell all 2,000, it would be:

# Ordered	# Sold	Income	Costs	Net	Times %	Expected Profit
2,000	1,000	1,000 x 20	2,000 x 10	0	60%	$0
2,000	2,000	2,000 x 20	2,000 x 10	20,000	40%	$8,000
						$8,000

If we order 3,000 shovels and there is a 60% chance of a mild winter in which we will only sell 1,000 shovels, and a 40% chance of a cold winter in which we would sell all 3,000, it would be:

# Ordered	# Sold	Income	Costs	Net	Times %	Expected Profit
3,000	1,000	1,000 x 20	3,000 x 10	(10,000)	60%	$(6,000)
3,000	3,000	3,000 x 20	3,000 x 10	30,000	40%	$12,000
						$6,000

Based on the numbers above and assuming that you're relatively risk adverse, I would have to suggest that you order 1,000 shovels. You are pretty much guaranteed a $10,000 profit. If you order 3,000 shovels, you have only a 40% chance of making $12,000 and a 60% chance of losing $6,000.

– Can you graph it?

Sure. It would look like this.

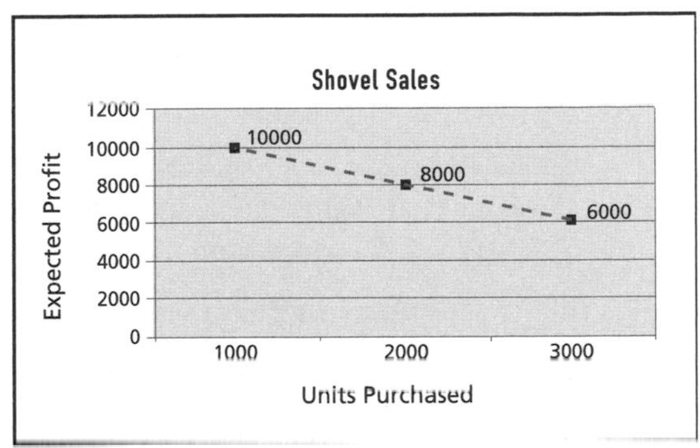

– Good recovery.

One last question. In this case, we assumed that the leftover inventory is a loss in the current period. It's really an asset unless they plan to throw it away.

– Good point. You're right, but in this case we don't want to deal with it.

- **Type of Case: Strategy**
- **Comments: This case is all about risk. The student tried to come to a fast answer, then pulled back and quickly rethought this strategy based on the interviewer's reaction. Estimated value may not be common knowledge to a lot of non-MBAs, so go back and reread the answer.**

N.B.: I've given this case 40 times to Harvard students and only 2 got the correct answer. On a scale of 1 to 10, this is probably a 9.

✢ North American Airlines*

◗ Case 23: In an effort to increase in-flight sales, North American Airlines (NAA) is contemplating partnering with JavaMoose, the world's leading coffeehouse, to sell several varieties of special blend coffee. From the perspective of NAA, would such a partnership prove itself to be profitable?

Okay. So, let me rephrase the scenario. NAA wants to sell several varieties of JavaMoose coffee on their flights to increase sales. We want to evaluate whether or not this is a good idea for NAA. Did I understand that correctly?

– That's right.

Besides making a profit, are there any other objectives I should be aware of?

– There is the possibility of a joint marketing campaign, but focus on the profits.

I'm going to need some additional information regarding the airline's routes, the products it currently sells, its clientele, its financial targets with this venture, as well as information about the JavaMoose products it intends to sell.

– Alright. What would you like to know?

Let's start with the routes. What routes does the airline serve? What is the duration of each of these routes?

– Okay. Eighty percent of NAA's routes are under two hours. These flights serve New York, Boston, Washington D.C., and Philadelphia. Recently, NAA has added two routes to its portfolio: one connecting New York to Los Angeles; the other linking New York with San Francisco. These routes comprise the other 20%. Each of these flights is direct and lasts about six hours.

I see. Could you tell me how many flights are under two hours and how many over two hours in a given day?

– Sure. NAA makes 50 flights daily.

Okay. So 40 of its flights are short and 10 of them are long.

– That's right.

Let's move on to the products it offers on its flights. Could you tell me what is complimentary, what is sold and what the markup is on the items that are sold?

– NAA offers complimentary soft drinks, bottled water, regular tea and regular decaf and caffeinated coffee on all its flights, regardless of duration or the time during which the flight takes place. On the early flights, NAA charges for specialty juices, bagels and breakfast rolls. Peanuts, chips and fruits are offered only on the two cross-

*Special thanks to Mukund Jain.

country routes. Beer, wine and champagne are sold on every flight. There is a 50% markup on these items.

Now I would like to know something about NAA's fleet, clientele, occupancy rate and the average sales per flight. More specifically, are all planes the same size? What types of passengers are on these flights? What percentage of each flight is full? What type of passenger makes in-flight purchases? Are purchases more prevalent during particular flights and/or particular times?

– Okay. All good questions. All of NAA's planes are the same size — with the capacity of 200 passengers. Its clientele consists of business travelers usually looking to make a day trip. The average occupancy rate per flight is 95%. Because they are mostly business travelers on these flights, these are the passengers making in-flight purchases. The average number of sales per flight depends on the flight's time of day and the length of the flight. Sales on morning and early afternoon short flights average $50 per flight. Sales on the long and early flights average $100 per flight. On the other hand, sales on the shorter evening and night flights average $150 per flight, while the later, longer flights average sales of $200.

That helps. Could you tell me how much the average passenger spends?

– Of those who purchase an item, it's $5.

Of the 50 daily flights, how many are early flights and how many are late flights? How many of the early flights are long, and how many are short?

– That's split even — 25 early and 25 late. In terms of long and short, 80% of the early flights are short, and 80% of the late flights are short.

Alright. I'm going to summarize this information in a table.

	Early			Late			Totals	
	# of Sales	Sales/Flight	# of Flights	# of Sales	Sales/ Flight	# of Flights	# of Flights	Sales
Short	10	$50	20	30	$150	20	40	$4,000
Long	20	$100	5	40	$200	5	10	$1,500
Totals	30		25	70		25	50	
Total Sales		$1,500			$4,000			$5,500

So on a given day, NAA's in-flight sales total $5,500, and with a mark-up of 50%, that's costs of $3,666 and $1,833 in profits.

– You're telling me something I already know. We're low on time. Could you move along?

Absolutely. What percentage of NAA's clientele are drinkers of special blend coffee?

– We don't know.

Okay. With 95% occupancy, that makes 190 potential customers per flight. We'll look at the short, early flight first. Ten drinks are sold on each of these 20 flights. I'm going to assume that each of the drinks is purchased by a different passenger. Since these are early flights

taken mostly by business travelers who are usually not too price sensitive, I'll suppose that only 10% of the remaining 180 passengers will purchase a JavaMoose product. I'm basing that assumption on a couple of facts. First, many passengers taking an early flight may want to take a nap on the flight rather than inject additional caffeine into their system. Secondly, for an appreciable number of customers, the complimentary coffee presently offered by the airline will satisfy their desire for caffeine. Third, several passengers might have already purchased a JavaMoose product at the terminal while waiting to board the aircraft. Thus, we can assume that 10% or eighteen passengers are potential customers on the short, early flights.

– Really? Let's move on.

The late, short flights will probably have an even lesser number of in-flight JavaMoose customers. I'm going to estimate this number at 5% of the passenger population not ordering a drink. Justifying this number are two similar facts. One, the sale of coffee generally declines as the day moves ahead. Substitute drinks such as sodas and bottled water contribute to this decline, as does a diminishing need to stay awake with less of a day remaining. Secondly, coffee is a drink that accompanies breakfast better than it accompanies lunch, an afternoon snack or dinner. Thus, 5% of 170 makes 8.5 potential passengers. To be conservative, let us say eight sales.

– Fascinating. Please continue.

In long, early flights, there are currently 30 sales of drinks per flight. That leaves 160 passengers, assuming that those purchasing specialty juices will not purchase coffee. Even though these flights are usually three times longer in duration, I am going to assume that still only 10% — rather than 30% — of remaining passengers will purchase a JavaMoose coffee. The same reasons justify this number as the ones I mentioned for the short, early flight. First, a longer flight affords a longer opportunity to sleep. Also, the complimentary coffee provided on the plane is a satisfactory substitute for many. Additionally, the opportunity to drink multiple cups for free on a longer flight is attractive to avid coffee drinkers. So, 10% of 160 is 16 passengers.

– We're running out of time.

Sure. That leaves us with the late, long flights. With 40 drinks sold, that leaves 150 passengers who might purchase coffee. Once again, I'm going to estimate that 5% of the passenger population not ordering a drink will purchase coffee. Premium coffee is not a drink that one drinks later in the day, especially with the availability of substitute drinks that go better with an afternoon snack or dinner. Thus, the total number of passengers who might purchase some JavaMoose coffee is 5% of 150, that is 7.5 or seven to be conservative.

The table below presents a summary of what we've discussed.

	Early			Late		
	# Sales/ Flight	# of Flights	Total # of Sales	# Sales/ Flight	# of Flights	Total # of Sales
Short	18	20	360	8	20	160
Long	16	5	80	7	5	35
Total	34	25	440	15	25	195
Total Sales			635			

Thus, the total number of cups of JavaMoose coffee that might be sold on a given day is 635.

– So, what do you think?

Well, there are a few concerns to selling JavaMoose coffee. First, JavaMoose might object, as it could cannibalize their sales at the terminal. This is a particularly serious concern to JavaMoose since customers who purchase coffee might also purchase something to eat. Second, serving JavaMoose coffee might require special preparation that could raise costs for both parties, particularly if we serve several varieties. Third, storing an additional beverage in an already space-constrained aircraft would be very difficult. Fourth, there is the risk of damaging the JavaMoose brand, a serious risk given JavaMoose's position as the market leader.

– You seem to be looking at this from the JavaMoose point of view, not our client's. So should NAA approach JavaMoose with this opportunity?

I think NAA can pilot this coffee on some of the earlier flights — long and short. To push adoption, they can halt serving the complimentary coffee and offer JavaMoose. Or, they can simply halt the complimentary coffee and charge for the JavaMoose, but that might upset the coffee drinkers looking forward to a free cup of joe. As far as preparation of JavaMoose is concerned, JavaMoose could help out by providing — pre-made — one or two varieties of their more popular flavors that would require minimal work on the part of the flight attendants. Looking at the table, if NAA were to charge $3 for a cup of coffee, they would raise revenues of $3 times 635 or $1905 on a given day. I assume JavaMoose would also get an appreciable piece of this pie, which would further reduce NAA's intake.

Thus, my recommendation is for NAA not to pursue this opportunity.

– Are you at all concerned about what the competition does? Whether other airlines sell JavaMoose or Starbucks coffee on their flights?

I was going to get to that, but we ran out of time.

– What about the fact that for every cup of JavaMoose we sell, not only do we make a profit on the cup of coffee, but we save some money on the complimentary drink we were going to give them for free. Did that positive cannibalism ever cross your mind?

No, but it's a good point.

– Did you think about whether customers would switch to NAA because we now serve JavaMoose on all flights? It could raise our occupancy rate up a percentage point. That's worth much more than the profit we'd make.

No.

– Did you consider the option of serving JavaMoose for free on all flights?

Given time ...

– Did you think about how our competition would respond to our serving or not serving JavaMoose on board our flights?

That would be an interesting analysis.

– It's clear to me that you are unfamiliar with the business traveler market. And I have my doubts whether you'll be familiar with it after graduation. Business traveler purchases are notoriously price inelastic because, for one, these are ends-oriented busy people who can not be bothered with a price differential under $5. And two, they are generally not paying for the coffee out of their own pockets — their companies are. As such, I can't imagine anyone who would hesitate before selecting the JavaMoose coffee over airline coffee.

And what about the "wake up" coffee — for people who rack out on the red-eye? Don't you think the percentage that would purchase a "wake up" coffee is relatively high? In addition, when I travel cross country, I just work or sleep as does everyone around me. I can't remember more than 10% of my flights being 95% full. And, finally, you paid zero attention to time zones and the jet-lag. Caffeine balance is extremely familiar to business travelers.

How do you expect me to move you on to the next round when you missed so many key points?

You told me to focus on profits and, given the time constraints, I think I did a good job at looking at the economics of the situation. I asked a lot of good and relevant questions — did I not?

– Yes, you did.

My quant skills were strong. I did most of the math in my head. I made easy-to-read charts and walked you through my thinking. I'm proud of my answer. Sure, I could have looked at those other things, but I needed to prioritize given the time constraints. Now, I'll be happy to work out a model to determine whether it makes more sense to give the JavaMoose coffee away if it will boost our occupancy by one or two percent. I can also look at the effects of a joint marketing program as well as investigate other options such as Starbucks. And I'll be happy to do a competitive analysis within our region as well as other regions of the country.

– No, that won't be necessary. You did do a decent job. I wanted to see if you could handle criticism. And you did a good job of that as well.

Type of case: New product and increasing sales – not a very good fit for either one

Comments: The student did do a good job with the economics of the case. And she defended herself without being defensive. This is an important point to remember. Sometimes the interviewer will bust your chops just to see if you can defend yourself without getting bent out of shape. Roll with the punches and don't take it personally. They're doing their job to see if you do yours.

✢ Texas Star Markets

Case 24: Our client is a large grocery chain throughout Texas. Their stores are concentrated in suburbs outside all the major cities in Texas: Dallas, Arlington, Fort Worth, Houston, Austin, Galveston, San Antonio, Amarillo, Corpus Christi, El Paso and Padre Island. They are looking to grow the company — but only in Texas. They feel that they have saturated the grocery market in the suburbs and have dismissed the idea of opening up stores downtown.

They already have an online grocery ordering and delivery service, so they are thinking of entering into the convenience store business. Is this a good idea? If so, how best to enter the market?

Basically, a large Texas-based grocery chain wants to explore the possibility of entering the convenience market. We need to determine if this is a good idea and, if it is, how best to enter this new market.

– That's right.

Besides the ones stated above, are there any other objectives I should be aware of?

– No.

Talking in broad strokes, I'd like to figure out why the company wants to expand, what the current convenience store market is like and then discuss ways to enter that market. Does that sound like a good idea?

– Possibly. I wouldn't have done it like that, but let's see how you make out.

I assume the reason or reasons Texas Star is entertaining this notion are: A) they have excess cash on hand and want to see if this is a better return on investment than a money market or other investments they've looked at; B) they want to increase their market share of the Texas in-store food business; C) there has been a decline in their existing business, maybe because of shrinking sales or higher costs; and/or or D) they see this as a growing market.

– Assumptions A, B and D are correct.

May I take a moment to jot a few ideas down?

– Sure.

The student takes a moment to draw a decision tree.

CURRENT MARKET
• SIZE
• GROWTH RATE
• CUSTOMER SEGMENTATION
MAJOR PLAYERS. MARKET SHARE, STRENGTHS AND WEAKNESSES
PRODUCT DIFFERENTIATION
BARRIERS TO ENTRY / BARRIERS TO EXIT

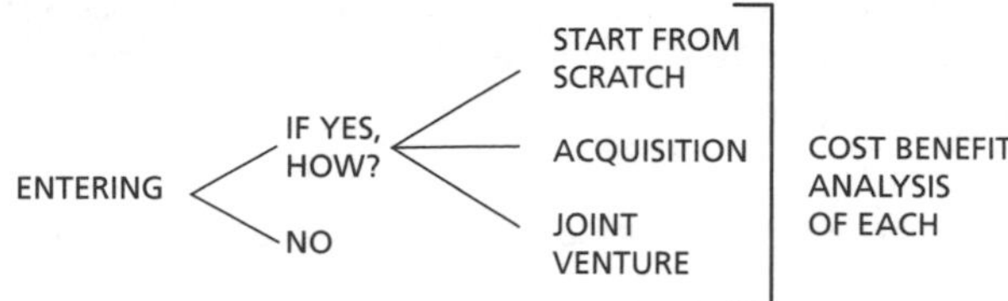

I know that there's plenty of competition with 7Eleven, Christy's, Dairy Mart, White Hen, The Red Apple, and Utote-um, just to name a few. Can you give me any market share information?

– I can tell you that the leader is 7Eleven and that they did over $3 billion in sales last year. That includes both in-store merchandise and gasoline sales, but I don't know what their market share is.

Do you know how many stores they have?

– Over 58,000 in the US and Canada. But I don't think that's relevant.

You're right. The proper question should have been how many of those stores are in Texas and how many convenience stores are there in Texas?

– That's right, but I don't have that information either.

I can't think of any barriers to entry, so I'll assume that's not a concern.

– What are the concerns?

While our grocery stores have name recognition, we need to figure out a way to capitalize on that and any other competitive advantage we might have. A convenience store is a convenience store. We'll probably be selling the same items as the 7Eleven around the corner. Why would people come to us? I can think of three reasons: location, price or loyalty to the grocery chain.

– Okay, I like that. Explore it some more.

Well, the first one was location. Which leads me to the next question. How do we plan to enter the market? We can start from scratch, buy our way in or do a strategic alliance.

– Texas Star doesn't want to do a strategic alliance.

I'd like to come back and visit this question in a minute. However, we would need to look at the real estate market and see what kinds of locations are available. We may want to see if there is a small chain of existing stores with good locations but poor management that we could take over.

– What else?

Next on the list is price. This is where I think we make our mark. People pay for convenience. Prices are high because costs are high because stores tend to buy many items in low volumes.

One of our advantages is that we already buy large amounts of all the products we would sell in the store, so we have economies of scale working for us. We should be able to leverage our current value chain components.

– What does that mean?

To be honest, I'm not sure.

– Let's call a time out for a second. Never use jargon or phrases that you don't understand. If you do it in an interview, then I'll assume that you will do it in front of a client. It's easy for the interviewer to lose trust in a candidate, because I can't trust you in front of a client. Now it just so happens that I like you and that you are doing really well on the question, so I'm going to pretend that I didn't hear that. Continue. Where were we?

We were discussing price. If we can price our items somewhere between what we charge in our grocery stores and what our competitors charge in their convenience stores, we could drive in traffic. For instance, if I buy a gallon of milk at the grocery store, it costs me $2.95. If I buy that same product in a convenience store, it costs me $3.95, a dollar more. If we could price it at $3.49, that's a significant enough difference where it would drive people into the store. In addition, I'm assuming that Texas Star, like most large grocery stores, has store-label items, such as their own brand of peanut butter. Those items sell for significantly less than the traditional name brands, so the price difference would be even greater. We could offer all the traditional convenience store items while adding things like a salad bar and prepared gourmet meals. This could change the genetic code of convenience store retailing.

– Let's not get carried away.

Let's look at the company's resources and capabilities. We buy in large volume; we have the management team, the marketing team, trained workers, name recognition; and we have an untraditional marketing channel through our existing stores. I don't think that there would be any cannibalization of existing grocery store sales, because items would still be less expensive in the grocery store. In fact, we could cross market and offer coupons to try our convenience stores.

The last thing on my list was brand loyalty. Texas Star obviously has a strong following, a commitment to Texas and, I'm guessing, to local communities.

– All right, summarize for me.

Texas Star is looking to expand. Their idea of getting into the convenience store market is a viable one. This market will continue to grow and there are no major barriers to entry. It will allow Texas Star to build on their name recognition and take advantage of the organization's existing resources and capabilities. They can offer lower prices and store-brand items, cross market with their grocery stores and offer new items to traditional convenience store fare.

The best way to enter the market is to look for a small chain that has good locations but bad management. Buy the chain, change the name and bring in your own management. All stores

should be in close proximity to a Texas Star grocery store. If they can't find a buy-out target, they should start from scratch.

And I just want to restate that it is a combination of name recognition, location and prices that will make this idea a success.

– Okay, that was pretty good. Now you got me thinking. Texas Star, as you can tell, is always looking for new ways to increase their revenue streams. They are also considering opening an in-store bank. No other competitors in their area are currently doing it. What do we need to be thinking about?

Again, they are entering a new market. There are a number of things that they need to figure and decide. First, do they have the space in their stores, or will they have to construct additional space? Also, if they do have the space, we need to think about whether that space can be used more effectively. How much space is needed?

– It's the equivalent of a florist department, and we already have one of those. And yes, we do have the space for this. It would take some remodeling, but nothing significant.

We need to look at who the major players are, what size market share they have, will our products or services be any different from our competition's and if there are any barriers to entry.

– What would you guess?

That there's plenty of competition and that our products or services might be basic compared to our competitors'. All we really have to offer them is convenience. Hopefully, there will be increased traffic at the grocery stores due to the bank. But now, with ATMs, debit cards and cash back, the basic services are easily covered. I'm thinking that we need to figure out how best to enter the market and determine if this makes sense.

There are three ways to enter the market: start from scratch, buy our way in and a joint venture. What are the costs in each of theses options? What are the potential revenue streams and how do they differ. And what is the risk associated with each?

– Do a quick cost benefit analysis for each.

Starting from scratch will be time consuming and somewhat expensive. We'd have to hire new people with experience in banking to run the organization. There might be some barriers due to federal and state banking regulations, which might take some additional time. And if it fails or doesn't live up to expectations, it could damage the overall Texas Star brand. On the other hand, we already have locations and our rent would be minimal. Revenues will come from bank transactions and possibly increased grocery sales. However, I'm not convinced that this is the best way.

Buying our way in would mean buying an existing bank and taking over its business. We would already have the people in place, a number of existing locations, and some brand recognition. It might be expensive. We would have to do due diligence on the entire bank and the banking industry. We might be able to sell some of the branches to other banks to help reduce any debt we would incur. This would be really jumping in with both feet.

The third way would be a joint venture with an existing bank. I think this is the simplest solution and holds the least risk to profits and our brand. We would just lease space to the bank for a monthly fee. We would have to weigh the rental income against the remodeling costs.

– So what are you saying?

I would tell Texas Market that if they feel that having a bank branch in their grocery stores would result in increased traffic and maybe higher sales, they should form a joint venture with an existing bank and keep risk to a minimum and lease out the space. Starting from scratch or buying an existing player is expensive and risky. We currently know nothing about the industry and a failure could hurt the Texas Star brand.

Type of Case: Entering a new market

Comments: Besides getting into trouble for using business jargon that he did not know, the interviewee did pretty well. He laid out his strategy up front and stuck to it, but also added ways that the client could differentiate itself from the competition. He seemed to roll into the banking part of the case with a little more confidence.

✢ Hector's Hard Lemrumade

Case 25: Our client is Hector's Hard Lemrumade. Hector's is a Puerto Rico-based manufacturer of alcopop beverages. Hector's Lemrumade is made with rum, lemonade and carbonated water.

Their biggest competitor is Mike's Hard Lemonade®. Mike's, a large Canadian manufacturer and distributor of wines, hard ciders and alcopops, also distributes Corona® beer in Canada.

Mike's, which is made with malt, has about 60% of the US alcopop market, Hector's has 20%. The remaining 20% is made up of regional players. Hector's has been growing by 10% a year, keeping even with the industry. There is enough of a taste difference between malt-based hard lemonade and rum-based hard lemonade to allow this growth.

Hector's just received word that Mike's will soon be manufacturing rum-based lemonade to compete directly with them. They will also enter this market with two other rum-based drinks – cranberry lemonade and apple lemonade.

Our client wants to know if they should respond by producing both a cranberry lemrumade and an apple lemrumade. What do you think?

Our client is Hector's Hard Lemrumade. They currently have 20% of the alcopop hard lemonade market, with the lion's share going to Mike's. Currently Hector's makes their lemonade with rum and Mike's uses malt. However, Mike's plans to enter the rum-based lemonade market competing directly against us with not one but three beverages.

– That's right.

Besides deciding if and how to respond, are there any other objectives I should be aware of?

– Profits.

You said that both the industry and Hector's was growing by 10%. Would we continue to grow by 10% if we did nothing?

– No. Hector's volume will fall 12% if they do nothing.

How many cases does Hector's sell a year?

– They sell 44,000 cases.

If Hector's responds by adding two new products, what will this do to his volume?

– If Hector's brings two new products to the market, their volume will remain at 44,000 cases, just divided between the three products.

What are some of Hector's costs? How much do they make per case?

– Hector's production costs are $5 a case. They make $10 a case.

What about marketing and distribution costs?

– Don't worry about them.

Are there any additional costs Hector's will face when bringing two new products to market?

– Minimum production of each new product is 5,000 cases. It will cost the company $10,000 to retool its productionline for each new flavor and two cents a bottle for new labels.

Let me take a moment to recap. If Hector's does nothing, their volume will fall 12%. Currently they produce 44,000 cases, so their new volume will be ... 10%. 10% is 4,400 plus an additional 2% is 880 cases for a total of 5,280. If we take 5,280 away from 44,000, we get a new volume of 38,720 cases.

– That's right.

If they come out with two new flavors to compete with Mike's, their volume will remain at 44,000 cases, but their costs will shoot up by $20,000 for retooling the factory and two cents a bottle. How many bottles in a case?

– There are 24.

So figure a minimum of the two new flavors. That 10,000 cases times 24 bottle equals 240,000 bottles times two cents equals ... $4,800. Hector's is facing $24,800 of new costs.

Currently Hector's produces 44,000 cases. They sell 44,000 cases. Their sales are $660,000, their costs are $220,000 and they net $440,000. If they make all three flavors, their sales stay the same, but their costs jump $24,800. So 440,000 minus 24,800 equals ... $415,200.

Let me ask you this. Does Hector's have to produce 44,000 cases a year? If their volume drops 12% to around 38 or 39,000 cases, can we manufacture ...?

– To the nearest thousand cases.

Our second objective was profits. What if we raised our prices?

– Okay, good. If Hector's raises their prices by five cants a bottle or $1.20 a case but doesn't bring in any new products, their volume will fall by 20%. If they raise their prices by $1.20 a case but bring in the two new products, their volume will fall by 10%.

We have five different scenarios going. I'd like to take a moment to draw up a quick chart.

– Good idea.

We already know the current numbers, the three product numbers and some of the 12% volume drop numbers. Let me plug those in. I can tell with the 20% volume drop that the numbers are going to be too small to make that the most profitable option, so I'll skip those calculations. Give me a minute to run the 10% drop numbers. I'm going to round off cases sold to the nearest thousand.

	Produced	Sold	Income	Cost	Net
Current	44,000	44,000	660,000	220,000	440,000
Mike enters no challenge: volume drops 12 %	387,200	39,000	38,720	580,800	193,600
Hector's makes 3 products	415,200	44,000	44,000	660,000	244,800
Raise prices and produce 3 products: 10% volume drop	40,000	39,600	641,520	224,800	416,720

As you can see, our best option is to raise our prices and produce the two new products.

– Quickly, four other things Hector's can do to grow the company.

They can increase their distribution channels; they can buy a regional player; they can diversify their product line to more than just drinks and they can develop a major marketing campaign.

– Nice job.

- **Type of case: Production, strategy and pricing case**

- **Comments: She got big points for coming up with the raising the prices strategy. She knew she struck gold when the interviewer had the answers to that question. He was probably hoping she'd ask. Her math was solid. She drew a simple chart when the options became confusing.**

✢ The Up-in-Smoke Cigarette Company

Case 26: The Up-in-Smoke Cigarette Company, a company that manufactures cigarettes, is considering outsourcing its distribution truck fleet to an independent company. If they want to continue providing this service in-house, they have to significantly upgrade their fleet due to new regulations requiring commercial trucks to provide electronic records of their itineraries — including average and maximum speed, time driven continuously and the length of driver breaks.

The Chief Operating Officer (COO) has hired you to help her decide: should they outsource or should they upgrade the fleet and continue to do it in-house?

Our client is a cigarette company that is trying to decide whether to outsource its delivery function. They've asked us to determine whether it is best to outsource the work or keep it in-house. Are there any other objectives we need to focus on?

– No. Do you have a problem with having a cigarette company as your client?

It wouldn't be my first choice, but no.

– We don't always get to pick our clients. If this is going to be problem, then tell me now.

It's not a problem.

– Okay, then proceed.

To help the COO decide, I will consider two main factors: the economics of such a move and associated risks.

Under the economic factors, I will compare the needed investments in the truck upgrade with the potential costs or savings from outsourcing.

Under the risks, I will look at both the internal and external risks. Internally, I will look at the cultural impact and impacts on labor – like the potential of a strike. Externally, I will look at the bigger macroeconomic risks – cost of gasoline, government regulations, future flexibility vs. competition.

– Okay, good. Where would you want to start?

I would like to start with the economics of the problem. I would like to figure out the costs for both the outsourcing and keeping it in-house. Also, I would like to know the estimated investments and the company's required payback period.

– It would cost the company about $1 million to upgrade its fleet, including trade-ins on the old trucks. Essentially, it would have to buy new trucks, as the current trucks are old and the COO figures they are due for replacement soon anyway. The company requires a four-year payback on all its investments.

– For a detailed table on the costs associated with both in-house deliveries and outsourcing, please take a look at the following table.

	In-house	Outsource
# of Deliveries	400	400
Average Cost of Delivery	?	$2,400
Labor Costs	?	N/A
Insurance	$200	$100
Gas	$200	N/A
Maintenance (per Delivery) (Includes oil change, tires, etc.)	$100	N/A
Cost per Delivery	?	?

In order to determine the difference between outsourcing and in-house deliveries, I need to determine the labor cost per delivery. Can you tell me more about labor costs? How many full-time drivers do we have and how much do we pay them on average?

– We have 10 full-time drivers that we employ for $5,000 per month, including benefits.

Great. That means the salary costs are 10 drivers times 12 months times $5,000 per month, which is $600,000 per year. We divide $600,000 by 400 and we now know that the labor cost per delivery is $1,500. When we add the additional costs, we have the total in-house cost per delivery of $2,000. In the case of outsourcing, the total cost is $2,500.

Overall, our client would save $500 per delivery or $500 times 400 deliveries, which equals $200,000 per year with in-house distribution.

However, when we compare that with the required investment of $1 million dollars, we get a payback of five years, which is longer than the required payback of our client.

– How'd you get five years?

I divided 1 million by 200,000 and got five.

– Okay, good. What's your final recommendation?

Just looking at the economics of the move, I would recommend outsourcing the delivery to the independent company. However, I would like to analyze some of the risks involved.

As I mentioned initially, the internal risks are worth analyzing. For example, I would like to analyze the potential impacts of this move to our internal culture – we'd be firing 10 drivers. Also, I would like to assess the potential for a strike should we decide to outsource this service.

– Those are good points, but our drivers are not unionized and we estimate the culture will not change significantly. Can you think of anything else?

Yes, actually. Looking at external factors, I can see some benefits in outsourcing. By outsourcing — especially if we sign longer-term contracts — we externalize the risk for the increase in the price of gas and the change in government regulations. These are important risks to a company like ours and are significant benefits to our company. Additionally, it would maintain the flexibility of the distribution in the event our company expands.

– Great answer. Now let's change hats and try to figure out how to make the in-house deliveries work. What would be some of your suggestions?

Well, we have a few variables. For the in-house deliveries to work, we would have to have:

Investment < Savings from In-house times Payback period.

Therefore, we can do several things.

1. **We can lower the needed investment. We can do this by leasing or renting the trucks instead of buying them.**
2. **We can increase the payback period beyond four years.**
3. **We can increase savings from in-house deliveries. Here, we have several options as well:**
   a. **We can increase the number of deliveries, either for our company or for smaller companies, in order to increase the utilization of our drivers.**
   b. **We can reduce the maintenance costs by outsourcing that job alone.**
   c. **We can introduce new software to determine more efficient routing for our trucks, thus saving us gas and maintenance.**

– Excellent. Thank you.

Type of case: Reducing Costs, in-sourcing v. outsourcing

Comments: You're not always going to get the clients you want and you need to think this through. Many consulting firms will try to reassign you if you have a legitimate reason for not wanting to be on the case, but they can't always control it because it has to do with scheduling. The student did well. He analyzed the simple chart and was able to fill in the blanks. He looked at both external and internal factors and came up with good recommendations on both sides of the issue.

+ Jamaican Battery Enterprise

Case 27: Our client is the Jamaican Battery Enterprise. Currently, they sell car batteries throughout the Caribbean, Africa and Central and South America. Over the past two decades they have been eyeing the Cuban battery market. However, Cuban Battery Enterprise, a state-owned battery company, currently has 100% of the secondary market. The reason they have 100% of the secondary market is because the Cuban Government has a 50% tariff on the manufacturing costs and shipping costs on all imported batteries.

The Cuban government has just announced it will be lowering the tariff on batteries by 5% a year for the next 10 years until the tariff reaches zero.

The Jamaican Battery Board of Directors wants to know the size of the Cuban market and if, when and how they should enter it.

The Board of Directors of the Jamaican Battery Company wants to know the size of the Cuban market and if, when and how they should enter it. We know that currently the Cuban battery market is dominated by the Cuban Battery Enterprise because of a 50% tariff on the manufacturing and shipping costs on all imported batteries. But we also know that the government is lowering the tariff by 5% a year for the next 10 years until the tariff reaches zero.

– Yes, that's right.

I'll assume that the objective is to gain market share and be profitable. Are there any other objectives that I should know about?

– No.

What is the market share that they would like?

– One hundred percent.

Let me rephrase. What is the market share that they can reasonably expect to gain and under what time table?

– Twenty five percent within five years of entering.

Let's start by estimating the size of the Cuban secondary car battery market. I'll assume that there are 10 million people in Cuba.

– That's a little low but a good figure to use.

I'll also assume that disposable income is limited and that only one in ten households has a car. So if we estimate that the average Cuban household is made up of five people —

– Where did you get five from?

I'm assuming that there are two generations living in a number of the homes.

– Okay.

So, if there are 2 million households and if only one in ten have a car, that means that there are 200,000 cars. I would also like to add in another 10,000 vehicles, which include taxis, trucks and government vehicles.

– So 210,000 vehicles.

Yes. I'll also assume that Cubans keep their cars for a long time and that the average car needs a new battery every three years.

– Three years? What were you thinking when you made that assumption?

I was assuming that this is a monopoly in a communist country, thus the quality of the battery might not be competitive with a Jamaican Battery, which probably lasts five years.

– Go on.

So 210,000 vehicles will need a new battery every three years. But there are two factors we need to figure in. First, let's say that half of the 10,000 "other" vehicles that we mentioned are government or military vehicles. So we need to subtract 5,000 from the total. Now it is 205,000 divided by every three years, which equals around 68,000 batteries.

Also, the number is going to be reduced over the long run because our batteries will last five years, not three. I'm not sure how to factor that in.

– That's okay. It's just important that you brought it up.

If we want 25% of that market, we're talking 17,000 batteries a year.

– Okay, what's next?

I'd like to know some costs and prices. What are our costs and prices compared to theirs?

– Prices are irrelevant, but costs aren't. It costs the Cuban Battery Enterprise $12 to produce a battery. Their raw material costs are 20%, their labor costs are 50% and their overhead and all other costs are 30%.

It costs us $9 to produce a battery. Our raw material costs are 20%, our labor costs are 25% and all other costs including overhead and marketing are 55%. It costs us $1 to ship it to Cuba.

Let me just write this out.

Cuban Battery Enterprise		**Jamaican Battery Company**	
Production costs:	**$12**	**Production costs:**	**$9**
Raw material 20%		**Raw material 20%**	
Labor 50%		**Labor 25%**	
All other costs 30%		**All other costs 30%**	
Shipping costs	**$0**	**Shipping costs**	**$1**
Tariff	**$0**	**Tariff $5**	
Total cost	**$12**	**Total cost**	**$15**

That means it costs us $9 manufacturing plus $1 shipping, which equals $10. Add in the 50% tariff and we're talking $15 a battery.

We now need to figure out when we will be competitive. In five years the tariff will drop from 50% to 25%, which is half. So, it will still cost us $10 to manufacture and ship the battery; however, the tariff will only be $2.50. That makes our total cost $12.50. So I would say, based on sheer numbers, we can enter and compete during Year 6. But if we can market and explain that for a little bit more our battery will last five years instead of three years, we might be able to charge a premium and that could justify entering the market in Year 5.

– Let's switch hats for a second. You now are advising the Cuban Battery Enterprise. What do you advise them?

My first step is to approach the government and try to get them to reconsider lowering the tariff.

– Castro's mind is made up. The tariff will be reduced.

Next, I would want to find out why our labor costs are so high.

– Why do you think?

The two things that jump to mind are technology and medical costs. Maybe our technology is old and our manufacturing process is very labor intensive.

– Yes, that's part of it. What else?

We are in a communist country where health care is free. That's the hidden cost in everything that's done, every service and every manufactured item. Even a country like Canada, with its national health care program has higher prices. If the Canadian dollar wasn't so weak compared to the US dollar, they would price themselves right out of the market in many items.

– We'll save that discussion for another time.

Well, we can't do much about the health care costs, but we can upgrade our technology. The upgrade would also make our batteries more competitive and able to last five years instead of three years.

– Say we upgrade our technology and we are now able to make a world-class battery for $9 a battery. How would that change things?

Well, the tariff becomes moot in the sense that we can be competitive without it. This is good, but we still have a perception problem. I think we need to launch a marketing campaign to show the Cuban public that we have a new battery that is world-class. I'd also like to review our customer service and our distribution channels. These are key functions that are often overlooked in a monopoly environment.

– Good point. Our customer service is pitiful and our distribution channels are restricted to two major warehouses, one in Havana and the other in Nuevitas. You said that you would launch a marketing campaign, and I'll assume that there will be a customer service aspect to that. What would you do about the distribution channels?

I'll make two assumptions. First, I'll assume that we have at least two years before the Jamaican Battery Company enters our market. Second, I'll assume that other non-American battery companies will also enter our market, probably about the same time and with a similar strategy to the Jamaican company.

– Both fair assumptions.

First, I would go to every gas station on the island, both in the cities and in the countryside. I would front them the cost of the batteries, give them a nice display rack, free t-shirts and maybe some cash. In return, they would have to sign an exclusive agreement to sell only our batteries.

Let me ask you this? Does the government make its own tires? And, if yes, how's the quality?

– Yes, they do, but the quality is poor. However, based on your advice, they will also upgrade their technology and launch a marketing plan because the tire tariff is being eliminated as well.

So you know what I'm getting at. We can open a service store where residents can get both a new battery and new tires, and maybe an oil change. We can snap up all the best locations before the foreign competitors come into our market.

– We're switching hats again. You are now back to advising the Jamaican Battery Company. You have seen that the Cuban Battery Enterprise has upgraded its plant, increased its distribution channels, formed a joint venture with the Cuban Tire Enterprise and has launched a nationalistic marketing campaign. Do you now enter the Cuban battery market, and if so how?

Whenever you enter a new market, there are several things you need to examine. Who are the major players? What size market share do they have? How are their products or services different from ours? And are there any barriers to entry? The major player is the Cuban Battery Enterprise. They have 100% of the market. Two years ago, their products were inferior, but today they are very similar. The tariff was a barrier to entry, but now it looks as if access to distribution channels could be a threat.

I've learned that there are three main ways to enter a market. Start from scratch, buy your way in or form a joint venture. I'd like to do a quick cost benefit analysis of each. Starting from scratch would be a fine strategy if we can define our distribution channels. If the Cuban firm has all the gas stations tied up and has built tire and battery stores, then our distribution means are limited. Plus, selling 17,000 batteries a year might not justify an investment of building our own battery stores.

The second strategy is to buy our way in. Since this is a communist country, there isn't a lot of buying opportunity. If we were going to buy anyone, it would have been the Cuban Enterprise, and we should have bought it when it was a mess and not a formidable competitor.

The third way is to form a joint venture. If I work under the assumption that there are no independent battery distributors, then my first choice is to form a joint venture with one of the tire companies that are entering the market. My guess is that there will be several tire companies and battery companies jumping in, so we need to be part of that coalition.

– So it all boils down to —

So it all boils down to distribution channels.

– Great job.

- **Type of Case: Strategy / entering a new market / market-sizing**

- **Comments: This was a long case and one that you'd get in the final rounds where you have about an hour to answer it. It had a market-sizing component to it, but probably the hardest thing was the switching of the hats. It forced the student to come up with counterstrategies to the strategies he had just developed.**

Most students would have tried to figure out the reduction in tariff fees year by year, but this student saved time and impressed the interviewer by picking a point in the middle and working from there. He made the math simple and was able to do the calculations in his head.

The student was very well-organized — he even wrote out the costs and percentages in a little chart. This impresses the interviewer and makes everything easy for the student to find when flipping back through his notes.

Cabaña Feet

Case 28: Cabaña Feet, LLC makes gel-flow flip-flops. These are like traditional flip-flops but have the comfort of a gel insole. They come in a variety of sizes and colors. Earlier this year, Brad Pitt wore them in his latest film and they have become all the rage. Now, Cabaña Feet is struggling to keep up with demand. Cabaña Feet is the only flip-flop maker producing its footwear entirely in the US. This has been a selling point in their advertisements for the last 10 years. Thus, it can't outsource production to other flip-flop makers. Take a look at the chart below and lay out for me in broad strokes some short-term and long-term strategies that it might review.

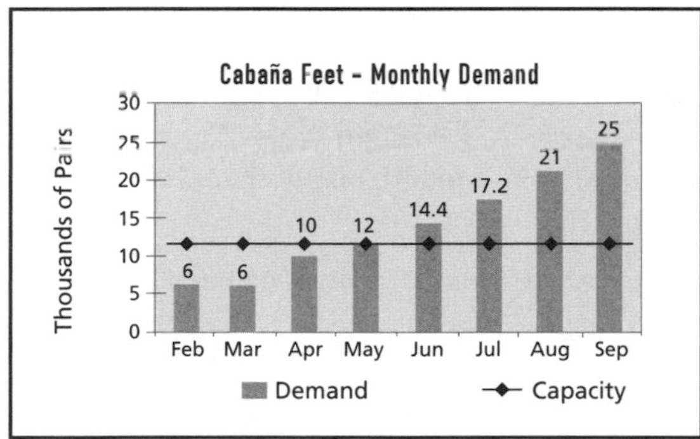

Our client is a company called Cabaña Feet. They make gel-flow flip-flops. It looks like they were producing about 6,000 pairs a month. Demand suddenly shot up when Brad Pitt wore their flip-flops in a movie. They can't outsource because they are the only flip-flop maker in the US and a big part of their advertising rides on the fact that their product is American made.

– That's right.

You want me to come up with some short-term and long-term strategies to help them meet demand. Are there any other objectives I should be aware of?

– No.

Can I ask a few questions?

– Absolutely.

Judging by the chart, our capacity is 12,000 pairs of flip flops a month.

– Yes.

I'm assuming that the movie came out in April.

– Yes.

What month are we in now?

– Early September.

So the 25,000 number is an estimate?

– That's right.

Have we been able to fill the orders up until now, or are there thousands of pairs backordered?

– We've been able to fill the orders because of inventory; however, we'll run out of inventory at the end of the month.

Do we expect the trend to continue? When does the DVD come out?

– The DVD comes out in December. What are your thoughts on the trend?

I would expect the trend to level off after the DVD's release. But our strategy must take into consideration two scenarios. First, what happens if Brad Pitt wears construction boots in his next movie and sales fall back to the 6,000 pairs a month number? And what can we do if it levels off at around 25,000 pairs?

– Okay, good. What are you thinking? How can we meet demand?

I have a couple of ideas. First, we put on more shifts if we haven't already. Ask employees if they want to work weekends and a third shift. If not, then hire new employees for those shifts. Second, I'd do a complete analysis of the current production line. See if there are any bottlenecks. See how we can squeeze more pairs out of each shift without compromising quality. Third, look for labor saving devices or technologies that would boost production without committing to another production line. Fourth, build another production line or even another factory. Fifth, econ 101 – raise our prices. And sixth, outsource production.

– There is no one inside the US that can help us. So the only option is to go outside the US.

Then go outside the US.

– And throw away our marketing campaign of the last 10 years? We'd get crucified in the press.

Not if we go to the business press and argue that this is a temporary measure, that for us to meet demand we need to go outside the US. Once we can meet demand with US manufacturing then we'll bring everything back home. Look, our sales jumped from 6,000 pairs a month to 25,000 pairs a month. Assume that 5,000 out of the original 6,000 customers bought our shoes because they were made in the US. I think that number is high, but let's assume it to be true. That means that we have 20,000 new customers who are more interested in looking like Brad Pitt from the ankles down than whether the flip-flops are made in the US.

We can't miss this opportunity. If we don't get those flip-flops on the market, someone else will. We have to worry about knock-offs and new competition.

– Alright. By what percentage did their demand grow from March to April?

It went from 6,000 pairs to 10,000 pairs. That's 10 – 6 =4 4/6 = .66 or 66%.

– I'm going to give you some additional information. At the plant, workers make $15 an hour. Supervisors make $20 an hour. Each shift uses 10 workers and one supervisor. Each shift is eight hours long. Assume 20 work days in a month. Got it?

Got it.

– What would be the labor costs of one shift if benefits equal 30% of wages and there is a miscellaneous cost of $232 per shift?

Workers' wages, $15 an hour times eight hours times 10 workers equals $1,200. The supervisor costs are $160. I got that by multiplying $20 by eight hours. Total wages are $1,360 times 30% equals ... 408. So $1,360 plus $408 equals $1,768 plus the miscellaneous cost of $232 equals $2,000 per shift.

– Good. Now assume that the total costs per shift, fixed and variable, equal $2,000. Cabaña makes $8 a pair up to production capacity. What is the shift breakeven point? How many pairs of flip-flops do they have to make each shift to breakeven?

That would be $2,000 divided by $8 equals ... 250 pairs of flip-flops.

– Capacity is 12,000 pairs of flip-flops a month. Capacity equals two shifts a day, five days a week. Given a normal eight hour shift, what is the maximum production per shift?

For a single shift?

– Yes, a single shift. I want you to think out loud when you do the math.

Okay. I'll take 12,000 pairs and divide that by two shifts. So each shift makes 6,000 pairs per month. Next I'll divide the 6,000 pairs by 20 work days in the month and I'll get 300 pairs of flip-flops per shift.

– How much would a third shift increase our capacity?

It would increase it by 6,000 pairs and push it from 12,000 to 18,000.

– If we started a third shift using our current employees, what would be the cost of the third shift? How much would our profits per pair of flip-flops change? Keep in mind that wages would go to time and a half. And you'll need to add in the miscellaneous cost as well.

Workers' wages at time and a half would jump to ... $1,800 ($22.50 x 10 x 8) and the supervisor's costs would be $240 (30 x 8). That totals to $2,040. Multiple 2,040 by 30% for benefits and that equals ... $612 so that's $2,652 plus the miscellaneous 232. So the total is $2,884. So $2,884 minus $2,000 equals $892 in additional costs. Divide the $892 by 300 pairs and it equals... $2.97. Thus we have $8 minus $2.97 equals $5.03 per pair.

– What are some of the pros and cons of adding a triple shift using our current workers?

Can I take a minute to think this through?

– Sure.

Student draws a line down the center of his page. Writes out the pros and cons and presents them in bulk – all the pros first, then all the cons.

Pros	Cons
Able to meet demand up to 18,000 pairs without major new investment	Possible worker burn out
More total profits	Lower profit per pair
Help keep competitors out	Higher wear and tear on the machinery
Save on hiring and training costs of new employees	Might lower quality of product, may have to throw out some pairs
Easy to get back to normal production levels	Less time for maintenance
Better utilization of equipment	Suppliers might not be able to meet our demand

– By adding a third shift we'll only be able to produce 18,000 pairs a month. You said earlier that you thought demand would level out at 25,000 pairs. If we add a new line that produces 800 pairs a day, this includes two shifts, is this enough?

Well, 800 pairs a day equals 16,000 pairs a month, given 20 work days in a month. Add to that the current capacity of 12,000 pairs and we total 28,000 pairs a month. If demand is greater than that, we can go as high as 42,000 pairs if we put on triple shifts on the new line and the old line.

– Summarize the case for me.

Our client, Cabaña Feet has seen demand for their flip-flops skyrocket from 6,000 pairs a month to 25,000 pairs within a six month period. While we'll assume that demand might continue to grow for a few more months, we're thinking that it will settle down at around 25,000 pairs a month. Current capacity is only 12,000 pairs a month. They've been able to meet demand because of inventory on hand; however, the inventory is now down to nothing. We came up with six short-term and long-term strategies to fix the problem. The main ones are putting on more shifts, streamlining our production process, and outsourcing production to another manufacturer outside the US.

We learned that our breakeven point is 250 flip-flops per shift and that our capacity is 300 pairs per shift. We talked about the pros and cons of putting on a third shift, including watching our profit per pair drop from $8 to about $5 a pair. And finally, we are considering adding a new line, which could increase our overall production to 42,000 pairs a month. That's a 250% increase over our current double shift capacity.

– Good. Thanks for coming by.

- **Type of case: Production and strategy case**

- **Comments: The student did very well. He was quick to come up with some long-term and short-term strategies. He held his own when the interviewer pushed him about the outsourcing question. His math skills were solid and he tried to quantify his answer when he could.**

+ Full Speed Ahead

Case 29: As a member of the MBA consulting club, your "team" has taken on a small, privately-held business. Your client is a retail company that sells nautical clothing, foul weather gear, sailing shoes and boots, half hulls, burgees, basically all things nautical except boats and boat parts.

They have 10 retail stores located up and down the east coast of the United States. Sales last year were $24 million, up 5%. The owner had a website built, but it only brought in $10,000 in sales, barely enough to cover the cost of the design.

He wants you to help him increase sales and profits. What do you tell him? What are some short-term and long-term strategies?

I'd like to repeat the question to make sure I got my numbers right. Our client sells all things nautical in his 10 retail shops up and down the east coast. He just spent $10,000 to build a website; however, web sales were disappointing. Besides coming up with both short-term and long-term strategies to increase sales and profits, are there any other objectives I should be aware of?

– No.

I'd like to lay out my structure then ask some questions.

The student writes E(P=R-C)M at the top of his sheet. (See page 45 for explanation.)

I'd like to start by investigating the industry, the market, their direct competition and the overall economy. Next, I'd analyze the company focusing first on their revenue streams. What are their established revenue streams and are there any new ones besides the website? I'd also like to know what percentage of the total revenue does each stream represent and whether those percentages have recently changed. In addition, I'd like to review their distribution channels and marketing plan.

Next, I'd like to examine their costs and identify the major variable and fixed costs. I'd like to know if there have been any major shifts or increases. We'd need to investigate to see if we can reduce costs without damaging the revenue streams, maybe even benchmarking our costs against our competitors.

Finally, I'd like to see if we can figure out ways to increase volume. We could possibly expand into new areas, and maybe increase our marketing campaign or our sales force. Because sailing is mostly done in the spring and summer, we could look at ways we can create some seasonal balance. Lastly, I'd look into our pricing strategy and customer service issues.

– That sounds like a plan.

Can I ask a few questions?

– Absolutely.

How is our client growing compared to the industry overall?

– Sales are growing by 5% a year, compared to a 7% increase in the overall industry.

Has that been constant over the last couple of years?

– Yes. And assume that if nothing changes, the client will continue to grow at 5%.

What's their market share?

– Not relevant. Okay, you laid out your structure and it seems pretty complete. I'd really like to focus on how we can drive sales to our website. Website sales were poor; part of the reason was that there was very little advertising. Assume we're starting from scratch. How would you drive sales to the website?

The first step is to put our web address on all our written material, stationary, bags, receipts, etc. and in all our advertising, print ads, handouts at boat shows. The second step is to do some online advertising – things like adwords and sponsored links on Google and Yahoo. We could try email marketing, buying relevant customer lists and emailing them. It's very inexpensive.

– You're gonna spam people? Two problems with that. First, the email would probably get caught up in spam filters; second, people hate spam and spammers. It would probably do us more harm than good.

We could create our own list. Ask customers if they want to receive emails about sales and special events.

– Okay. What else?

I can't think of anything else.

– Nothing?

Maybe ask for links to our page on some of our manufacturers' web pages. Like, if someone goes to the Sperry Topsider® webpage, they could tell customers that we sell them.

– I was looking for the word catalogs. Did you know that last year the number of catalogs mailed grew by 5.5% to 19.2 billion? Catalogs have been recognized as the best way to get consumers to go to your website? I'm talking about the small and glossy, magazine-like ones that convey a lifestyle to the consumer. Did you know that last year Victoria Secret's shipped 400 million catalogs — resulting in online growth of 10%? That's more than double the 4% increase in their stores.

Catalogs.

– Catalogs. I've done some research and for our client to buy the mailing list, design, publish and mail catalogs, it will cost him $1.25 each for a million catalogs, $1 each if he sends out 5 million catalogs and 50 cents each if he sends out 10 million catalogs. Look at this chart.

Number of Catalogs	Costs	Total costs	Increase in sales
1 million	$1.25 each	$1.25 million	7% (5%+2%)
5 million	1.00 each	$5 million	9% (5%+4%)
10 million	$0.50 each	$5 million	12% (5%+7%)

– The last column shows how much our sales would grow. The number is made up of the 5% growth that we would have without the website and the remainder is how much the website would add to our growth. Assume that sales will increase at the same rate as above in Years 2-5. What are your thoughts?

A couple of things come to mind. If we send out 1 million catalogs, we will increase our sales by 2%. Two percent of $24 million is $480,000. We'd be laying out $1.25 million and only bringing in $480K. The 5 million is not an option, because we can send out 10 million for the same price. A 7% increase equals around $1.5 million, maybe a little more.

– I want you to work out the numbers for the 10 million catalogs and make a chart comparing the growth without catalogs to growth with and growth with catalogs minus the costs of the catalogs. For the next five years. Assume Year 1 sales are $24 million.

Can I take a minute to do the math?

– Certainly.

Student takes about four minutes to do the calculations and build a table, and from the table a column chart.

Estimated Sales			
	w/o Catalog	w/ Catalog	w/ Catalog net costs
Y1	$24m	$26.8m	$21.8m
Y2	$25.2m	$30.1m	$25.1m
Y3	$26.5m	$33.7m	$28.7m
Y4	$27.8m	$37.7m	$32.7m
Y5	$29m	$42.3m	$37.3m

The chart makes it clear, that even when we take the cost of the catalog into account, we'll break even around Year 2. We will certainly have an increase in sales of $2.2 million by Year 3, and it continues with an increase of over $8 million by Year 5. Because we are a private company, we can take the initial hit to the bottom line without worrying about what Wall Street thinks. It looks like catalogs are the way to go.

– Okay, can you summarize the case for me?

Our client, a nautical retailer with 10 stores and sales of $24 million, is looking for ways to increase sales by driving traffic to its new website. We discussed adding the website address to all printed materials and ads, doing some online advertising by way of adwords and sponsored links. However, the big push would come from the publishing and mailing of 10 million catalogs a year. This would increase our sales an additional 7% a year. We'd take a $2 million dollar hit the first year, break even the second year, and then we have clear sailing with additional sales of around $2 million in Year 3, $5 million in Year 4 and $8 million in Year 5. Since we're a private company, we can afford to take the risk.

– Not bad.

- **Type of case: Increasing sales**
- **Comments: Started out as a typical P&L case. Student did a good job structuring her answer upfront, remembering to look at outside factors first. The case then switched to driving business to their website. Her answer was okay and then she hit a brick wall. She recovered a bit with the analysis and table of the profit growth.**

+ Playing It Smart

Case 30: Our client is a multi-national corporation, much like GE, which has many divisions. Their biggest are financial services, computer chip manufacturing, development and production of medical devices, auto insurance and laser security technologies. They want to get into the smart card market; they want to know where in the value chain they should enter and how they should enter. The CEO wants to utilize as many different divisions as possible in overall strategy.

Our client is a large multi-national corporation that has many divisions including financial services, computer chip manufacturing, medical device development and production, auto insurance and laser security technologies. They want to enter the smart card market, incorporating as many different divisions as possible. They want us to advise where along the value chain they should enter. Is that right?

– Yes, that's right.

Are there any other objectives?

– No.

Can you explain to me what a smart card is?

– The typical debit or credit card used in the US has a magnetic strip on the back of the card. The strips are coded with customer information and it allows the merchant to quickly authorize a purchase by swiping the card through a reader. The current smart card, which is popular in Europe and Asia, is a debit or credit card that contains a tiny microprocessor chip that stores encrypted customer information and requires a personal identification number, a PIN. The use of the PIN makes it more secure.

Are they used in the US?

– No.

Why not?

– It's expensive. The microchip costs $2 and the magnetic strip about 85 cents. In addition, the US has better telecommunications links to cash registers that can authenticate information quickly, keeping the fraud levels low. Besides, Americans don't want to remember another number. Smart cards also allow for use of contactless payment, which allows the consumer to pay by holding their card near a special reader. You've probably seen the ad of the marathon runner going into a convenience store during a race. It's quick, easy and very secure.

Are there any new technologies that would differentiate our card from the competition?

– Assume no.

I'd like to know the different facets of the smart card value chain.

– What do you think they are?

Thinking it through logically, I would imagine that the main areas would be card development, terminal manufacturing, processing the transactions and terminal maintenance.

Student draws.

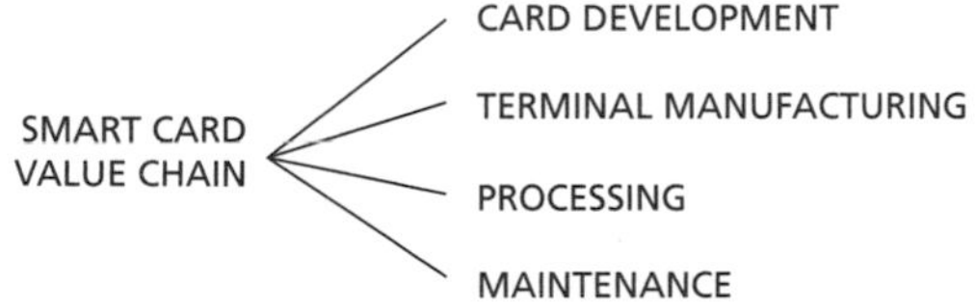

Those are the key areas, but why did you draw a decision tree instead of a chain?

That was my next step.

– I see.

I'd like to learn more about each.

– Good.

The consultant hands him the chart below.

	Card Development	Terminal Manufacturing	Processing	Maintenance
Competition	3 players with equal share	10 players with equal share	10 players with equal share	Highly fragmented
Competitive Tactic	Patented technologies	Products are mfg based with little intellectual property	Major IT consulting firms	Geographically based
Profit Margins	15%	10%	20%	10%
Share of $1 Spent in Industry	25%	30%	20%	25%

Can I take a minute to review this more closely?

– Certainly.

I'd like to analyze the expected profits and corporate alignment – how it fits in with the rest of the company, the competition, the risk and the entry strategy. I'll start with card development. The expected profit would be $1 times the 25% share of the industry dollar times the 15% profit margin. With card development, it equals $0.0375. Next I'd look at corporate alignment, the competition, the risk to starting this and how we'll enter the market. Let me make a chart.

Student takes several minutes to work through the numbers and draws up a chart.

	Expected Profits	Corporate Alignment	Competition	Risk	Entry Strategy
Card Development	$1 * 25% * 15% = $0.0375	Medium / High	Low	M	Acquisition or Internal Development
Terminal Manufacturing	$1 * 30% * 10% = $0.03	High	Medium	M	Acquisition
Processing	$1 * 20% * 20% = $0.04	Medium	Medium	L	Acquisition or Internal Development
Maintenance	$1 * 25% * 10% = $.025	Low	High	L	Acquisition

Processing is more profitable, with less risk and with average competition. We can gain market share through acquisition or by expanding our current financial services processing centers. The thing that bothers me here is the corporate alignment. I'd probably want to explore more about the card development – profit is just a little less, corporate alignment is high, competition is low and the risk is manageable.

Note: There is no right answer as long as you can justify your choice.

– Here's a market-sizing question for you. How many credit cards do you think are issued in the US?

I'm going to start with the population of the US at 300 million. I'm going to break that population down by four generations – 0-20, 21-40, 41-60 and 60+. I'll assume that there are even numbers of people in each generation. So 300 divided by four equals 75 million people per generation.

Generation	Population per	Number of cards
0-20	75 m	5 m
21-40	75 m	70 m
41-60	75 m	120 m
60 +	75 m	105 m

In the first group, most teenagers don't have their own card, so I'm going to estimate that at maybe 5 million, which is around 7%. The second group, I'd assume that maybe a little more than 40 million have a least one card and of that number 20 million have two and that 10 million have three cards. That totals up to 70 million cards. The third generation has more money and more debt, so I'll assume that 60 million have at least one card, of that 60 million, 40 million have two cards, and 20 million have three cards. That totals up to 120 million. The last generation is probably a bit more conservative. I'll say that 60 million have one card and 45 million have a second card. That totals 105 million. The grand total on the consumer side is 300 million credit cards.

On the business side...

– That's okay. I get your logic and we're short on time. But I'll tell you that there are approximately 1 billion credit cards floating around this country doing $2 trillion in business every year. And I'll tell you that 14% of US consumers have 10 credit cards or more.

Now you seemed disappointed that the smart card wasn't anything more than what it was. What if I were to tell you that we have developed a new biometric security feature that could be placed on smart cards as well as on credit cards? The consumer has to hold his thumb over an embossed thumb print on the card in order for the card to be accepted. The problem is that consumers would have to have their thumb prints scanned. What can we do about that?

While I think the consumer would like the idea of a thumb scan for better security, it would be a logistical nightmare as well as expensive to scan and process the thumb print.

– That's right. Figure that's $100 a card to process the scan and for the new microchip.

That's a $100 a card compared to $2 a card for a smart card.

– Yes, but this technology is much safer. I said credit cards sales are $2 trillion a year. What would 5% of that number be?

Ten percent would be $200 billion, so 5% is $100 billion.

– That's right. So if we can save half of that in fraud charges, we've more than paid for it. But that still leaves the original questions: how can we scan people?

My birthday is next month.

– That's terrific. What does that have to do with anything?

I have to get my driver's license renewed every five years. I have to get a new picture, why not a thumb scan? This is my idea. Figure it costs the State of California $25 on top of the fee they charge me to renew my license. What if we provided them with finger print scanners and covered the $25 for the state and in return they scan the driver's thumb? They might even want to use this technology for their own use. They could download the scans into a large database. We could offer to use the driver's license for more than just a driver's license. One side can be the driver's license, and on the other, we can make it a credit or debit card. It could hold not only customer loyalty programs but medical information in case you are injured. It would be up to the consumer. And we'd be able to reach all the new drivers for their first credit card.

– That's a great idea; however, the civil libertarians would be all over us for scanning people's thumb prints and keeping them in a data base. We would have to have them sign a waiver, not to mention the groups of activists who think it would be wrong to offer a credit card to 17 year olds. But say we can get by with that, how much of an investment are we talking about?

California has 36 million people. I'm going to divide them into four generations. I'll assume an equal number of people per generation and age group.

Age	People per generation	# that would drive legally
0-20	9	1m
21-40	9	8m
41-60	9	8m
60 +	9	8m
	36	25m

In the first age group there are 9 million people. But only people who are 17 and older can drive. So I'll divide 9 million by 20 and I get 450,000 per year. The number of people eligible to drive in that first generation is 4 times 450,000 or 1.8 million. For a variety of reasons, not everyone drives, so I'll round that number down to 1 million.

In addition, I'll assume that 8 million out of the 9 million eligible drivers will have licenses for the other generations. That gives us a population of 25 million drivers. Drivers renew their licenses every five years, so 5 million drivers renew every year. It costs the driver $100 to renew his license, and it costs the state $25 per driver for processing. If we paid the state, $25 times 5 million equals $125 million. I doubt that everyone would do it, but the beauty of it is that the Division of Motor Vehicles already has offices and employees. So instead of paying $100 to scan the thumb, we're only paying $25. Of course we would have to pay for the scanners. If California has 100 Division of Motor Vehicle offices around the state, and if we bought five scanners for each office and scanners cost $300, that's another $150,000.

We could roll this out to all 50 states. And within five years we'll have everyone covered, except the new drivers of course. And of course this would take a new type of biometric processing terminal that we would have to design and manufacture. If we decided to process the payments and service the machines, we could be in every link of the smart card value chain.

- Type of case: Entering a new market

- Comments: Good use of charts and good idea about the California drivers' licenses. So much of consulting is brainstorming, and if you can come up with a good idea and develop it in short order, that counts for lots of points.

✣ Partner Cases

Partner cases are cases that you can do with your friends, regardless of whether they know how to give a case. There are four easy Level 1 cases, two medium Level 2 cases and four hard Level 3 cases. Your partner first needs to read the Roommate's Guide found on the next page and then read the case all the way through, twice. The case gives your partner plenty of advice and information to make it easy and fun for them to grill you.

For some of the cases there are charts in the back of the book (see Partner Case Charts starting on page 219 that need to be photocopied beforehand; if you can't photocopy, then some of the charts can be hand drawn in a few minutes' time.

There is flexibility built into these answers and, as usual, there is no one right answer. Have fun with these. After you have answered the case, turn around and give it to another friend. You learn just as much giving a case as you do answering one. The average student, serious about a career in consulting, will do at least 30 'live' cases. Nothing beats live case practice.

✣ Partner Cases

✣ The Roommate's Guide

If you have been begged, bribed or blackmailed into helping your friend(s) prepare for case questions, here are some suggestions.

Your prep

- Read the question and answer all the way through before giving the case.
- Be aware that there are multiple "right" answers.
- It's alright to give them help if they lose their way.
- Don't cop a know-it-all attitude.

Things to watch for at the beginning

- Are they writing down the case information?
- Is there a long silence between the end of the question and the beginning of their answer?
- Are they summarizing the question?
- Are they asking about the client's objective(s)?
- Are they asking clarifying questions about the company, the industry, the competition, and the product?
- Are they laying out a logical structure for their answer?

Things to watch and listen for during the course of the question

- Are they enthusiastic and do they project a positive attitude?
- Listen for the logic of their answer. Is it making good business sense?
- Is their answer well-organized?
- Are they stating their assumptions clearly?
- Are they being creative?
- Are they engaging, bringing you into the question and turning the case into a conversation?
- Are they asking probing questions?
- Are they quantifying their answer?
- Are they asking for help or guidance?

Review list

- Was their answer well-organized? Did they manage their time well?
- Did they get bogged down in details?
- Did they seem to go off on a tangent?
- Did they ask probing questions?
- Did they use business terms and buzzwords correctly?
- Did they have trouble with math, multiplying, and percentage calculation?
- Did they try to get you to answer the question for them?
- Were they coachable? Did they pick up on your hints?
- Did they speak without thinking?
- Did they have a positive attitude?
- Did they summarize their answer?

Final analysis

- Did they take your criticism well?
- Did they defend themselves without sounding defensive?

Aftermath

- Go out on the town.

+ The Ripple Effect

Problem Statement

Because of plunging sales and tighter credit, a large electronics retailer with 560 stores nationwide closed its doors and filed for bankruptcy. What is the ripple effect? Who gets hurt? Who loses money?

Guidance for the Interviewer

The student should summarize the question and verify the objective (determine the ripple effect). She should also ask if there are any other objectives she should be concerned with – in this case the answer is no. Next, we are trying to see if the student sees the complete picture, that the effects of closing the store go much further than just the store employees who lost their jobs. We are also looking to see how the student approaches this, whether there is any logic to her thoughts or whether she is just throwing out whatever pops into her head.

Data Bank

- Store employees and office employees at the headquarters lost their jobs. The cleaning service, for both the headquarters and the stores, lost their jobs, too.

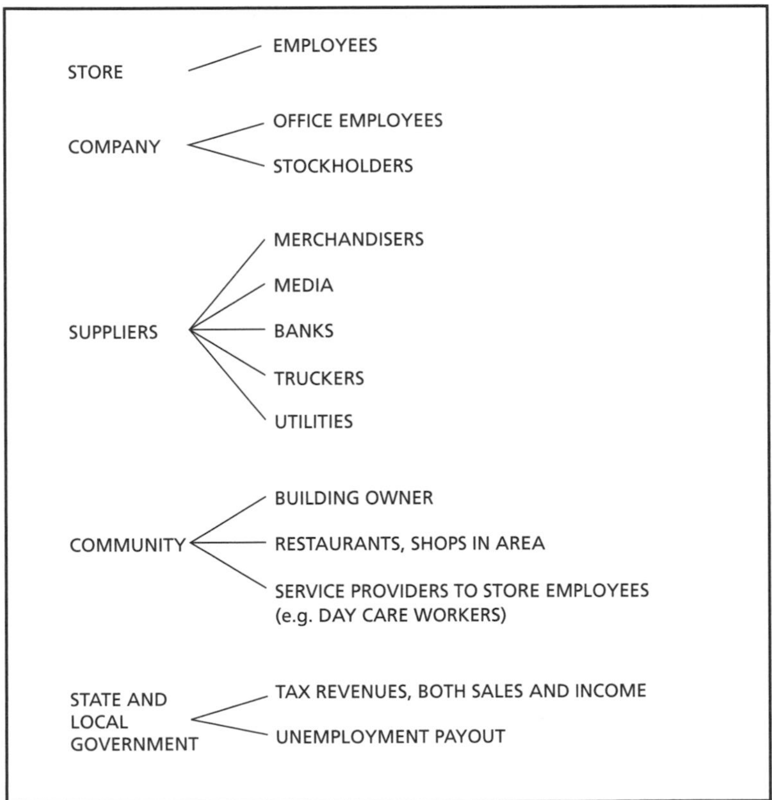

- Stockholders who have seen prices nosedive will never see their investment back.
- Merchandise suppliers who sent their products to the stores will never receive payment for it. They may even have to lay their own workers off.
- Media outlets that ran the stores' ads in newspapers, on television and on the web are losing revenues and have lost outstanding balances.
- Banks that have outstanding loans with the company may never receive their money back.
- Truckers who delivered the merchandise to the stores will lose business.
- Utility companies that provide light and heat will lose revenues and won't get compensated for outstanding bills.
- Local restaurants and stores that serviced employees and customers have lost revenues.
- The owner of the building who rented to the retailer has lost rent revenue and now has to try to rent it in a bad economy.
- Other service providers like day care providers will suffer as ex-employees now have less disposable income.
- States are losing tax revenues, sales tax and income tax. They will also have to pay unemployment to those laid off.

Mark of a Good Case Discussion: A good candidate should have determined and separated the different constituencies. If she drew a decision tree like the one above or made some sort of chart, then she would have impressed the interviewer. Remember, the interviewer is looking to see how she thinks, the logic of her thought. Regardless, she should have gotten at least eight of these points and discussed them in detail.

✣ High Speed Train

Problem Statement

Our client wants to start high-speed train service from Toronto to Montreal. Is this a good idea?

Guidance for the Interviewer

Make sure that the student summarizes the question and verifies the objective. In this case, the objective isn't stated but the student should surmise that it is profits. She should also ask if there are any other objectives she should be concerned with – in this case the answer is no.

A good student will know quickly that she will have to figure out what the price of a high-speed ticket should be.

Give this information to the student if she asks for it.

Data Bank

- The client does not own any other train line or ships; he does own a hotel in Toronto and one in Montreal.
- Currently there is train service between these two cities, but it takes three hours. Our high-speed train would take an hour and 15 minutes.
- Other ways to get between the cities: drive a car three to four hours, bus five hours or fly for one hour.
- The cost of flying is $500 roundtrip.
- Most passengers would be business travelers.
- On weekdays 5,000 people travel back and forth (5,000 each way). On weekends 1,000 passengers travel each day.
- There are 40 one-way flights each day. They run every half an hour during peak times and once an hour during slow times. The planes hold 100 passengers.
- The client's train station would be located right in the city. It is a half-hour drive from the airport to the city. A taxi cab ride into the city is $50.
- We would have to build the track and it would take a year.
- The cost per trip is $50,000. That takes into account all the costs, both fixed and variable, associated with the new train line. The client is planning 10 trips per day – five each way.
- A train can hold 500 passengers.
- A survey showed that 75% of business travelers said they would take the train at a price equal to or less than the plane.

The Numbers

Give this information to the student if she asks for it.

Our cost per trip is $50,000. If we charge the same as the plane ($250 one way) our breakeven would be 200 passengers or 40% occupancy rate.

If we ran at 50% occupancy rate, we would be carrying 250 passengers per trip. Our profits per ride would be 50 passengers times $250 equals $12,500.

Because the cab would take the passenger to their selected location, our passengers would also have to take a cab ride, albeit much shorter – say $25.

Five thousand people travel back and forth daily between cities. Seventy-five percent said they would take the train if the price was equal to the plane. Say we got 40% of the market. Forty percent of 5,000 equal 2,000 customers.

Problem, cont.

Have her determine a list of reasons why taking the train is better than flying. When you ask her, see if she asks for a moment to jot some ideas down. This will allow her a little time to think and it gives her some place to go.

In real case interviews the interviewer has probably given the case ten times. He knows every answer that the student can think of and he's heard them all before. There is a good chance that he will cut her off as soon as he knows where her answer is headed. It is very difficult for a person to drop their secondary thought and then come up with a new thought right away. When cut off in mid-thought, people tend to panic, scramble and then shut down.

If she takes the time to jot down some ideas and gets cut off, then she can just look at her notes and give another idea. It takes a lot of stress out of the process and these interviews can be stressful enough.

As soon as she mentions a reason, cut her off and ask "What else do you have?" Do it over and over again until she comes up with at least five reasons.

- Less hassle to get to the train station
- Train drops you off in the city
- Train has Wi-Fi
- Passengers can use their cell phones the whole time
- You can walk around and stretch
- Club car with food or drink
- There will be a quiet car
- There can be a smoking car
- Service animals are allowed and more easily accommodated
- Open seating

Summary

The interviewee needs to jump right into this without any down time to collect her thoughts. A good summary is about a minute, minute and a half long. It is not a rehash of everything you spoke about; it is a short recap of the problem and two or three main points that the student wants the interviewer to remember.

Did the interviewee...

- repeat the question, verifying the objective and asking about other objectives?
- make math mistakes?
- figure out the breakeven without your help?
- get flustered when you cut her off and asked "What else?" (This is a crucial element of the interview since clients will be demanding and sometimes rude.)
- come up with good ideas and features?
- identify the synergies of the hotels?
- determine other considerations like competitive response?
- produce a good, short summary touching on the most critical points?

Mark of a Good Case Discussion: This case is mostly about the numbers. Did she figure out the breakeven point without being asked? That said, the candidate should also touch on the synergies – owning both the train and the hotels.

✛ Gator Vator

Problem Statement

Our client, Gator Vator, is an American elevator manufacturer. Traditionally, their revenues come mainly from two sources – manufacturing elevators and service contracts to maintain them. Management feels the need to expand across the border into Canada. They have targeted some growth opportunities in Canada. How should Gator Vator go forward thinking about their options?

Guidance for the Interviewer

Make sure that the student summarizes the question and verifies the objectives (should Gator Vator enter the Canadian market and how). This case is designed to elicit two things. First, the candidate must walk through the classic entering a new market options for a company looking to expand into Canada. (See page 36 for info on entering a new market.) That is straightforward. Second, a great candidate will also create sub-framework to analyze whether or not the company should focus on manufacturing elevators, servicing them or both. There is certainly no one correct answer, but based on the information you can provide them below, it should be more than evident what a logical path forward for the company will be.

Data Bank

If prompted by the interviewee, you can offer the following information on the client. If the student asks you a question you don't have the answer for, tell him that either you don't have the information or that his question isn't relevant.

- **What types of elevators does the company make?** Residential and commercial.
- **What types of markets does Gator Vator typically sell into?** Gator Vator has had success in all markets. However, they tend to focus their business in urban centers rather than the suburbs.
- **In the US market, what is the revenue breakdown between elevator sales and service contracts?** The split is roughly 50/50.
- **Which business lines have the higher profit margins?** Service contracts, by nearly a factor of two; however, the company services contracts only for its own elevators.
- **Who typically buys Gator Vator's products?** High-rise apartments and, on the commercial side, office buildings, department stores, factories and other industrial customers. The split here is also 50/50, but in Canada, Gator's management sees more promise in the commercial market.
- **How has the US elevator market been doing?** Over the last decade it had seen growth of between 8 and 12% a year. Last year it dropped down to 3%.
- **What does the US market look like?** Otis Elevator has 50%, Gator has 20% and three other players share the remaining 30%
- **Is the Canadian market competitive?** Not really. In the US, the market is saturated, but there are not any companies at Gator Vator's scale in Canada. The Canadian market

breaks down this way: Otis® (a US company) has 40% market share and three small Canadian companies equally share the remaining 60%. The Canadian companies focus on structures less than five stories tall.

N.B.: You can instruct the candidate to assume that there are no major barriers to entry in the Canadian market, only a small tariff and shipping costs.

Suggested Approach

There are many elements to this case. The student should first build an understanding of the US market and where we sit. Once that is done, he should focus on entering a new market.

- Who are the major players in the Canadian market? What market share do they have? And how do their products and services differ from what we offer?
- What is the customer segmentation?
- Are there any barriers to entry? What about barriers to exit?

The market should look promising. The student now needs to tell you how he plans to enter this market. Each strategy should be accompanied by a cost benefit analysis.

- Start from scratch. Should the client import into Canada? Do they set up their own factory? Do they just service other companies' elevators?
- Acquisition. Should they buy a Canadian manufacturer?
- Joint venture. Have him discuss the merits.

Chances are he'll want to buy a Canadian manufacturer. If so, what do they need to consider?

- Why do they want to buy it? (Make him give you several reasons.)
- Can they afford to buy it? Do they have to take on much debt? If the economy gets worse can they still make their payments?
- How is the Canadian elevator industry doing? What kind of due diligence should the company be doing?
- How is the real estate market doing?
- How will the competition view this acquisition? What steps might they take? (Competitive response.)
- What is the company's exit strategy?

You can always look on page 36 for a more detail account of an entering a new market case and page 38 for M&A.

Summary

The interviewee needs to jump right into this without any down time to collect his thoughts. A good summary is about a minute, minute and a half long. It is not a rehash of everything you spoke about; it is a short recap of the problem and two or three main points that the student wants the interviewer to remember.

Did the Interviewee…

- repeat the question, verifying the objective and asking about other objectives?
- make math mistakes?
- touch on the main points of entering a new market and an acquisition?
- determine other considerations like competitive response?
- produce a good, short summary touching on the most critical points?
- have well-organized and easy-to-read notes?

Mark of a Good Case Discussion: This is a case that can go one of a hundred ways, but it is also hard to mess up. If the interviewee gets bogged down by asking for hard numbers, you can steer him away and remind him that this is about an overall growth strategy for the Canadian market. A good interviewee will make sure to cover the possible growth opportunities in the country, such as mentioning the possibility of acquiring an existing company (both for manufacturing and servicing), setting up a joint venture, a general business expansion and/or hiring away talent from either US-based or Canadian competition. The interviewee should also be touching upon the fact that there could be barriers to entry in the foreign market, even though they are not important in the case itself. An even better candidate will be diving deeper into a framework to think about how the company should enter, and whether Gator Vator should focus on manufacturing, servicing or both. Each of these could be presented with a short cost benefit analysis per option. This case encompasses growth, entering a new market and M&A.

✛ Tate Pharmacueticals

Problem Statement

Our client, Tate Pharmaceuticals, produces drugs designed for those who suffer from chronic arthritis. Their most successful drug, RumaX66, is not only the company's most popular product but also is the market leader for patients who suffer from a specific type of knee-related arthritis. Tate has seen their market share dominance remain steady, and although sales have been up, profits have been falling slightly. What is the world-wide market size (the US has 20%), and what is happening with Tate's profits?

Guidance for the Interviewer

The student should repeat the question to make sure everyone is on the same page, verify the objectives (determine why profits have been falling) and then attempt the market-sizing aspect of the question.

Market-sizing

Since we know that the US makes up 20% of this market, the student should figure out what the US market is first, then add 80%. Because this is a general population problem, the student might want to build a chart. The general population of the US is 300 million.

Age	Population	% w/ arthritis	# w/ arthritis
0-20	75m	0%	0
21-40	75m	1%	.75m
41-60	75m	6%	4.5m
61-80	75m	20%	15m
	300m		20.25m

N.B.: Regardless of the assumptions he makes, use the 20 million number.

We see that 20 million Americans have this type of arthritis and the US represents 20% of the market so, 20 million times 5 = 100 million

This case is designed to test the interviewee's ability to conduct an industry analysis, to determine the industry's competitive dynamics, to evaluate threats and to walk through Tate's options moving forward, either for growth or market exit. (To learn more on market analysis, turn to page 37.) The student will probably fall back on the P&L framework E(P=R-C)M. While this is important for any P&L case, make sure that he just touches on this and spends more of his time coming up with short-term and long-term strategies.

The candidate can ask questions about the size of the company, the market and so forth. For some of these, the answers are listed on the next page; other numbers can be made up by you. Hopefully, the candidate will ask the following questions, to which you may provide the following answers:

Data Bank

Why are profits down? The student should try to determine if this is an industry problem or a Tate problem. All of the pharma companies are seeing their profits dip because of higher costs (e.g. rising costs of ingredients, utilities and other energy). This is an industry problem.

- **Who else makes drugs similar to RumaX66?** There are two main competitors who produce rival drugs: Drug 2 and Drug 3.
- **What part of the revenue stream does each drug represent for their respective companies?**
  RumaX66 = 10% of Tate's company sales
  Drug 2 = 20% of its company sales
  Drug 3 = 60% of its company sales (forecasted)
- **What are the differences between RumaX66, Drug 2 and Drug 3?** RumaX66 is currently the cheapest for consumers at $5 per dose with limited side effects. Drug 2 is more expensive with only limited side effects (concentrated in males over 50 years old). Drug 3 is currently in the FDA approval process, and industry reports indicate that their company will price it at $2 dose with no side effects whatsoever.
- **What is Tate's position in the industry?** Tate currently has about one-half of the prescription market for arthritis drugs, with RumaX66 leading the way. The maker of Drug 2 commands one-quarter of the market. Currently there are five other arthritis drugs making up the remaining 25%. However, we feel that once Drug 3 enters the market they will quickly pick up at least 25% of the market, forcing many of the smaller players out and possibly stealing some of our market share. Tell the student that the other competitors costs are $7 and their drugs have three side effects. As you give this information to the student, look to see if he draws up a chart similar to the one below.

	Cost	Side effects	Mkt share
Tate's RumaX66	$5	2	50%
Drug 2	$5+	1	25%
Others	$7+	3	25%
Drug 3	$2	0	

Tate's options: the basic three options are to keep Drug 3 out, protect market share and get new customers. Some ways to do that are the following:

Short-term options

- Try to keep Drug 3 out of the market – petition FDA.
- Protect what's ours, shore up relationships with distributors and doctors, maybe lower the price.
- Increase marketing to the public and to the medical community.
- Increase distribution channels in developing markets. When Drug 3 enters the market, they are less likely to go after these smaller markets first.
- Buy Drug 3's company.

Long-term options

- Improve RumaX66: reduce costs, reduce side effects.
- Sell division.

Summary

The interviewee needs to jump right into this without any down time to collect his thoughts. A good summary is about a minute, minute and a half long. It is not a rehash of everything you spoke about; it is a short recap of the problem and two or three main points that the student wants the interviewer to remember.

Did the Interviewee...

- repeat the question, verifying the objective and asking about other objectives?
- make math mistakes?
- touch on the main points of entering a new market and an acquisition?
- determine other considerations like competitive response?
- produce a good, short summary touching on the most critical points?
- have well-organized and easy-to-read notes?

Mark of a Good Case Discussion: A good candidate will set up a matrix or table comparing and contrasting the three drugs against each other in terms of price, efficacy, side effects and other characteristics. Second, a good candidate will conduct a light analysis of the industry; analyze the competition and offer hypotheses of what the client faces down the road. Finally, a good interviewee will walk through Tate's options moving forward, such as whether they should lower their prices, purchase the competitor, do nothing, grow in other markets by increasing channels and advertising or sell the company as a preemptive move. Ultimately, this is a multi-pronged strategy case that should test the candidate's ability to analyze a specific industry, to understand the nature of a competitive threat and to opine on the costs and benefits of all the options on the company's table. By using the few questions and facts above, the rest should flow as a good discussion, which can walk you down any number of paths.

✢ Nerves of Steel

Problem Statement

Our client is the second largest maker of steel filing cabinets and desks in the US. They are nearing the end of a four-year rolled-steel contract which expires at the end of Year 7. Our client signed their steel contract in Year 4.

The CFO wants to know if it makes sense to stockpile two year's worth of steel at the end of the contract at the Year 4 price or sign a new contract at Year 8's price.

You can assume that the company uses 12,000 tons of steel a year and will continue to do so over the next five years.

Guidance for the Interviewer

Make sure that the student summarizes the question and verifies the objective. The student is looking at two options. Option one is to sign a new contract at Year 8 prices. Option two is to stockpile steel for two years, then sign a new contract in Year 10.

Ask the student what he needs to know. He should ask about:

- Cost of steel in Y4 contract — $600/ton
- Current Y7 cost of steel — $810/ton
- Amount of steel to stockpile — 24,000 tons (12,000/year)
- Time value of money — $FV = PV (1+i)^n$
- Current interest rates — 5%
- Inventory storage cost — $50/ton per year paid at the beginning of each year
- Steel price forecast — Economic conditions

While the student may not ask for all this information up front, give him some time to discover what he needs.

Steel Pricing Trends

Y1	Y2	Y3	Y4	Y5	Y6	Y7	Y8
$263	$554	$615	$600	$610	$750	$810	?

Hand the student this chart. (You can photocopy it from page 220 in the back of this book.) You are looking to see what conclusions the student can derive from this chart – not much. The numbers are all over the place and there is very little consistency. The most it can do is anchor the Year 8 price for him.

Ask him what he thinks the Year 8 price will be. He has a starting point of $810 (the Year 7 price). He should take into consideration the economic conditions around the world, particular in the three top industries that use rolled-steel: autos, airplanes and appliances (which are tied to housing starts).

Remember that there is no right answer. Students are often reluctant to go out on a limb and give a number, but you need to force him to come up with a price. (Let's assume he comes up with a Year 8 price $850 per ton.) Once he comes up with a price for Year 8, look to see what he does with it. Give him big points if he draws up the final slide.

The Final Slide

This is critical. If the student has the foresight to build the final slide, he will stand out from all the other candidates. Whenever you have a case that compares two or more strategies, options or ideas and you are applying the same criteria, you should build "the final slide" almost immediately. As you calculate the numbers, fill them in on the final slide; it keeps all relevant information in one place and makes it easier for the interviewer to follow. Once all the information is filled out, the student turns the final slide towards the interviewer and walks her through it. It is the best summary. It is similar to the final slide of a deck that a consultant would present to a client.

In this case it would look like this (assuming he came up with an Year 8 price of $850):

	Y8	Y9	Y10	Y11
Option 1 – new contract	$850	$850	$850	$850
Option 2 – stockpiling				

The student should also conclude that he needs to come up with a price for Year 10. If he stockpiles for two years, then the company will have to sign a new contract. Again, he should talk about where he thinks the economy and those three industries in particular are headed. Let's say he comes up with a Year 10 price of $900 per ton.

	Y8	Y9	Y10	Y11
Option 1 – new contract	$850	$850	$850	$850
Option 2 – stockpiling			$900	$900

The only two squares left open in the final slide are the stockpiling squares.

They would stockpile 24,000 tons, enough for two years. Because they are stockpiling, they would need to pay for all of it up front.

Inventory Costs

Inventory costs are paid on a yearly basis at the beginning of each year. When money is laid out at the beginning of the year, you need to figure the "cost of money." Remember $50 per ton per year.

Year 1 / (24,000 x 50) = 1,200,000
$FV = PV (1+i)^n$ ($n = 1$)
FV = 1,200,000 x 1.05
FV = 1,260,000 or $1.26m

Year 2 / (12,000 x 50) = 600,000
$FV = PV (1 + i)^n$ ($n = 1$)
FV = 600,000 x 1.05
FV = 630,000 or $0.63m

Y1 = $1.26m
Y2 = $0.63m
Total Storage and Inventory Costs = $1.89m

Steel Costs

24,000 tons x $600 = $14,400,000
Interest rates are at 5%

$FV = PV (1 + i)^n$
$FV = 14,400,000 (1.05)^2$
FV = 14,400,000 x (1.10)
FV = 15,840,000 or $15.84m

Stockpiling = $15,840,000 + $1,890,000 (inventory costs)
Stockpiling = $17,730,000 or round off to $18,000,000

$18,000,000 / 24,000 tons = $750/ton (it always comes out to $750/ton)

	Y8	Y9	Y10	Y11
Option 1 – new contract	$850	$850	$850	$850
Option 2 – stockpiling	$750	$750	$900	$900

Summary

The interviewee needs to jump right into to this without any down time to collect his thoughts. A good summary is about a minute, minute and a half long. It is not a rehash of everything you spoke about; it is a short recap of the problem and two or three main points that the student wants the interviewer to remember.

Did the Interviewee...

- repeat the question, verifying the objective and asking about other objectives?
- make math mistakes?
- design the final slide?
- draw the interviewer into a discussion?
- produce a good, short summary touching on the most critical points?
- have well-organized and easy-to-read notes?

Mark of Good Case Discussion: The key things to look for are the student's knowledge of the current economic conditions, the realization that they will have to sign another contract two years later if they stockpile and of course the use of the final slide. Not only that the slide is filled in, but the student should turn it toward the interviewer and walk through his analysis and decision.

+ Brazilian Soda Manufacturer

Problem Statement

You are working for BSM, a Brazilian Soda Manufacturer that has been experiencing declining profits over the last two years. Why do you think this is occurring? What are the company's options for improving profitability? What are the possible effects of a change in the soda's price? And estimate the size of the Brazilian soda market.

Guidance for the Interviewer

Before determining the market size, make sure that the student summarizes the question and verifies the objectives (determine the reason for declining profits and how to fix it, analyze effects of a price change and estimate the market size). She should also ask if there are any other objectives she should be concerned with – in this case the answer is no.

Data Bank

Brazilian soda market: major players and market share

- Coke and Pepsi make up 80%
- Our client BSM has 10%
- Two generic brands have 5% each
- Market share has remained the same over the last five years

Pricing – 12 oz. size

- Coke and Pepsi sell for 80 cents each
- BSM sells for 60 cents and makes 25 cents per bottle
- The generic brands sell for 35 cents each

Product mix

- Coke and Pepsi have a full array of products
- BSM has two products: cola and guarana (it's like a fruit soda)
- Generic brands only sell colas

The soda market grew by 5% last year. It has been growing by 8% a year for the last five years. It is important that the student ask for trends in the market.

The Brazilian economy has been growing by 8% a year for the last two years.

❑ **Market-Sizing**

If the student doesn't know the population of Brazil, let her guess, then tell her to use 200 million people. The easiest way to solve this is by breaking the market down by generation, assuming an equal number of people in each generation with a life expectancy of 80 years. Also assume a 50-week year.

Age Group	# of People	Soda Drinkers	Sodas/Week	Sodas/Year
0-20	50m			
21-40	50m			
41-60	50m			
61-80	50m			
	200m			40b

The student should draw a chart similar to this. **Regardless of what she comes up with, have her use 40 billion as the number of sodas consumed in Brazil every year.** Thus, if the market is 40 billion sodas and we have a 10% market share, we manufacture 4 billion bottles of soda a year. If we make 25 cents per bottle, our profits are $1 billion.

❑ **Profit and Loss Case**

The student has been taught to use the framework E(P=R-C)M.

The E stands for the economy which is growing at 8% a year. So the problem is not with the economy. The M stands for the market and the market has been growing at 5% a year. So we can assume that it is not a market problem; it is a company problem.

The student will then look inside the parentheses, first at the revenues. You can tell them it is not a revenue problem. She will then go through a whole list of costs problems. You can tell her no for most of those.

The problem is that our distributor has raised his fee by 1 cent a bottle this year. That means our costs will go up by $40 million.

The student should suggest we look at raising our prices, which addresses one of the original objectives.

Ask the student to run the numbers, then tell you what she wants to do and why. What would be some additional benefits to their decision?

Assumptions:

The current price is 40 cents and the current volume is 4 billion bottles.
If BSM increases their price by 5 cents, they can expect a 5% loss in volume.
If BSM leaves their price the same, they can expect a 5% increase in volume.

If BSM lowers their price by 5 cents, they can expect a 10% increase in volume. Check to see if the student makes a similar chart.

Present Volume	Δ in Volume	New Volume	New Price	Revenues
4b	-5 %	3.8 b	$0.45	$1.71 b
4b	+5 %	4.2 b	$0.40	$1.68 b
4b	+10 %	4.4 b	$0.35	$1.54 b

As you can see, the best option is to raise our prices. We produce 400 million fewer bottles and make $30 million more. In addition, BSM will save on production costs (i.e. labor and raw materials), shipping and distribution fees.

Summary

The interviewee needs to jump right into to this without any down time to collect her thoughts. A good summary is about a minute, minute and a half long. It is not a rehash of everything you spoke about; it is a short recap of the problem and two or three main points that the student wants the interviewer to remember.

Did the Interviewee...

- repeat the question, verifying the objective and asking about other objectives?
- make math mistakes?
- develop a logical and well-thought-out market-sizing process?
- draw the interviewer into a discussion?
- produce a good, short summary touching on the most critical points?
- have well-organized and easy-to-read notes?

Mark of a Good Case Discussion: The student's math needs to be perfect. She needed to draw the chart on the market-sizing section, the chart on the change in volume and she should have exhausted the possible cost reasons behind the fall in profits.

+ Statin Blue

Problem Statement

Our client is a large pharma company similar to Johnson & Johnson. They have developed a new cholesterol drug called Statin Blue. Because Statin Blue is on the lower end of the Statin chain (meaning that it is weaker than traditional prescription cholesterol drugs), the company has the option of releasing this drug as either an over-the-counter product or prescription drug.

You need to:

- determine which market they should enter, as a prescription drug or as an over-the-counter product.
- figure the breakeven in terms of the number of customers for both markets.
- calculate the estimated profits for both markets.
- list the pros and cons of entering the prescription market.

Guidance for the Interviewer

Make sure that the student summarizes the question and verifies the objectives (determining which market to enter, figuring the breakeven in terms of customers for both markets, calculating the estimated profits for both markets and listing the pros and cons of entering the prescription market). She should also ask if there are any other objectives she should be concerned with. In this case the answer is no. After the student summarizes the question and verifies the objectives, have her start with the pros and cons.

When she lists the pros and cons, check to see if she asks for a moment to write down her thoughts. By asking for a moment (up to 30 seconds), she can list the pros and cons any way they pop into her head; however, when it comes time to tell them to you, she should list all the pros first, then all the cons. Make sure she doesn't ping-pong back and forth between pros and cons.

Prescription:

+ Price – can charge more
+ Insurance coverage
+ Perceived higher value
+ Good established sales force
– Highly competitive market
– One dominant player (Lipitor with 49% of market)

Over-the-Counter

+ Easy access – don't need to see a doctor
+ High volume
+ Easier to market

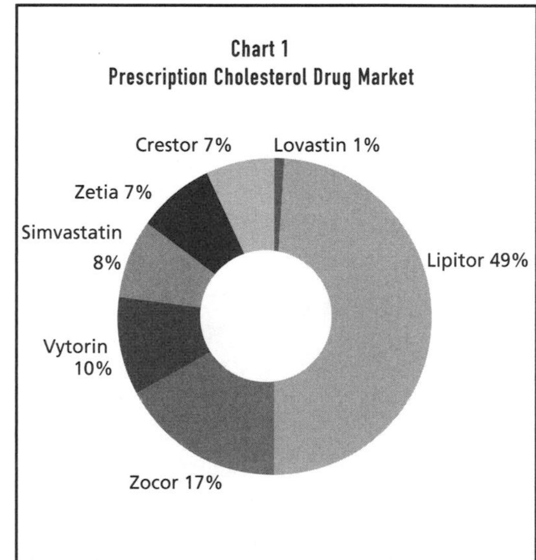

Hand this chart to the student when she asks about the Rx market.

+ Company brand name recognition
+ Potentially huge untapped market
– Patients in the high-risk category already on prescription drug
– Viewed as less effective (which it is – 10%)

❑ **Entering the Market**

After listing the pros and cons, the student should ask about the market. Force her to ask about the prescription market first. What does the student need to know about entering a new market? (For more on entering a new market, you can turn to page 36.)

Who are the major players?
What market share do they have?
How do their products differ from Statin Blue?
Are there any barriers to entry? (Have they received FDA approval for both markets?)

Special note – our company does not produce any of the other Statin products

Data Bank

Our Client

- Large pharma with a large drug portfolio. Fifty percent of their products are over-the-counter and 50% are prescription drugs. This should tell the student that our distribution and marketing channels are well-established in either market.

Prescription Market (Rx)

- Current market size: 14 million Americans and $14 billion in sales. Hand the student a copy of the donut chart. (Photocopy it from the back of the book. See page 221.)
- Covered by insurance, the patient pays a $15 a month co-pay.

Over-the-Counter Market (OTC)

- No such market exists.
- The OTC version of Statin Blue would cost the consumer $15 for a month's supply.
- No insurance coverage.

Statin Blue

- Think of it as Lipitor Light — it's less effective.
- Similar side effects as regular Statin drugs, just less intense. Side effects include muscle pain, diarrhea, sexual dysfunction, cognitive impairment and possible liver damage.

Costs

- Costs are $40 million a year. This is the only cost number the student needs to know.

Pricing

- The cost to the end user will be the same regardless of which market we use. Prescription, the patient will pay a $15 a month co-pay. OTC, the patient will pay $15 for a month's supply.

Profits

- The company makes a $20 profit per bottle sold in the prescription market. The patient would use one bottle a month, 12 bottles a year. Yearly profit is $240 per patient per year.
- The company makes a $5 per bottle profit sold in the OTC market. The patient would use one bottle a month, 12 bottles a year. Yearly profit is $60 per patient per year.

❑ **Rx Markets**

Walk the student through a copy of the chart below. Explain that if your cholesterol is less than 180, you are very healthy. If it falls between 180 and 200, the doctor will tell you to exercise more and eat some Honey Nut Cheerios. Patients with cholesterol levels between 200 and 220 are the prime target for Statin Blue. This group makes up 10% of the overall prescription market. However, we think that we will be able to get only 4% of the overall 14 million person prescription cholesterol market (which is 560,000 patients). If your cholesterol levels are over 220, then the doctor will prescribe one of the seven drugs in the first chart.

Before there was Statin Blue, if your level was 210 or above, the MD would most likely prescribe one of the seven current drugs; however, you would be over-medicating and at risk for the side effects.

250	**Big Trouble** **(represents 10% of the overall prescription cholesterol market)**	
220	**Other Prescription Cholesterol Drugs** **(represents 80% of the overall prescription cholesterol market)**	
200	**Statin Blue** **(We believe that the patients whose cholesterol levels fall between 200 and 220 make up 10% of the overall cholesterol market.)**	10%
180	**Honey Nut Cheerios & Exercise**	
<180	**Healthy**	

❑ **OTC Market**

The market-sizing of the OTC market is the hardest part of the case.

Assumptions:

- There are 300 million Americans.
- There is an 80/20 spilt between Americans with health insurance (the ones who would have access to the prescription market) and those without health insurance (the ones who wouldn't have access to discounted prescriptions).

- Of the 240 million Americans with health insurance (300 million times 80% = 240 million), we know that 14 million or 5% of them have a cholesterol problem (14/240 = 5.8% or round-off to 5%),
- That leaves an uninsured population of 60 million (300m * .2 = 60m). Thus, we can assume that at least 5% of the uninsured, or 3 million people, have a cholesterol problem (60 million times 20% = 3 million). I would add in an extra 1 million because the uninsured don't receive constant healthcare and have a higher rate of obesity, heart attacks and strokes.
- Out of the 4 million uninsured that likely have a cholesterol problem, we'll assume that 25% or 1 million people would buy this drug. Many have higher priorities (like feeding their families or paying rent) than spending $15 a month on a drug for a problem that they can't see or feel.
- To that 1 million I'd add a group of people ages 20–40. These are people who don't have a cholesterol problem, but their parents or relatives do. Since cholesterol levels are tied into genetics, they know that they are on the same path as their parents and may want to take something now to prevent problems later.
    - Three hundred million Americans divided into four even generations of 75 million each. Thus there are 75 million Americans ages 20–40.
    - Assume that 5% of their parents have a cholesterol problem. five percent of 75 million is 3.75 million or 4 million. Out of that 4 million I'll assume 25% will take this preventative measure and buy Statin Blue. That equals 1 million preventers.
- Total of 2 million customers for the OTC drug. (This number is not set in stone.) It is not critical that the student use the same assumption numbers, just the same logic – even then, as long as there is logic to her thought then that is fine.

❑ **Breakeven Calculations**

- **Prescription Breakeven**
  $40 million in costs divided by $20 profit per bottle equals 2 million bottles divided by 12 months equals 166,667 customers
- **OTC Breakeven**
  $40 million in costs divided by $5 profit per bottle equals 8m bottles divided by 12 months equals 667,000 customers

❑ **Profit Calculations**

- **Prescription:** 560,000 customers x $240 = $134.4 million
- **OTC:** 2,000,000 customers x $60 = $120 million

What would you do?

The Final Slide

This is critical. If the student has the foresight to build the final slide, she will stand out from all the other candidates. Whenever you have a case that compares two or more strategies, options or ideas and you are applying the same criteria to both, you should build the final slide almost immediately. As you calculate the numbers, fill them in on the final slide; it keeps all relevant information in one place and it makes it easier for the interviewer to follow. Once all the information is filled out, the student turns the final slide towards the interviewer and walks him through it. It is the best summary. It is similar to the final slide of a deck that a consultant would present to a client. (Show the student this chart at the end of the case when you are walking through her analysis.)

	Prescription	OTC
Market Size		
Breakeven		
Profit		
Market Choice		
Other Concerns		

Summary

The interviewee needs to jump right into to this without any down time to collect her thoughts. A good summary is about a minute, minute and a half long. It is not a rehash of everything you spoke about; it is a short recap of the problem and two or three main points that the student wants the interviewer to remember.

Did the Interviewee...

- repeat the question, verifying the objective and asking about other objectives?
- make math mistakes?
- design the final slide?
- develop a logical and well-thought-out market-sizing process?
- draw the interviewer into a discussion?
- produce a good, short summary touching on the most critical points?
- have well-organized and easy-to-read notes?

Mark of a Good Case Discussion: Besides the final slide, students should bring up ...

- Competitive response to our entry in either market.
- Entering both markets.
  - Which market would they enter first? (Prescription)
  - What are some of the pros and cons?

Synergies include a common manufacturing plant. We can also take advantage of already established distribution channels and marketing strategies.

Notes: Make sure the student's notes are neat, well-organized and easy-to-read. At the very least she should have divided her notes into prescription and OTC. Did she draw a line down the middle of her paper? Did she do her prescription and OTC calculations on separate sheets of paper?

+ Bottled Water

Problem Statement

Last year Americans bought more than 4 billion gallons of bottled drinking water. Our client sold 1 billion bottles of spring water in the .5 liter size. In the past, our client has purchased the empty bottles from a guy named Ed for 5 cents each. These bottles are made from PET (polyethylene terephthalate), which is a combination of natural gas and petroleum.

Ed wants to raise his price by one penny, which would increase the client's costs by $10 million. The client is considering in-house bottle production but currently does not have the resources to do it. The CFO wants you to determine whether this makes sense. The CFO requires a two-year payback (breakeven) on investments and wants to know if they should in-source the bottle production.

Besides determining whether to in-source bottle production, can you tell me what market share our client has of the US bottled water industry?

Guidance for the Interviewer

Make sure that the student summarizes the question and verifies the objective (determining whether to in-source bottle production) before determining market share. He should also ask if there are any other objectives he should be concerned with. The answer is that there are no other objectives to be concerned about in this case.

How to figure out market share
It needs to be done by volume of water. Tell the student to assume that one pint equals .5 liters.

If he asks (and most students do) ...

2 pints = a quart
4 quarts to the gallon, thus 8 pints = a gallon

Easiest way is to turn everything into pints;

4b gallons = 32 billon pints
1b .5 liters = 1 billion pints
1b pints / 32b pints = about 3% of the market

Ask the student: Before we get into the numbers, just off the top of your head, can you layout the pros and cons of in-house production?

Pros	Cons
Possible lower price	Added risk
More control over costs in the future	No experience
Produce & sell to competitors	Big investment setup costs
	Economic variables out of our control

If the student misses any from the list above, don't tell him what he missed. He'll figure it out later.

Hand the student this chart. Photocopy it from page 223.

Y1	Ed	Client
COGS	60m	?
Building	N/A	$6m
Equipment	N/A	$4m
Labor	N/A	?
Utilities & Maintenance	N/A	$.04m
Transportation	N/A	?
Admin	N/A	$1m
Cost per bottle	$0.06	?

Explain that the left hand column represents the costs associated with bottle production. The middle column represents what the client would pay Ed (1 billion bottles times 6 cents each equals $60 million). The right hand column represents the client. Some of the numbers have been filled in; others are still a mystery and need to be figured out.

Data Bank

COGS – The cost per gallon of PET pellets is $5. It takes 10 gallons to make 1,000 bottles. We want to make a billion bottles.

Answer: $50 / 1,000 = $0.05 per bottle
$0.05 x 1 billion bottles = $50 million

Labor – Twenty people x $4,000 a month each equals $80,000 a month.

Answer: $80,000 x 12 months = $960,000 per year (don't round up)

Transportation – It costs $0.005 to transport one bottle.

Answer: $0.005 x 1 billion = $5 million

The completed chart should look like this:

Y1	Ed	Client
COGS	$60m	$50m
Building	N/A	$6m
Equipment	N/A	$4m
Labor	N/A	$.96m
Utilities & Maintenance	N/A	$.04m
Transportation	N/A	$5m
Admin	N/A	$1m
Cost per bottle	$0.06	$0.067

$67 million / 1 billion bottles = $0.067 per bottle

Client $0.067
Outsource – $0.060
$0.007 x 1 billion bottles = $7 million

The first year we pay $7 million more than if we had purchased the bottles from Ed.

Tell the student:

For Year 2 – assume that production is up 5% to 1.05 billion bottles.
COGS should increase by 5%; the building and equipment are one-time charges and can be zeroed out. Labor, utilities and maintenance and administration remain the same, but transportation is up by 5%.

The new chart should look like this:

Y2	Ed	Client
COGS	$63m	$52.5m
Building	N/A	N/A
Equipment	N/A	N/A
Labor	N/A	$.96m
Utilities & Maintenance	N/A	$.04m
Transportation	N/A	$5.25m
Admin	N/A	$1m
Cost per bottle	$0.06	$0.056

Have the student come up with the new dollar total, which is $59.75 million.

(52.5 + .96 + .04 + 5.25 +1 = $59.75)

I never make the student divide 59,750,000 by 1,050,000,000 just tell him that it equals around $0.056 per bottle.

Thus $0.06 - $0.056 = $0.004 less than what we would pay Ed.

However, make him figure out that $0.004 x 1.05 billion = $4.2 million.

To summarize so far:
Year 1: down $7 million
Year 2: up $4.2 million (so we are still down $2.8 million)

Remember: the CFO wanted a two-year payback.

Tell the student that in Y3 the company will end up with $3.31 million profit, so we are $510,000 in the black.

What do you tell the CFO?

The student will most likely say that we won't breakeven in two years; however, if we stay the course, we become profitable in Year 3.

Tell the student that the CFO wants a two-year payback and that he needs to figure out (1) a way to breakeven through increasing revenues and (2) a way to breakeven by lowering expenses.

Revenues side: produce more bottles to sell to competitors.

Expense side: lease the building and equipment.

Summary

The interviewee needs to jump right into to this without any down time to collect his thoughts. A good summary is about a minute, minute and a half long. It is not a rehash of everything you spoke about; it is a short recap of the problem and two or three main points that the student wants the interviewer to remember.

Did the Interviewee...

- repeat the question, verifying the objective and asking about other objectives?
- make math mistakes?
- know how to value a company?
- produce a good, short summary touching on the most critical points?
- have well-organized and easy-to-read notes?

Mark of a Good Case Discussion: One thing that I look for that the students never do is to stop before they go into the meeting with the CFO and say, "If I go into the meeting now, I will have to tell the CFO that we can't do it in two years. Before I go in, I want to figure out a way to do it in two years. That way I can tell the CFO yes we can!"

This shows great forethought and a can-do attitude that any consultant would love.

Smackdown Rivals*

Problem Statement

Our client, Smackdown Rivals, is a publicly-traded sports entertainment company. Smackdown has successfully conceived and developed a very popular genre of wrestling that has cultivated an impassioned international fan base as it is marketed and distributed globally across live and televised events, digital media platforms and a wide variety of consumer products.

Smackdown had revenues of $526.5 million last year, with an operating profit of $70.3 million and a net profit of $45.4 million. Smackdown has 72.85 million shares outstanding, and it has been paying dividends of $1.44 per share. The company has enjoyed a good growth trajectory and has been expanding internationally. In fact, in the past few years international revenue has been growing at twice the rate of domestic revenue. Smackdown currently employs almost 600 people, not including the approximately 150 wrestlers who are contractors under exclusive agreements with the company.

The COO has asked for your advice. Analysts have praised Smackdown's ability to generate cash, its lack of debt, its healthy revenue trajectory and its generous quarterly dividends. Yet, a few analysts have voiced concerns that costs have been rising out of proportion to growth. In addition to pleasing analysts, the COO knows the company needs to be as efficient as possible in its operations so it can fuel strategic investments that allow international expansion and other growth possibilities.

The COO wants to keep growing the company aggressively, but he needs to make really solid choices on where and how to grow. If a future creative idea doesn't work out, it could be an expensive loss for the company. On the other hand, if Smackdown is too conservative in their growth investments, their fan base could begin spending their entertainment dollars elsewhere.

I need you to take the following five steps:

1. Determine whether costs are rising out of proportion to growth.
2. Explain whether analysts have a valid concern about costs.
3. Based on your observations, tell me what you would advise the COO to do, if anything, regarding costs.
4. Give your opinion about how a COO should determine the appropriate cost structure for this business.
5. Give your opinion on Smackdown's recent dividend payments.

Guidance for the Interviewer

- Make sure that the student summarizes the question and verifies the objectives before starting to answer your questions.

*Written by Lynda Knoll Cotter

Questions 1 and 2

1. Calculate if costs are rising out of proportion to growth.
2. Explain whether analysts have a valid concern about costs.
    - Give the student Chart 1 (see page 224) and give her time to review the statement.
    - Using Chart 1, the student should be able to calculate the YOY (year over year) growth and cost percentages to answer Question 1.
    - The student might ask for more detailed data. If so, give the student Charts 2 and 3 (profitability ratios and headcount on page 225) and Chart 4 (a breakdown of the revenues by business unit on page 225).
    - The student should calculate the YOY percentage growth for revenue and costs as in the table below:

YOY Percentage Growth

Area	2006–7	2007–8
Revenue	17.0%	8.4%
Total Costs	19.6%	8.6%
Cost of Revenue	22.0%	4.4%
Selling/Gen./Admin.	13.5%	20.3%

- From the data provided, the student should be able to make the following observations:
    - We have revenue data by line of business but not cost data, so it is difficult to make observations by line of business.
    - At a high level, total costs and revenue are staying roughly in sync. At a more detailed level, SG&A costs just took a big jump, 50%+, in proportion to other costs and revenue. **The concern of analysts appears to be valid.** The student may speculate that some analysts could be worried SG&A costs will continue to rise more quickly than revenue, and the company needs to have plans to ensure that the rising SG&A will not become a trend.
    - The student might point out that the number of employees did not rise in 2008, yet SG&A costs as a percentage of revenue increased by almost 10%.
    - The "All Other" bucket of expenses is a high number for a catch-all category, and the student will hopefully ask what is included in the "All Other" expenses. You can tell the student that it's good she asked, but the details are not available.
    - The student should note that there was a dramatic increase in advertising and promotion (over 100%) in the last year.
    - Revenue from studios appears to be a new revenue stream, and it is growing the most rapidly, at over 50% from 2007–08. The student might hypothesize that the growth in advertising and promotion could possibly be coming from this new venture.
    - The student should comment on the increase in bad debt, and the student may wonder whether credit policies need to be tightened. The student may realize that the increase

in bad debt might not be from ignoring credit policies, but instead from paying closer attention and being more aggressive in writing off uncollectible debt.

Question 3

3. Based on your observations, tell me what you would advise the COO to do, if anything, regarding costs.

- It would be difficult for the student to make detailed recommendations on cost-cutting without more detailed information on what the costs represent and how they are allocated to each line of business.
- The student should understand that costs are an investment made to grow the company. The Smackdown leadership team, analysts and investors want to ensure that the company is using their investments in the parts of the business that have the most potential.
- The student should suggest that the COO perform further investigation in the areas where costs have increased the most (i.e., advertising and promotion, bad debt, all other).
- On Chart 2, the student should be able to explain the difference between the two profitability ratios. The definitions are as follows:
  - **Gross Margin:** The percentage of revenue remaining after subtracting the cost of goods sold.
  - **Operating Margin:** The proportion of revenues remaining after taking out costs of goods sold and SG&A expenses.
- The student should be able to explain that the operating margin is going down, presumably due to the increase in SG&A costs.
- It would also be good if the student asked to see the costs of other companies in the industry to get benchmark information. Although benchmark data is usually fairly easily available, with this particular company you would need to benchmark the different areas of the business separately, and you can tell the student that this information isn't available right now, but benchmarking in general is a good practice to follow.

Question 4

4. Give your opinion about how the COO should determine the appropriate cost structure for this business.

- The student might suggest that Smackdown should control costs differently for a growing part of the business than for a non-growing part of the business.
- The student should consider that a new business could require substantial startup costs and may lose money in the first year or two.
- These are good points, but regardless of whether or not a business unit is experiencing growth, the key is to control costs. A business unit leader shouldn't ever have a "no-holds-barred" approach to hiring and other expenditures, regardless of how fast her area is growing.

- The student should suggest that the cost structure for the business should be based on the results of ROI analyses for new areas of growth, and that leadership should reduce costs for those lines of business that are not in a growth mode.

Question 5

5. Give your opinion on Smackdown's dividend payments.

- The student should note that Smackdown is currently using all their profits for dividends, which is not a sustainable policy in the long run.
- The student should also mention that growth companies tend not to pay dividends and generally use that money to fuel the growth instead.
- The student should understand that dividends can be a very important part of shareholder value, and she should speculate as to why this company has such a high dividend. The student may surmise that since the company is in a non-traditional business, the dividend could be used as the backbone of their stock valuation.

Data Bank

Smackdown Chart 1

Smackdown Rivals
Trending Schedules
Statement of Operations
($ in millions, Unaudited)

	2006	2007	2008
Revenues	**$ 415.3**	**$ 485.7**	**$ 526.5**
Cost of Revenues	244.9	298.8	311.8
SG&A	96.1	109.1	131.3
Dep. & Amortization	8.7	9.4	13.1
Operating Income	**$ 65.6**	**$ 68.4**	**$ 70.3**
Interest and Other, net	9.8	8.0	(1.0)
Income before Taxes	**$ 75.4**	**$ 76.4**	**$ 69.3**
Interest and Other, net	26.6	24.3	23.9
Effective Tax Rate	**35%**	**32%**	**34%**
Income from Continuing Operations	**$ 48.8**	**$ 52.1**	**$ 45.4**
Discontinued Ops			0.0
Net Income	$ 48.8	$ 52.1	$ 45.4
EPS - Continuing Operations	**$0.68**	**$0.72**	**$0.62**
EPS - Net Income	$0.68	$0.72	$0.62
Memo:			
EBIDTA	$ 74.3	77.8	83.4
EBIDTA margin %	18%	16%	16%

Smackdown Chart 2

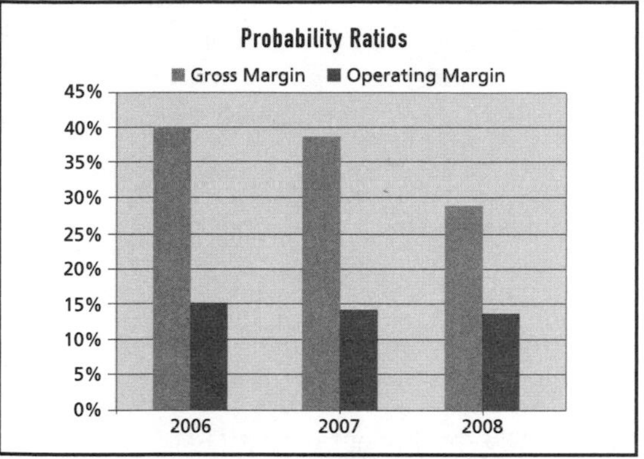

Smackdown Chart 3

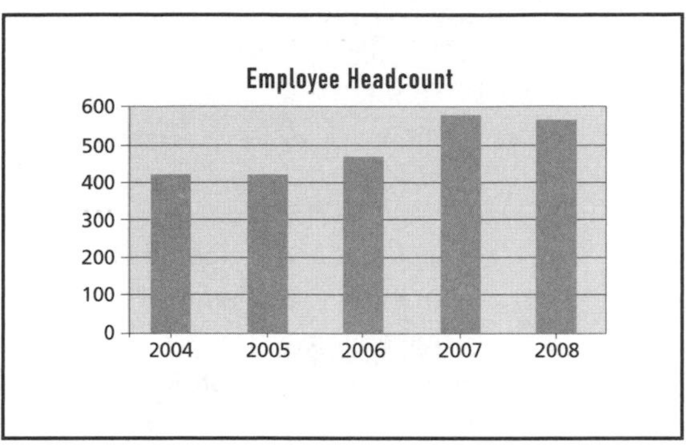

Smackdown Chart 4

Revenues	2006	2007	2008
Live & TV Entertainment	$292.2	$316.8	$331.5
Consumer Products	95.0	118.1	135.7
Digital Media	28.1	34.8	34.8
Smackdown Studios	0.0	16.0	224.5
Total revenues	$415.3	$485.7	$526.5

	2006	2007	2008
Staff related	$44.7	$50.3	$55.2
Legal accounting and other professional	10.9	14.0	16.6
Stock compensation	4.7	7.8	8.0
Advertising and promotion	5.2	5.4	11.6
Bad debt	0.5	0.1	2.5
All other	30.1	31.5	37.4
Total SG&A	**$96.1**	**$109.1**	**$131.3**
SG&A as a percentage of revenue	23%	23%	25%

Summary

The interviewee needs to jump right into to this without any down time to collect her thoughts. A good summary is about a minute, minute and a half long. It is not a rehash of everything you spoke about; it is a short recap of the problem and two or three main points that the student wants the interviewer to remember.

Did the Interviewee...

- repeat the question, verifying the objective and asking about other objectives?
- quantify their findings?
- make math mistakes?
- produce a good, short summary touching on the most critical points?
- have well-organized and easy-to-read notes?

Mark of a Good Case Discussion: This is a tough case. Did the student get rattled by what was asked of her, or did she jump right in? Did she know to ask for more data and what information to pull out? With this case, it is easy to get overwhelmed, so award extra points for staying calm and working through it.

+ Cowabunga*

Problem Statement

An entrepreneur from Northern California opened a surf-themed ice cream shop named Cowabunga Creamery. The creamery is located in the downtown area in a town of 30,000 and is surrounded by mostly small shops and restaurants. At least 20% of the potential customers in the town are within walking distance, and the parking is easy for the other 80%. The main competition in the neighborhood is an organic yogurt shop down the street. The average temperature in the area is 60 degrees.

Serving Marianne's ice cream, a local brand with a loyal following, the store also features frozen yogurt, coffee drinks, cow pies, as well as ice cream cones and sundaes. Cowabunga has received great reviews and sales have grown since it opened six months ago. With the goal of keeping costs low, the owner has been manning the counter. The shop is open from noon to 10:00pm, seven days a week.

A tub of ice cream is three gallons, and it contains 50 servings of ice cream. The ice cream store owner pays $25 per tub, and he charges $2.75 per serving. The cones (or cups) cost 25 cents each.

Below are Cowabunga's rough monthly expenses:

Hand this chart to the student. (You can find a copy to photocopy on page 225.)

Fixed Costs	
Rent	$2,800.00
Utilities	$500.00
Insurance	$50.00
Property Taxes	$250.00

What is the average gross margin on an ice cream cone? And how many ice cream cones does the owner need to sell an hour in order to break-even?

Guidance for the Interviewer

Make sure that the student summarizes the context of the case and verifies the objectives (determining average gross margin and the number of cones to break even) before starting the calculations. She should also ask if there are any other objectives she should be concerned with—in this case the answer is no.

Calculations

- Gross Margin:
  - Cost of the ice cream: $25 per tub / 50 servings = $0.50 per serving
  - Cost of each cup or cone: $0.25
  - Gross margin: $2.75 – .50 – .25 = $2.00 per serving

*Written by Lynda Knoll Cotter

- Breakeven point
  - $3,600 total costs per month / $2.00 per serving = $1,800
  - $1,800 / 30 days = 60 ice cream servings per day
  - 60 ice cream servings / 10 hours a day = 6 servings per hour

Problem Statement, (cont.)

Cowabunga has proven to be a great concept, but the current income won't sustain the owner over the long run. What are three options to grow the business? Determine which is the best.

Guidance for the Interviewer

Cowabunga's owner could grow the business in a number of different ways. To consider different growth opportunities, it's important for the interviewee to consider the trade-offs of each. The interviewee should know to pick one strategy and make a case as to why her recommendation is what the owner should follow right away.

Growth Strategies

1. *Increasing Distribution Channels:* Since Cowabunga serves ice cream that comes from a supplier, this strategy is unlikely, unless the owner franchises the operation or opens additional locations. If the owner were to open additional Cowabunga locations without franchising, he would need to find some private investors or a business partner, as he has limited funds available right now.
2. *Increasing the Product Line:* Cowabunga could offer additional products that are a good fit with ice cream, like other confectionary items or snacks. Cow pies have been selling, so he could be more aggressive in moving sales of pies or other "to go" items in the display freezer. Increasing his product line will certainly help the owner make additional profit, but it's unlikely to be a long-term growth strategy.
3. *Investing in a Major Marketing Campaign:* Increasing the marketing of Cowabunga could also help drive foot traffic. However, since the owner has limited funds, he would need to be creative with his marketing budget. Additionally, the store is located in a small town, and the creamery is downtown, so many townies already know about Cowabunga. The marketing campaign might serve to draw customers from outside areas, but the owner should do a competitive scan first.
4. *Diversifying Products and Services:* Cowabunga is a relatively new concept, so diversifying the products and services wouldn't make perfect sense until the owner increases awareness more broadly of the Cowabunga brand. For diversification ideas that might work down the road, ensure that the interviewee has firm logic behind her product and service ideas.
5. *Acquiring Competitors:* The use of this strategy may make sense, depending on how much business the owner is losing due to the organic yogurt shop or other stores in the area. But, again, the owner has limited money to invest right now. If the owner found a partner/investor, he could investigate opportunities consistent with his strategy.

Problem Statement, (cont.)

Cowabunga has just found out that the supplier of their ice cream, Marianne's, is up for sale because its owner wants to retire. In addition to producing ice cream, Marianne's has one retail location in Santa Cruz, California, about a two-hour drive from Cowabunga.

How should Cowabunga figure out if it makes sense to vertically integrate through buying its ice cream manufacturer? What should Cowabunga think about? What should it do in order to make a decision? And what are the possible ramifications of not buying Marianne's?

Guidance for the Interviewer

The owner of Cowabunga should use the same framework as he would to consider any potential merger or acquisition. In considering whether or not to buy Marianne's, he should think through the following acquisition considerations and do some research to determine if his instincts make sense. (For more on M&A see page 38.)

Acquisition Considerations

1. *Determine What His Goals and Objectives are:* Does he want to ensure that he can continue selling Marianne's ice cream in his store? Is he afraid the organic frozen yogurt store down the street will buy Marianne's, so he wants to preempt his competition? Would it provide the owner with some tax advantages? What type of synergies would exist for Cowabunga if it were vertically integrated? Would the owner retain both store brands, or would he re-brand one of the stores or the ice cream itself?

2. *Analyze the Asking Price:* Is the price fair? How would he pay for the store? How much debt would he be willing to take on? Can he find a partner or other investor to work with him? If the economy gets worse, would he still be able to make his debt payments?

3. *Do Due Diligence on the Company and Industry:* What shape is Marianne's in? What shape is the Santa Cruz store in? Marianne's has a loyal following, but how loyal are the customers, and why are they loyal? How loyal are they likely to remain with the ownership change? How is the industry doing? Does the present economic trouble have any effect on ice cream sales? Is Marianne's a leader in ice cream manufacturing? Do they have any advanced technology or other equipment that is valuable? What are the margins like? How many extra ice cream cones would Cowabunga need to sell per day in order to service the debt? Is it realistic to sell this many? How will competitors respond? What legal ramifications might exist? What are the upfront assumptions the owner would need to make, and how would he track those assumptions?

4. *Understand Potential Exit Strategies:* How long would the owner plan on keeping Marianne's? If the owner needed to sell Marianne's, how might he do on the sale? Would he sell it whole, or would he break it up and sell parts of it?

The student should not be expected to mention every question listed above in her thinking, but she should be able to fairly easily cover each of the four categories of the merger and acquisition framework covered in this book. The student should also be able to ask a few good questions that represent each area of the framework.

The Possible Ramifications of Not Buying Marianne's

- Marianne's ice cream is a big draw to Cowabunga, especially to those customers who live outside the main downtown area and could easily go elsewhere for their ice cream fix.
- If a competitor buys Marianne's or if no one buys Marianne's, the owner of Cowabunga may be forced to find another ice cream supplier, and he believes that would be detrimental to his ice cream sales.

Problem Statement, cont.

Strategically, owning the ice cream supplier may make sense, but much of the long-term business value from acquiring Marianne's would be based upon the acquisition cost. How much should Cowabunga offer for the business? The owner of Marianne's has set a price based on his opinion of value and what he thinks he needs to retire, which is $1.2 million. The seller is not open to financing any part of the deal.

Marianne's is not computerized. Although Marianne's has well over 100 wholesale clients, no written contracts exist. Marianne's has long-term leases (10+ years with options) at both the retail and wholesale facilities. The recipes are unique to Marianne's and will be sold with the business.

(Copy the charts found on pages 226 and 227 and hand them to your interviewee.) Here is some information on Marianne's net profit, monthly sales and assets. How should the owner of Cowabunga value Marianne's? If you were in his shoes, how much would you offer for the business?

Data Bank

There are many different ways of valuing a small business exist, and the process of valuing a small business is much more of an art than a science. What is most important in a case interview of this type is for the student to be able to reason soundly through at least one method of determining the price that the interested buyers should offer the seller.

Valuation Approach

There are usually three general methods used for the basis of valuing a restaurant business: assets, gross annual revenue or cash flow multiples.

The asset-based method is appropriate for an unprofitable or closed location. Since Marianne's is a profitable, ongoing business, the assets-based method isn't ideal. Plus, the list of assets is pretty much an inventory of used equipment, and what's relevant is how much business value (through revenue) the seller will derive from the equipment. How significant are assets? Marianne's lists $195,000 of assets. This is about 15% of sales. In other words, the argument could be made that even if there were no assets, the price would only be altered by 15%.

The gross annual revenue (or sales) method makes more sense if the business has no profits, or if it is not run properly. In this case, Marianne's has turned a profit each year for the last five years (albeit a small one in 2006).

Cash flow is what matters most to this valuation. Future income is needed to pay for debt incurred when buying the business, and the buyer of the business has to estimate what his annual income will be as well as how fast that would allow him to retire his debt. The income can also be considered as interest income on a financial investment. For example, he could invest $1 million and make 3% on US Treasuries, 8% on corporate bonds or 12% on ice cream.

Another consideration: in this business, is income or cash flow more important? For a small restaurant, income and cash flow are pretty much the same, since cash is received when the sale is made and expenses are paid evenly throughout the year.

MARIANNE'S NET PROFIT STATEMENTS:

Year 1: Gross Sales	$	787,838
Net Profit	$	156,717
Year 2: Gross Sales	$	1,003,659
Net Profit	$	170,074
Year 3: Gross Sales	$	1,040,238
Net Profit	$	146,663
Year 4: Gross Sales	$	1,043,636
Net Profit	$	105,411
Year 5: Gross Sales	$	1,189,471
Net Profit	$	2,765
Year 6: Gross Sales	$	1,168,097
Net Profit	$	168
Year 7: Gross Sales	$	1,329,867
Net Profit	$	65,646
Year 8: Gross Sales	$	1,486,528
Net Profit	$	108,486

MARIANNE'S MONTHLY SALES COMPARISON:

OCTOBER LAST YEAR		
Retail Sales:	$	49,140.33
Wholesale Sales:	$	69,385.06
TOTAL:	$	118,525.39
OCTOBER THIS YEAR		
Retail Sales:	$	57,155.29
Wholesale Sales:	$	82,942.28
TOTAL:	$	140,097.57
OCTOBER INCREASE:		**$21,572.18**
NOVEMBER LAST YEAR		
Retail Sales:	$	42,354.09
Wholesale Sales:	$	56,687.89
TOTAL:	$	99,041.98
NOVEMBER THIS YEAR		
Retail Sales:	$	48,251.00
Wholesale Sales:	$	60,266.31
TOTAL:	$	108,517.31
NOVEMBER INCREASE:		**$9,475.33**

MARIANNE'S EQUIPMENT LIST:

Production

- 2 Cherry Burrell 80 gph ice cream machine - $2,500 (new $ 6,000)
- 2 50-gallon stainless mixing vat with piping - $1,500
- 1 packaging machine - $5,000
- Production equipment - $20,800
- 1 80-pound grease trap and pump- $8,000
- 2 40-gallon hot water heaters - $800
- 1 18 x 28 ft freezer box (17 degrees) - $20,000
- 1 6 x 8 ft passageway (room to freezer) - $5,000
- 1 10 horsepower compressor (for ice cream machine) - $6,000
- 2 5 horsepower compressor (for freezer box) - $10,000
- 1 1 horsepower compressor refrigerator box- $3,000
- 20 transportation freezers - $10,000
- 11 freezers on loan to customers - $5,000
- Office equipment - $8,000
- Other miscellaneous equipment - $1,850
- Delivery vehicles: 2 GMC Savannas and 1 Ford Van - $15,000
- 1 double-door freezer - $3,500
- Chocolate dipping tank - $5,000

Total: $130,950

Retail Store

- 8 x 11 ft (2 horsepower) walk-in freezer - $8,000
- 5 dipping cabinets - $15,350
- 2 cash registers - $1,000
- 2 milkshake machines - $1,100
- 3 fudge warmers - $500
- 1 Champion dishwasher - $3,000
- 1 20-pound grease trap - $1,000
- 18-foot back bar - $5,000
- 31 chairs ($35 each) - $1,085
- 9 tables - $1,000
- 1 neon-painted sign - $5,000
- Assorted signs and lights - $1,000
- Other miscellaneous equipment - $1,900
- 1 4-foot ice cream ready-pack merchandiser - $5,700
- 1 under-counter refrigerator (1/4 horsepower compressor) - $1,000
- Flavor rail with 8 pots - $2,500
- Safe and strong box - $550
- 28-foot counter - $600
- Drop ceiling and lights - $10,000

Total: $65,385

Summary

The interviewee needs to jump right into to this without any down time to collect her thoughts. A good summary is about a minute, minute and a half long. It is not a rehash of everything you spoke about; it is a short recap of the problem and two or three main points that the student wants the interviewer to remember.

Did the Interviewee...

- repeat the question, verifying the objective and asking about other objectives?
- quantify her findings?
- make math mistakes?
- produce a good, short summary touching on the most critical points?
- have well-organized and easy-to-read notes?

Mark of a Good Case Discussion: The student identified different growth strategies and acquisition considerations. She was able to discuss the ramifications of not buying the property, and not get mired in the extraneous charts.

+ Frameworks

Case questions have been popping up in marketing interviews for years. While there are many similarities between a consulting case interview and a case given in a marketing interview, there are differences as well.

I always tell the consulting students to stay away from "cookie-cutter" frameworks like the 5Ps, but in marketing interviews you are encouraged to employ them.

To truly stand out from your peers, it is best to incorporate the 5Ps into the overall structure and then to fill in your answer with concepts from the Ivy Case Method™. You'll find that out of the 12 Ivy Case scenarios you'll most often use (i) entering a new market, (ii) developing a new product, (iii) pricing and (iv) growth strategies.

In marketing interviews the 5Ps are: Price, Product, Promotion, Placement and Packaging.

On the following pages I have laid out some working structures for you to review. Keep in mind that these might vary depending on if the case is about a product or a service and what industry it belongs to.

+ New Product Launch

1. Customer needs
   - Do customers want or need this product?
   - Benefits to the consumer
2. Segmenting the market
   - Market-sizing – How big is the market?
     - Market growth rate (past, present and future forecast)
   - Competition and substitutions
     - Who are the competitors and what is their market share?
     - How do their products and services differ from ours?
     - Will they launch a competitive response?
   - Determine strategic opening
     - Entering the market
       - Start from scratch, buy your way in or form a strategic alliance
     - Barriers to entry
       - Government regulations, access to distribution channels, access to capital, access to raw materials
     - Barriers to exit
3. Choose target
   - ID heavy users
     - Why would they be interested in this product?
4. Positioning
   - Differentiate – How different is it from the competition?
5. 5Ps
   - Product – Why is it good? What's our niche? How is it packaged?
   - Price – Competitive analysis, cost-based pricing, price-based costing (what is the customer willing to pay for it)
   - Place – Distribution channels
   - Promotion – How best to market
   - Packaging
6. Evaluate financials
   - Do we have the funding we need to launch and support this product?

To launch or not to launch? Make a decision.

+ Competitive Defense

Assess the threatening product

- How similar is it to our product?
  - Does it do a better job meeting the customer's needs?
  - What are its strengths and weaknesses?
  - What kind of market share can it expect?
    - Curiosity about a new product – will it last?
    - Will it cannibalize our sales or will it steal sales from another competitor instead?

What kind of resources does it have behind it?

- Parent company – large or small
  - How committed is it to this division or product?
- Introduction strategy
  - Major marketing campaign
  - Incentive discounts
    - 2-for-1 offer
    - Low interest financing

Defense strategies

Defense strategies will differ depending on product or services offered. Below are a few well-tested ideas that you should think about to determine if they are appropriate for that particular case.

STRATEGY
KEEP COMPETITION OUT
PROTECT MARKET SHARE
GET NEW CUSTOMERS
RAISE BARRIERS TO ENTRY
RAISE SWITCHING COSTS
VISIT CUSTOMERS / CREATE LOYALTY PROGRAMS
LONG TERM CONTRACTS
INCREASE MARKETING EFFORTS
INCREASE SALES COMMISSION
STEAL STAFF AND CUSTOMERS AWAY FROM COMPETITION
WHAT IF THE ECONOMY SOURS?

+ 5 Ps

- Pricing – Can you adjust your price to maintain or even gain market share and profitability?
- Product – Can we upgrade our product or options offered? How long will it take and at what cost? Will it cannibalize existing products?
- Promotion – Reinforce brand with advertising, promotions and PR.
- Place – Increase exposure within current distribution channels, also increase number of channels.
- Packaging – Can you improve or update your packaging?

✢ Key Measures

In these cases the main key measures are market share, sales and profits. If you are given a case with an existing product, identify where that product is in its life cycle – emerging, growth, maturing or declining.

Things to consider:

- If market share is constant but sales are flat, that could indicate industry sales are flat and your competitors are experiencing the same problem.
- If market share declines and it is determined that market share is more important than profits, then consider lowering price; if not, then upgrade the product, increase promotions and expand distribution channels.
- If your case includes a decline-in-sales problem, analyze these three things:
  - Overall declining market demand (soda sales have dropped as bottled water sales climb)
  - The current marketplace might be mature or your product might be obsolete (CDs give way to digital)
  - Loss of market share due to substitutions (Netflix DVD rentals give way to Internet downloads, pay-per-view, DVD purchases, and competitors such as Blockbuster entering their market.)
- If sales and market share are increasing, but profits are declining, then you need to investigate whether prices are dropping and/or costs are climbing. However, if costs aren't the issue, then investigate product mix and check to see if the margins have changed.
- If profits are declining because of a drop in revenues, concentrate on marketing and distribution issues.
- If profits are declining because of rising expenses, concentrate on operational and financial issues.
- If profits are declining, but revenues went up, review:
  - changes in costs
  - any additional expenses
  - changes in prices
  - the product mix
  - changes in customer needs
- If a product is in its emerging growth stage, concentrate on R&D, competition and pricing.
- If a product is in its growth stage, emphasize marketing and competition.
- If a product is in its mature stage, focus on manufacturing, costs and competition.
- If a product is in its declining stage, determine the strength of the brand, then define niche market(s), analyze the competition's play, grow category, and maintain at more profitable levels or think about an exit strategy
  - Can this product be reinvented or changed to meet new consumer needs?
  - Can this product be produced at a lower cost?
  - Can this product have new uses?
  - Can new distribution channels be created?

+ Common Marketing Interview Questions

1. How would you develop and introduce a new product?
2. There are two ideas in the company pipeline. Which one would you choose?
3. Critique this ad.
4. Define a successful ad.
5. Your competition is attacking your product. How would you respond?
6. Give me an example of good marketing.

Most of this is psychological. The biggest assets a candidate can bring are a measure of confidence, a perspective of self-worth and a good night's sleep. The interview structure is daunting, the people generally intimidating, and the atmosphere tense, but you can slay all these dragons immediately when you choose to arm yourself with a positive self-image. In the end, it's not whether you are right or wrong, it is how you present yourself, your information, and your thinking. This is the measure of marketability for the firm and it is what they seek to determine through an imperfect process.

Finally, it's only you against the beast (the case question, not the interviewer). We can't be there with you, but we've given you the tools to feel confident and to have a good time. If you're excited about the challenge and the interview, then you're headed into the right profession. If you dread what's coming, you may want to re-evaluate your career choice. When discussing career choices, Winston Churchill advised his children, "Do what you like, but like what you do." It's all about having fun.

It's easy to forget that the firms know you can do the work — they wouldn't be interviewing you if they didn't think you were smart enough to succeed. Now it's just time to prove them right.

Case closed!

Just in case
If you need more practice, check out CQ Interactive at casequestions.com.

Back-of-the-envelope question : A type of case question, most often a market-sizing question, that asks you to make an educated estimate of something. The back-of-the-envelope question received its name because the questions used to start with, "You're on an airplane, with no books, phone, or any resources. On the back of an envelope figure ..." An example: "How many pairs of boxers are sold in the US each year?"

Barrier to entry: Factors (such as capital requirements, access to distribution channels, proprietary product technology, or government policy) that would inhibit a company when entering a new market.

Benchmark: Continuously analyzing the industry leaders and determining what they do better. A comparison against the best to provide targets for achievement.

Bottom line: Gross sales minus taxes, interest, depreciation, and other expenses. Also called net profit, net earnings, or net income.

Brainteaser: A type of case question in which the interviewee is asked to solve a riddle or logic problem.

Cannibalize: To take (sales) away from an existing product by selling a similar but new product usually from the same manufacturer; also: to affect (an existing product) adversely by cannibalizing sales.

Capital: Cash or goods used to generate income.

Case question: A fun, intriguing, and active interviewing tool used in consulting interviews to evaluate the multi-dimensional aspects of a candidate.

COGS: See costs of goods sold.

Core competencies: The areas in which a company excels.

Cost of goods sold (COGS): On an income statement, the cost of purchasing raw materials and manufacturing finished products.

Cost-based pricing: A pricing strategy in which a product or service is priced according to the cost of producing, manufacturing, or otherwise creating the product or service. R&D and COGS are the major determinants in this pricing strategy.

Cost-benefit analysis: A technique designed to determine the feasibility of a project or plan by quantifying its costs and benefits.

Depreciation: A decrease in estimated value.

Distribution channel: Means by which a producer of goods or services reaches its final users.

Economy of scale: Reduction in cost per unit resulting from increased production, realized through operational efficiencies.

Fixed cost: A cost that does not vary depending on production or sales levels, such as rent, property tax, insurance, or interest expense.

Framework: A structure that helps you organize your thoughts and analyze a case in a logical manner.

Gross sales: Total value of sales, before deducting for customer discounts, allowances, or returns.

Growth phase: A phase of development in which a company experiences rapid earnings growth as it produces new products and expands market share.

Initial Public Offering (IPO): The first sale of stock by a company to the public.

Interest expense: The money spent on the fee charged by a lender to a borrower for the use of borrowed money.

IPO: see Initial Public Offering.

Joint venture: An agreement between firms to work together on a project for mutual benefit.

Market share: The percentage of the total sales of a given type of product or service that are attributable to a given company.

Market-sizing question: A type of case question that is often called a back-of-the-envelope question. This type of question asks you to estimate the size of a specific market. An example: "How many pairs of boxer shorts are sold in the US each year?"

Maturity phase: A phase of company development in which earnings continue to grow at the rate of the general economy.

MECE: Borrows from the 80/20 tradition in espousing a "mutually exclusive, collectively exhaustive" approach to engagements. In other words, the consultant / interviewer must take care to ensure that, simultaneously, (1) each issue discussed is separate and distinct ("mutually exclusive") and (2) that the totality of issues discussed comprehensively addresses every conceivable aspect of the problem ("collectively exhaustive"). Likely, upon your admission to the firm, MECE will become such an instinctive element of your mentality and such a governing dynamic of your production (memos, reports, presentations, strategy), that you will be well served to evidence a familiarity and appreciation for it at some point in the hiring process. You will also be well served to remember that, when iterating your ideas, an "other issues" category can afford you a simple means to ensure you always remain at least attentive to the principle, if not genuinely MECE in your approach.

Net sales: Gross sales minus returns, discounts, and allowances.

Niche market: A focused, targetable part of a market.

Overhead: The ongoing administrative expenses of a business, such as rent, utilities, and insurance.

Price-based costing: A pricing strategy in which a product or service is priced according to what the market will bear, or what the consumer is willing to pay.

Profit: The positive gain from a business or operation after subtracting for all expenses.

Proprietary: Something that is used, produced, or marketed under exclusive legal right of the inventor or maker; specifically: a drug (as a patent medicine) that is protected by secrecy, patent, or copyright against free competition as to name, product, composition, or process of manufacture.

R&D: see Research & Development.

Research & Development (R&D) : Discovering knowledge about products, processes, and services and then applying that knowledge to create new and improved products, processes, and services that fill market needs.

Revenue: Same as sales. The total dollar amount collected for goods and services provided.

Substitution: A product or service that fills a consumer's need in the same or similar way as another product or service (e.g., Nutrasweet is a substitution for sugar).

Supply and demand: The two key determinants of price. Supply is the total amount of a good or service available for purchase, while demand is the desire and ability by individuals to purchase economic goods or services at the market price.

Transition phase: A phase of development in which the company's earnings begin to mature and decelerate to the rate of growth of the economy as a whole.

Unit cost: Cost per item.

Variable cost: A unit cost that depends on total volume.

VC: see venture capital.

Venture capital (VC): Funds made available for start-up firms and small businesses with exceptional growth potential. Managerial and technical expertise are often provided.

10 : Partner Case Charts

✛ Nerves of Steel

Hand the student this chart.

Y1	Y2	Y3	Y4	Y5	Y6	Y7	Y8
$263	$554	$615	$600	$610	$750	$810	?

+ Statin Blue

Statin Blue Chart 1

Hand the student this chart.

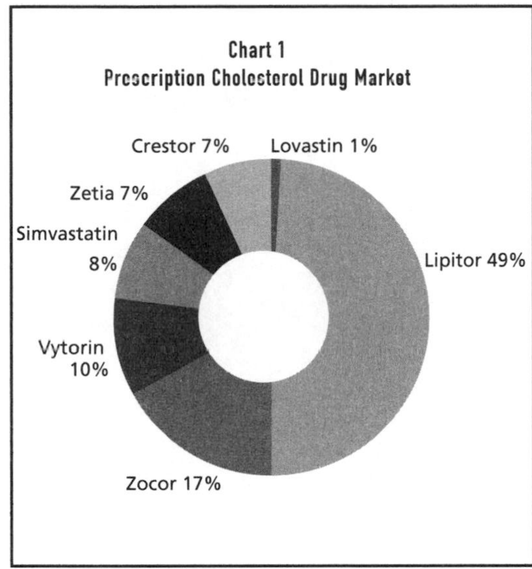

Statin Blue Chart 2

Walk the student through this chart.

250	Big Trouble (represents 10% of the overall prescription cholesterol market)	
220	Other Prescription Cholesterol Drugs (represents 80% of the overall prescription cholesterol market)	
200	Statin Blue (We believe that the patients whose cholesterol levels fall between 200 and 220 make up 10% of the overall cholesterol market.)	10%
180	Honey Nut Cheerios & Exercise	
<180	Healthy	

Statin Blue Chart 3

Show the student this chart during your analysis.

	Prescription	OTC
Market Size		
Breakeven		
Profit		
Market Choice		
Other		

+ Bottled Water

Bottled Water Chart

Hand the student this chart.

Y1	Ed	Client
COGS	60m	?
Building	N/A	$6m
Equipment	N/A	$4m
Labor	N/A	?
Utilities & Maintenance	N/A	$.04m
Transportation	N/A	?
Admin	N/A	$1m
Cost per bottle	$0.06	?

Smackdown Rivals

Smackdown Chart 1

Smackdown Rivals
Trending Schedules
Statement of Operations
($ in millions, Unaudited)

	2006	2007	2008
Revenues	**$ 415.3**	**$ 485.7**	**$ 526.5**
Cost of Revenues	244.9	298.8	311.8
SG&A	96.1	109.1	131.3
Dep. & Amortization	8.7	9.4	13.1
Operating Income	**$ 65.6**	**$ 68.4**	**$ 70.3**
Interest and Other, net	9.8	8.0	(1.0)
Income before Taxes	**$ 75.4**	**$ 76.4**	**$ 69.3**
Interest and Other, net	26.6	24.3	23.9
Effective Tax Rate	**35%**	**32%**	**34%**
Income from Continuing Operations	**$ 48.8**	**$ 52.1**	**$ 45.4**
Discontinued Ops			0.0
Net Income	$ 48.8	$ 52.1	$ 45.4
EPS - Continuing Operations	**$0.68**	**$0.72**	**$0.62**
EPS - Net Income	$0.68	$0.72	$0.62
<u>**Memo:**</u>			
EBIDTA	$ 74.3	77.8	83.4
EBIDTA margin %	18%	16%	16%

Smackdown Chart 2

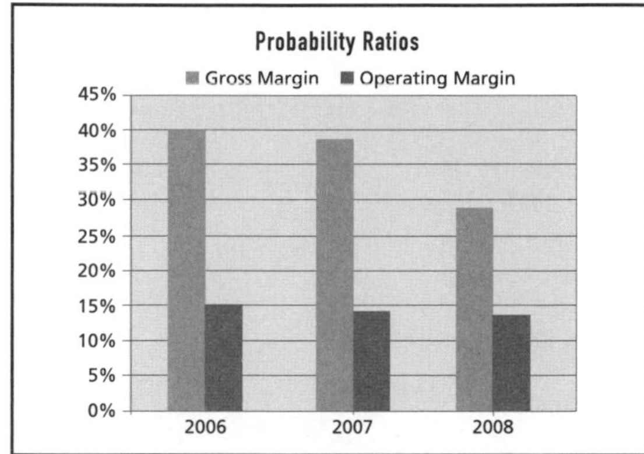

Smackdown Chart 3

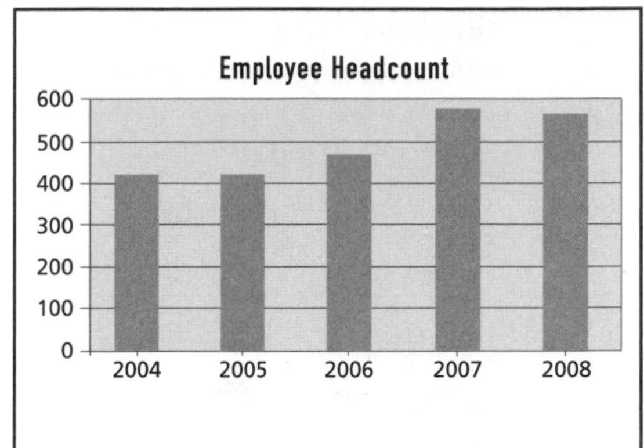

Smackdown Chart 4

	2006	2007	2008
Revenues			
Live & TV Entertainment	$292.2	$316.8	$331.5
Consumer Products	95.0	118.1	135.7
Digital Media	28.1	34.8	34.8
Smackdown Studios	0.0	16.0	224.5
Total revenues	$415.3	$485.7	$526.5

Smackdown Chart 5

	2006	2007	2008
Staff related	$44.7	$50.3	$55.2
Legal accounting and other professional	10.9	14.0	16.6
Stock compensation	4.7	7.8	8.0
Advertising and promotion	5.2	5.4	11.6
Bad debt	0.5	0.1	2.5
All other	30.1	31.5	37.4
Total SG&A	**$96.1**	**$109.1**	**$131.3**
SG&A as a percentage of revenue	23%	23%	25%

✛ Cowabunga

Cowabunga Chart 1
Hand this chart to the student.

Fixed Costs	
Rent	$2,800.00
Utilities	$500.00
Insurance	$50.00
Property Taxes	$250.00

Cowabunga Charts 2 – 4
Hand all three charts to the student all at once.

MARIANNE'S NET PROFIT STATEMENTS:

Year 1:	Gross Sales	$	787,838
	Net Profit	$	156,717
Year 2:	Gross Sales	$	1,003,659
	Net Profit	$	170,074
Year 3:	Gross Sales	$	1,040,238
	Net Profit	$	146,663
Year 4:	Gross Sales	$	1,043,636
	Net Profit	$	105,411
Year 5:	Gross Sales	$	1,189,471
	Net Profit	$	2,765
Year 6:	Gross Sales	$	1,168,097
	Net Profit	$	168
Year 7:	Gross Sales	$	1,329,867
	Net Profit	$	65,646
Year 8:	Gross Sales	$	1,486,528
	Net Profit	$	108,486

MARIANNE'S MONTHLY SALES COMPARISON:

OCTOBER LAST YEAR		
Retail Sales:	$	49,140.33
Wholesale Sales:	$	69,385.06
TOTAL:	$	118,525.39
OCTOBER THIS YEAR		
Retail Sales:	$	57,155.29
Wholesale Sales:	$	82,942.28
TOTAL:	$	140,097.57
OCTOBER INCREASE:		**$21,572.18**
NOVEMBER LAST YEAR		
Retail Sales:	$	42,354.09
Wholesale Sales:	$	56,687.89
TOTAL:	$	99,041.98
NOVEMBER THIS YEAR		
Retail Sales:	$	48,251.00
Wholesale Sales:	$	60,266.31
TOTAL:	$	108,517.31
NOVEMBER INCREASE:		**$9,475.33**

MARIANNE'S EQUIPMENT LIST:

Production

- 2 Cherry Burrell 80 gph ice cream machine - $2,500 (new $ 6,000)
- 2 50-gallon stainless mixing vat with piping - $1,500
- 1 packaging machine - $5,000
- Production equipment - $20,800
- 1 80-pound grease trap and pump- $8,000
- 2 40-gallon hot water heaters - $800
- 1 18 x 28 ft freezer box (17 degrees) - $20,000
- 1 6 x 8 ft passageway (room to freezer) - $5,000
- 1 10 horsepower compressor (for ice cream machine) - $6,000
- 2 5 horsepower compressor (for freezer box) - $10,000
- 1 1 horsepower compressor refrigerator box- $3,000
- 20 transportation freezers - $10,000
- 11 freezers on loan to customers - $5,000
- Office equipment - $8,000
- Other miscellaneous equipment - $1,850
- Delivery vehicles: 2 GMC Savannas and 1 Ford Van - $15,000
- 1 double-door freezer - $3,500
- Chocolate dipping tank - $5,000

Total: $130,950

Retail Store

- 8 x 11 ft (2 horsepower) walk-in freezer - $8,000
- 5 dipping cabinets - $15,350
- 2 cash registers - $1,000
- 2 milkshake machines - $1,100
- 3 fudge warmers - $500
- 1 Champion dishwasher - $3,000
- 1 20-pound grease trap - $1,000
- 18-foot back bar - $5,000
- 31 chairs ($35 each) - $1,085
- 9 tables - $1,000
- 1 neon-painted sign - $5,000
- Assorted signs and lights - $1,000
- Other miscellaneous equipment - $1,900
- 1 4-foot ice cream ready-pack merchandiser - $5,700
- 1 under-counter refrigerator (1/4 horsepower compressor) - $1,000
- Flavor rail with 8 pots - $2,500
- Safe and strong box - $550
- 28-foot counter - $600
- Drop ceiling and lights - $10,000

Total: $65,385

Photo: Martha Stewart 2005

About the Author

Cosentino is the president of CaseQuestions.com. Over the past 24 years he has advised and coached over 10,000 Harvard students and alumni through the university's Career Services centers. He has written three books involving cases and consulting. *Case in Point* is now published in three languages. Cosentino has traveled around the country giving workshops to students at colleges and graduate programs and has held training sessions for career services professionals. He has consulted with and designed cases for private sector firms, government agencies and non-profits.

Marc has a Master's in Public Administration from Harvard University and a BSBA from the University of Denver.